COGNITIVE SCIENCE

A Primer

COGNITIVE SCIENCE

A Primer

John Parrington

University of Oxford, UK

World Scientific

NEW JERSEY · LONDON · SINGAPORE · BEIJING · SHANGHAI · HONG KONG · TAIPEI · CHENNAI · TOKYO

Published by

World Scientific Publishing Europe Ltd.
57 Shelton Street, Covent Garden, London WC2H 9HE
Head office: 5 Toh Tuck Link, Singapore 596224
USA office: 27 Warren Street, Suite 401-402, Hackensack, NJ 07601

Library of Congress Control Number: 2025026672

British Library Cataloguing-in-Publication Data
A catalogue record for this book is available from the British Library.

COGNITIVE SCIENCE
A Primer

ISBN 978-1-80061-780-3 (hardcover)
ISBN 978-1-80061-799-5 (paperback)
ISBN 978-1-80061-781-0 (ebook for institutions)
ISBN 978-1-80061-782-7 (ebook for individuals)

For any available supplementary material, please visit
https://www.worldscientific.com/worldscibooks/10.1142/Q0524#t=suppl

Desk Editors: Nambirajan Karuppiah/Gabriel Rawlinson

Typeset by Stallion Press
Email: enquiries@stallionpress.com

About the Author

John Parrington is an associate professor in molecular and cellular pharmacology at the University of Oxford, a tutorial fellow in medicine and joint head of research at Worcester College, Oxford, and a college lecturer at Exeter College, Oxford. His research focuses on how chemical signals regulate important processes in the body and how better understanding of these processes might be harnessed to create new types of drugs. He has published over 110 peer-reviewed articles in reputed science journals, including *Nature, Current Biology, Journal of Cell Biology, Journal of Clinical Investigation, The EMBO Journal, Development, Developmental Biology*, and *Human Reproduction*. He has extensive experience writing popular science, having published articles in *The Guardian, New Scientist, Chemistry World, The Biologist, Psychology Today*, and *Aeon*. He is the author of *The Deeper Genome* (Oxford University Press, 2015), *Redesigning Life* (Oxford University Press, 2016), *Mind Shift* (Oxford University Press, 2021), and *Consciousness* (Icon Books, 2023).

Contents

Introduction

What is consciousness? How does human consciousness differ from those of other species? What is the basis of personality, and why does it seem to differ so much between individuals? What causes mental distress in some individuals: is it a product of a diseased mind or rather due to adverse life experiences? Such questions have been debated since human beings first learned how to write down their thoughts five and a half thousand years ago and probably for hundreds of thousands or even millions of years before that, depending on how far back in time we want to go in considering the prehistory of the human species.

In the modern age, thanks to advances in the biological sciences, we have become aware that human consciousness is primarily a product of our brains. But that has not stifled the continuing debate about the basis of human consciousness. For instance, despite our greatly increased understanding of the individual components of the human brain and how they work, major questions remain about the ways the different brain regions interconnect, how the brain works as a whole organ, and how this then gives rise to our inner thoughts.

Another unresolved question is what causes mental disorders, with some seeing these as primarily a matter of 'faulty' genes and others as more due to the environment. A further issue of debate is whether human consciousness is unique compared to those of other species or merely one end of a spectrum. An ongoing dispute among philosophers of mind is about whether, despite advances in neuroscience, we will ever be able to fully explain consciousness in the sense of that subjective feeling of what it means to experience the world around us in all its detail.[1]

The aim of this book is to address all these questions in a unified fashion that connects the philosophy of mind with insights that have been emerging from the diverse fields of molecular and cellular biology, physiology, pharmacology, psychology, and philosophy. A key aspect of the model of consciousness we will be developing in this book is that, ultimately, the human mind is underpinned by a biological entity – the brain – and its interactions with the rest of the body, as well as the wider natural and socially constructed environment outside that body.

Box 0.1.   The Hard Problem of Consciousness

A major debate among philosophers of mind was initiated in 1995 by David Chalmers with his proposal of a 'hard problem of consciousness'. Chalmers argued that neuroscience may soon allow us to understand how we learn, store memories, perceive things, react instantly to a painful stimulus, or hear our name spoken across a room at a noisy party, these being the 'easy' part of understanding the material basis of consciousness. In contrast, Chalmers believes that explaining in scientific terms the subjective sense we all have as human individuals of being us, with all that implies in terms of our specific responses to, say, a sunset or work of art, the particular way we felt when we first fell in love, or any highly subjective feeling, is likely to be much more difficult, if not impossible. Chalmers' distinction of a 'hard' problem of consciousness has triggered much debate, primarily among philosophers of mind, but also among some neuroscientists and psychologists. One criticism of Chalmers' proposal is that it is simply an updated version of 17th-century philosopher René Descartes' view that while we should be able to explain some aspects of human behaviour in purely material terms, such as unconscious nervous reflexes, our inner 'soul', being of a supernatural form, will always be impenetrable to scientific enquiry. The philosopher Daniel Dennett is particularly critical of views of the human mind that envisage a little 'homunculus' at its centre, for that then raises the question of who controls the mind of the homunculus, and so on. Instead, Dennett argues for a 'bottom-up' approach, which sees the mind as the product of unconscious, evolved processes that somehow manage to combine to provide the appearance of an individual 'I', yet in reality has no conscious entity at its core, or, for that matter, a specific place in the brain where 'it all comes together'. According to this viewpoint, human consciousness can essentially be thought of as a kind of illusion. This viewpoint has its own critics. For instance, the philosopher Galen Strawson has called the idea that consciousness is an illusion, 'the silliest claim ever made.' Strawson's main objection is linked to Descartes' great insight: 'I think, therefore I am'. Whatever else we might doubt about the reality of the outside world, that feeling we have when we wake in the morning of immediately being aware of ourselves as a unified individual consciousness is surely a key certainty of life that is hard to square with this simply being an illusion. Throughout the rest of this book, we will be looking at the question of whether advances in neuroscience and psychology are beginning to allow us to explain human consciousness in terms of molecular and cellular mechanisms that don't disregard this important feature of our minds or ignore the complexity of subjective feelings.

Because biology is central to human consciousness and because many other species on Earth also have varying forms of consciousness, we will be looking into what we can learn from studies of such species' brains and nervous systems about our own minds. The importance of experimental studies of other species – which include non-human primates and other mammals as well as 'lower' organisms like fruit flies and zebrafish – stems partly from the technical and ethical limits to the type of studies that can be performed in humans. But it is also the case that the relative simplicity of the brains and nervous systems of some species and the varied ways by which they can be genetically manipulated provide ways to understand not only the molecular and cellular basis of other species' brains but also of our own minds.[2]

Despite the importance of animal studies for neuroscience and experimental psychology, another key aspect of the model of consciousness we will be exploring in this book is that, while many of the molecular and cellular mechanisms that underpin human consciousness have similarities to those in other species, there are also fundamental differences between human consciousness and that of such species. In particular, given the fact that the evolution of humans from apes has followed a unique trajectory based on the use of tools, the development of language, and the subsequent enlargement and restructuring of the human brain, a central proposal of this book is that human beings have undergone a 'mind shift' that has transformed our consciousness.

Importantly, we will be exploring the idea that human language – with its framework of abstract symbols linked by grammatical rules – gives our species the unique power of conceptual thought. We are so used to think-ing in concepts as human beings that we can often take this ability for granted, yet it underpins our ability to comprehend the past, present, and future, the ideas of location and distance, ourselves as individuals versus others, and all the other complex ways that we understand the world around us and express this to others.

Another unique aspect of human beings compared to other species which is linked to our twin capacities for language and tool use is that human society evolves with each generation. This has implications for human consciousness because it means that new technologies, for instance the invention of writing or the development of the internet, continually alter over time the ways that human beings can express themselves to others, and this has implications for the way that ideas themselves come into being in our heads.

A key question to address is how language and tool use affect brain function, both in terms of the mechanisms by which the human brain has evolved over millions of years of evolution and through the influence of social interaction on the brain during its development in each individual as they progress from birth through childhood to adulthood. Here though, we face a challenge due to the difficulties involved in studying brain func-tion and the molecular and cellular mechanisms underlying this in a living human being.

In this book, we will be looking at some of the ways that modern neuroscience is tackling this challenge, ranging from molecular and cel-lular analysis of human brain tissue from deceased people who have donated their bodies to science, to electrophysiological analysis of neurons in living individuals undergoing brain surgery, to non-invasive brain imag-ing of human patients and volunteers. But it also means that in addition to insights from neuroscience, we will be looking at those from psychology and philosophy of mind to help us understand human consciousness and what makes it different from that of other species.

We will also discuss mental disorders, both with a view to finding bet-ter ways to diagnose and treat such disorders and because understanding their biological as well as their social basis may help us better understand the material basis of human consciousness as a whole.

As part of this discussion, we will look at the view that some human conditions that are labelled as 'disorders' and have been primarily viewed in a negative way – such as autism spectrum disorder (ASD) or attention deficit/hyperactivity disorder (ADHD) – also have positive aspects.[3]

This new viewpoint is part of a broader reconsideration that rejects the idea of the 'normal' versus 'defective' mind and instead stresses the importance of neurodiversity when assessing mental conditions defined previously primarily as disorders.

In fact, this viewpoint is not without its own problems, given that some forms of ASD can be seriously debilitating, and it also raises the question of whether it is even justified to group different conditions as ASD if they are so different in severity and may have different biological roots. A fundamental problem here might be that labelling mental conditions in such a broad way may be blurring differences between conditions that could be quite different in character and genesis, despite having overlapping symptoms. Indeed, this may be true not only of ASD and ADHD but also of some psychiatric and personality disorders.

For this reason, not only could a more case-by-case approach to diagnosing mental conditions be fruitful, but so could one that seeks to relate this to biomarkers that may reveal important clues about the biological roots of a specific condition in a particular individual. Importantly, there is increasing recognition that many mental conditions may have their roots in changes in the brain that occurred long before symptoms become apparent. This is true not only of conditions with an obvious biological link but also of ones where the environment is clearly a major factor in the genesis of the condition. This raises the question of how much is due to nature and how much to nurture. In fact, we will be challenging the validity of trying to separate the influence of biology and environment in this way. Instead, by assimilating insights from new fields of research such as epigenetics, we will look at how even the genome is not a fixed entity but open to environmental influence.

In the final part of this book, we will be looking at what lies ahead in the future. We will look at the effectiveness and safety of the various types of drugs that have been developed to treat psychiatric disorders, such as clinical depression, schizophrenia, and bipolar disorder. We will also compare the relative merits of drugs compared to different types of psychotherapy and ask what might be done to improve treatment of these disorders by these twin routes.

Modern neuroscience has created a bewildering array of novel ways to study the brain, ranging from a variety of sophisticated imaging methods to diverse ways to edit the genomes of brain cells to optogenetics – a method for activating or inhibiting neurons with light. While currently employed mainly for research purposes, we will look at the question of whether some of these technologies might one day be used for therapeutic purposes.[4]

Another rapidly changing area of human endeavour is computer technology. A very topical debate at the moment is whether the so-called 'artificial intelligence', that is, computer programs, are on the verge of attaining a form of consciousness that matches and later surpasses that of human beings, with potentially life-changing, and possibly even life-threatening, consequences for our species. We will look at this question by comparing the workings of a computer with those of the brain.

A linked question is whether mechanical and computer implants might one day be used to enhance human perception and consciousness. In fact, such implants are already beginning to change the lives of people who were born deaf and blind or who developed loss of sight or hearing later in their lives. We will look at how not only new technologies but also a better understanding of perception by the human brain is enabling progress in this area. We will also discuss whether the use of such approaches to treat disabilities might, one day, lead further to attempts to artificially enhance the potential of human consciousness.

Before we do any of this though, we need to define what we mean by human consciousness, and to do so, it is time to look at the origins of consciousness by studying how it arose from the lifeforms that first evolved on Earth over four billion years ago. For any discussion of human consciousness that seeks to explain it as a material phenomenon occurring in an organic structure, the brain, needs to be aware of the origins of that brain. And if we also want to include in such awareness the detailed molecular and cellular components of this organ, we need to go surprisingly far back to the origins of life itself.

Chapter 1

Cells and Organelles

Key Concepts

- Channels, pumps, and proteins called receptors, which detect 'signals' from the environment, first evolved in unicellular bacteria, but they play key roles in the human body, including the functions of the human brain and nervous system.
- G-protein-coupled receptors (GPCRs) are a particularly important class of receptors involved in a variety of bodily functions, including all the main sensory processes. Our sense of smell is mediated by odorant receptors, which are GPCRs.
- Neurotransmitters are released at neuronal synapses, and they can either excite or inhibit neurons. An important excitatory neurotransmitter is glutamate, while an important inhibitory one is gamma aminobutyric acid (GABA).

Life first arose on our planet about four billion years ago. We can only speculate about how exactly it did so. What we do know is that the first lifeforms had a number of challenges to overcome to become distinguished from the non-material world around them.

A major initial challenge was for lifeforms to separate themselves spatially and energetically from the non-material world. The second law of thermodynamics states that entropy, the measure of disorder in a system, will tend to increase over time. In contrast, a central feature of lifeforms is that they are ordered systems amidst the disorder of the non-material world, at least until death occurs and disorder rapidly sets in.

To maintain their ordered state, a crucial step in the development of the first single-celled lifeforms was the evolution of a cell membrane, a structure that could protect the cell from its environment.[5]

One illustration of the unity of life is that lifeforms ranging from single-celled bacteria to multicellular organisms, such as a human being, all have the same type of membrane surrounding their cells, namely a double-layered structure called a phospholipid bilayer.[6] This protects the cell from injury and prevents its contents from dispersing. However, it also creates a potential problem in that a central way the cell maintains its ordered state amidst the disorder around it is by maintaining a more energetic and structured state than its surroundings. To maintain its internal order, the cell, on the one hand, needs to take in nutrients to be used for generating both energy and the building blocks of life, and, on the other hand, it needs to expel waste and toxic products.

To some extent, the phospholipid bilayer allows this. For instance, small uncharged molecules like oxygen, carbon dioxide, and water can cross the bilayer, as can fatty molecules like steroids, but large, uncharged molecules like glucose cannot, nor can charged molecules. For this reason, early during the evolution of lifeforms, the cell membrane began to acquire protein molecules that could act as channels or pumps. While channels allow large molecules, including charged ones, to enter or exit the cell in a passive fashion along their concentration gradient, pumps make it possible for the cell to either sequester a useful substance within itself or completely eliminate from the cell an unwanted one.

Unwanted cellular substances include not only waste products from the cell's activity but also toxins that may be present in the environment, such as antibiotics. Talking about antibiotics in the context of a discussion about the origins of life may sound odd given that we tend to think of antibiotics as artificial chemical substances used in medicine to treat infections. In fact, many antibiotics, including a well-known one, penicillin, occur naturally because they are produced by lifeforms in order to harm and destroy competing species. Exactly when this 'red in tooth and claw' aspect of nature first emerged during the evolution of life is unclear, but we can assume that it was rapidly followed by bacterial species not only developing their own weapons to attack their foes but also finding ways to nullify the latter's weapons, and pumps formed part of this.[7]

Channels and pumps are not the only proteins on the surface of the cell. Other types of proteins, called receptors, can detect 'signals' from the environment. One of the very first types of receptors to evolve was a 'photoreceptor' called rhodopsin.[8] This protein made it possible for bacteria to not only detect light but also harness its energy. Rhodopsin is a channel that opens when it senses light, allowing charged atoms, also known as ions, into the cell. This movement of ions can then be linked to processes that generate energy.

Prior to the evolution of rhodopsin, bacteria relied for their energy needs on the breakdown of organic substances, as well as energy from heat. But rhodopsin made it possible for them to begin to extract energy from light photons. This allowed lifeforms to tap for the first time the almost limitless energy from the sun. As such, it was one of the major steps in evolution that led to life thriving everywhere on the planet, even in the most inhospitable places on Earth.

While the controlled transport of substances into and out of the cell is a central part of life, we should not neglect what happens within the cell interior. Of key importance here is what is known as metabolism.[9] This is divided into catabolism, the controlled breakdown of complex organic molecules into simpler ones to generate energy and building blocks for cell activities, and anabolism, which uses energy to transform those building blocks into substances that can be used as future energy sources and also the structures of the cell.

Metabolism is performed by enzymes, the proteins that catalyse chemical reactions. In both anabolism and catabolism, the three key substances are carbohydrates, fats, and proteins, which explains why we learn at school that these are the basis of a healthy diet.

You may be wondering at this point what any of this has to do with consciousness, or even with brain function. So, it is now time to reveal some interesting connections that exist between the channels, pumps, receptors, and metabolic processes that first evolved in bacteria and brain function in more complex species, including that in humans.

Take rhodopsin. We have seen how the appearance of this protein allowed life for the first time to directly harness light as a practically unlimited source of energy. As such, it allowed bacteria to colonise almost every environment on Earth. This in turn led to the evolution of plants, which use a different type of light-sensitive protein, chlorophyll, to harness the energy of light, but the principle is the same. However, bacterial rhodopsin also evolved into a variant form that is the main light-sensitive receptor in our eye.

Even more surprising than these connections between different light-sensitive proteins is that bacterial rhodopsin is the direct ancestor of many receptor proteins that play vital roles in cell signalling in humans, including the signalling mechanisms that regulate the brain, the sensory structures that provide inputs to it, and the other organs it controls.

One of the ways that rhodopsin evolved into a much greater diversity of forms was to switch from light-sensing to detection of chemicals while retaining its basic function of acting as a channel for ions. Such proteins are called ionotropic receptors to signify that the flow of ions through them triggers some activity within the cell.

A big difference compared to the original bacterial rhodopsin is that the ionotropic receptors that play diverse roles in the human body not only each respond to a different activating chemical but also act as channels for various different ions. An example of an ionotropic receptor is the nicotinic acetylcholine receptor, which is activated by the neurotransmitter acetylcholine and plays a particularly important role in the stimulation of muscles by nerves (Fig. 1.1).[10]

The second way that bacterial rhodopsin evolved into receptor proteins that play central roles in the human body was to lose its character as an ion channel and evolve to become activators of diverse metabolic processes that involve an enzyme reaction. Such proteins are known as metabotropic receptors to reflect this characteristic.

Among the main types of metabotropic receptors are the G-protein-coupled receptors (GPCRs; Fig. 1.2).[11] These get their name from the fact that they activate a type of protein called a G-protein, which acts like a kind of molecular on/off switch that can regulate a variety of enzymes whose identity depends on the specific type of GPCR that is their activator.

An illustration of how important GPCRs are in terms of bodily function is that around half of all clinically used drugs target them. This reflects the fact that GPCRs regulate sensory processes in the body as diverse as taste, smell, vision, and pain. GPCRs also play important roles in organs, including the heart, lungs and brain, and in cell recognition processes, hormone secretion, and immunity.

One class of GPCRs relevant to cognition are the adrenergic receptors, which respond to the hormone adrenaline and the neurotransmitter noradrenaline and play roles in the brain.

Each receptor in the brain and the rest of the nervous system is activated by a specific neurotransmitter. These can either excite or inhibit neurons. An important excitatory neurotransmitter is glutamate, while an important inhibitory one is gamma aminobutyric acid (GABA).[12] In the

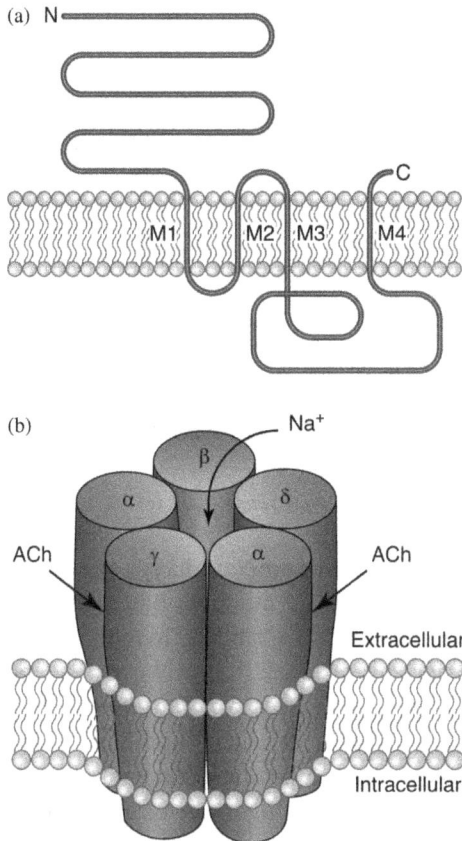

Fig. 1.1. Structure of nicotinic acetylcholine receptor (nAChR). (a) Threading pattern of receptor subunits through membrane. (b) Schematic representation of 3D structure, showing arrangement of subunits, location of two acetylcholine (ACh)-binding sites, and cation-conducting channel.

Source: Reproduced from Karlin, A. (2002) *Nature Reviews Neuroscience*, 3:102–114, with permission.

brain, it is vital to maintain a balance between excitation and inhibition, for too much excitation can stress and even kill neurons by over-stimulation, but too much inhibition can lead to sedation and even death by shutting down brain function.

A sign of how important it is for normal brain function to maintain a balance in the actions of glutamate versus GABA is shown by what happens when the concentrations of these chemicals are altered by disease

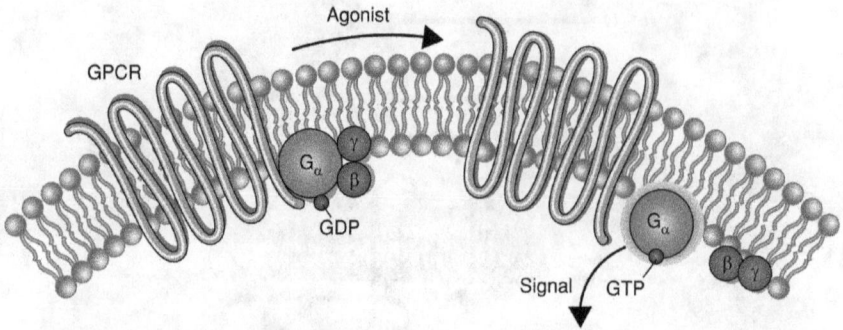

Fig. 1.2. Activation of Gα subunit of a G-protein-coupled receptor. Upon receptor stimulation by a ligand called an agonist, the state of the receptor changes. Gα dissociates from the receptor and Gβγ, and GTP is exchanged for the bound GDP, which leads to Gα activation.

Source: Reproduced from Li, J. *et al.* (2002) *Nature*, 420:716–717, with permission.

or drugs. For instance, when someone has a stroke, the dying neurons resulting from this release huge amounts of glutamate, which will then overexcite other neurons, and this can lead to their death. This may greatly exacerbate the adverse effects of the stroke on the brain. Meanwhile, drugs like alcohol or gamma hydroxybutyrate (GHB), which act on GABA receptors, can cause so much inhibition if taken in excessive amounts that this may lead to unconsciousness and even death.

Given the central, and opposing, roles of glutamate and GABA in the brain, it is interesting that GABA is a metabolic by-product of glutamate. Not only that, but glutamate is also an amino acid and, as such, a subunit of proteins and important in the metabolism of proteins in the body. GABA is far from the only neurotransmitter derived from amino acids. Other examples are adrenaline, noradrenaline, dopamine, and serotonin, whose actions in the brain we will look at later in this book.

What all this demonstrates is that many types of receptors, as well as some of the key neurotransmitters that mediate brain function, are descendants of proteins and metabolites that originated in simple bacteria. This shows that although we think of consciousness as specific to complex organisms and, in its highest form, only present in humans, its material components stem from the very origins of life itself.

Despite these real material links between simple lifeforms like bacteria and more complex ones like humans, major differences between lifeforms began to develop during our ancestors' evolution into the first multicellular organisms, and these changes are highly relevant to both understanding how the human brain works and human consciousness.

Sometimes adversity can generate opportunities that prove transformative. This has definitely been the case during the evolution of life on Earth. We have seen how the evolution of rhodopsin played a crucial role in evolution, for it allowed unicellular organisms for the first time to harness the energy of light. This in turn led to the development of photosynthesis.[13] This process uses light's energy to rearrange atoms in carbon dioxide and water to make oxygen and sugar molecules. The effect of this sugar rush was to allow photosynthetic bacteria to spread across the planet. However, as the oxygen generated by such lifeforms increased in concentration, it created a problem.

Being aerobic lifeforms, it is natural that we humans tend to see oxygen in a positive light. However, when it first appeared in large amounts on Earth, oxygen posed a challenge. Because of its tendency to form reactive free radicals that can degrade proteins and other cell structures, oxygen can be a very toxic substance. Indeed, there is evidence that the global rise in oxygen levels led to the extinction of many of the first bacterial species. Those that survived did so by finding ways to counter the toxic effects of oxygen.[14]

One strategy was to move to habitats where there was no oxygen, such as deep underground. Another strategy involved finding a way to detoxify oxygen by metabolising it. In all multicellular organisms, including humans, the majority of energy is generated by structures called mitochondria. We now believe that mitochondria were originally free-living bacteria that became incorporated into other bacteria to form a bigger unicellular lifeform (Fig. 1.3).[15]

From that point on, the two lifeforms existed symbiotically, with the proto-mitochondrion gaining protection, and the larger cell first using the mitochondrion to detoxify oxygen by converting it into water and this process then eventually being adapted to link it to energy production. The vast majority of energy in the human body is produced in mitochondria, as demonstrated by the effects of a fatal dose of cyanide, which blocks the end stage of this process and immediately ends life.

Although mitochondria were originally free living, we now refer to them as organelles to make it clear that they are subcellular structures within another cell. In addition, our cells have many other types of organelles.[16] These include the endoplasmic reticulum, in which proteins destined for the cell surface or secretion from the cell are produced. The Golgi apparatus,

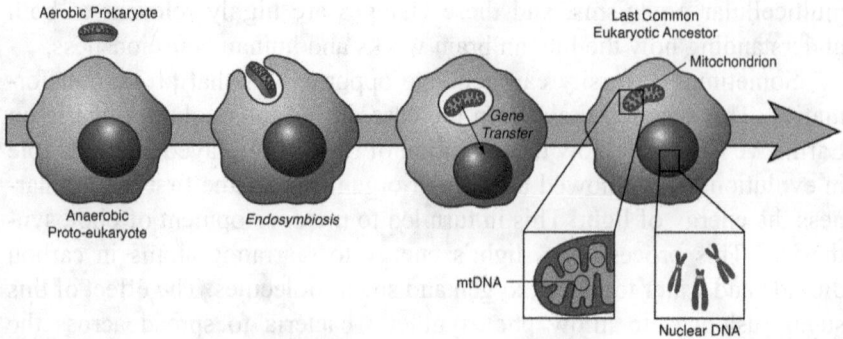

Fig. 1.3. The universally accepted theory of mitochondrial origins posits that the anaerobic proto-eukaryote engulfed the aerobic prokaryote. The acquisition of the mitochondria resulted in the last common eukaryotic ancestor, from which all current eukaryotes evolved.

Source: Reproduced from Read, A.D. *et al.* (2021) *Redox Biology*, 47:102164, with permission.

named after the Italian scientist who discovered it, is where proteins are sorted before being distributed to different cell regions. Lysosomes are often referred to as the 'dustbin' of the cell because unwanted cellular components are destroyed in them, but they also play important roles in sensing nutrient levels in the cell.

Then, there is the nucleus. Cellular lifeforms are defined as either prokaryotes or eukaryotes, the latter term meaning a type of lifeform with a cell nucleus and the former a lifeform without a nucleus. However, eukaryotic cells also contain all the other organelles mentioned above. While all prokaryotic lifeforms are unicellular bacteria, eukaryotic lifeforms can also be unicellular, yeast being an example. But all multicellular organisms, which of course includes humans, are eukaryotic.

There is a good reason for this. A multicellular organism requires huge amounts of energy to power its existence, and only mitochondria can provide this. Similarly, the other organelles all introduce a complexity into cellular function that is vital for multicellular lifeforms. This is because a major challenge for such organisms is that they must not only regulate the activities of each individual cell in the body but also coordinate interactions between cells in the organism.

While this is true of the human body as a whole, it is a particularly important issue for the brain, the most complex entity in our bodies and indeed in the known Universe. Later in this book, we will look at how different organelles can play important and distinctive roles in different aspects of brain function. But first, it is time to focus on the role of one particular organelle, the nucleus, in such a function.

In particular, let us now focus on a primary function of the nucleus, the storage of genetic information. Importantly, far from being a static 'blueprint', the genome within each brain cell is a dynamic entity that is highly responsive to changes in the cell's own internal environment, that of the brain as a whole, and to the body and its surroundings.

So, with that in mind, let us now look at genomes, the genes of which they are composed, and how this is relevant to human brain biology and function and to human consciousness.

Quiz

Which of the following is an ionotropic receptor?
A. Oestrogen receptor
B. Beta adrenergic receptor
C. Nicotinic acetylcholine receptor
D. Insulin receptor

Around how many odorant receptors are present in the human genome?
A. 10
B. 100
C. 1,000
D. 10,000

Which of these neurotransmitters is inhibitory?
A. Glutamate
B. GABA
C. Histamine
D. Aspartate

Chapter 2

Genes and Genomes

Key Concepts

- DNA works as a sort of code of life. First, the DNA base sequence is converted into messenger RNA (mRNA) by the process of transcription. The mRNA then serves as a template for the production of proteins.
- Extensive regions of the non-protein genome are devoted to the production of RNA species that are not destined to be translated into proteins, as is the case for mRNA, but which instead play important roles in the control of gene expression.
- Different mRNAs can be produced from a gene by alternative splicing. At synapses, different types of neuronal stimulation can generate different spliced mRNAs and thus different proteins, which introduces flexibility into neuronal circuits.

All species on Earth, from the simplest virus to a complex multicellular organism, such as a human being, share one thing in common, and that is their possession of a nucleic acid genome. While genomes are generally composed of DNA, some viruses, such as HIV, the influenza virus, or SARS-CoV-2, have an RNA genome. DNA is a polymer composed of a sugar phosphate backbone and four bases, adenine, cytosine, guanine, and thymine, generally abbreviated to A, C, G, and T, respectively. DNA has two strands, which together form the famous double-helix structure, within which the bases point inwards, A paired with T, and C with G.

This pairing lies at the heart of life on Earth, as when the two strands separate during DNA replication, a mirror image of each is produced by base pairing, thus propagating a replica double helix in each daughter cell.[17] DNA also works as a sort of code of life (Fig. 2.1). First, the DNA base sequence is converted into messenger RNA (mRNA) by the process of transcription. Unlike DNA, RNA usually occurs as a single strand.

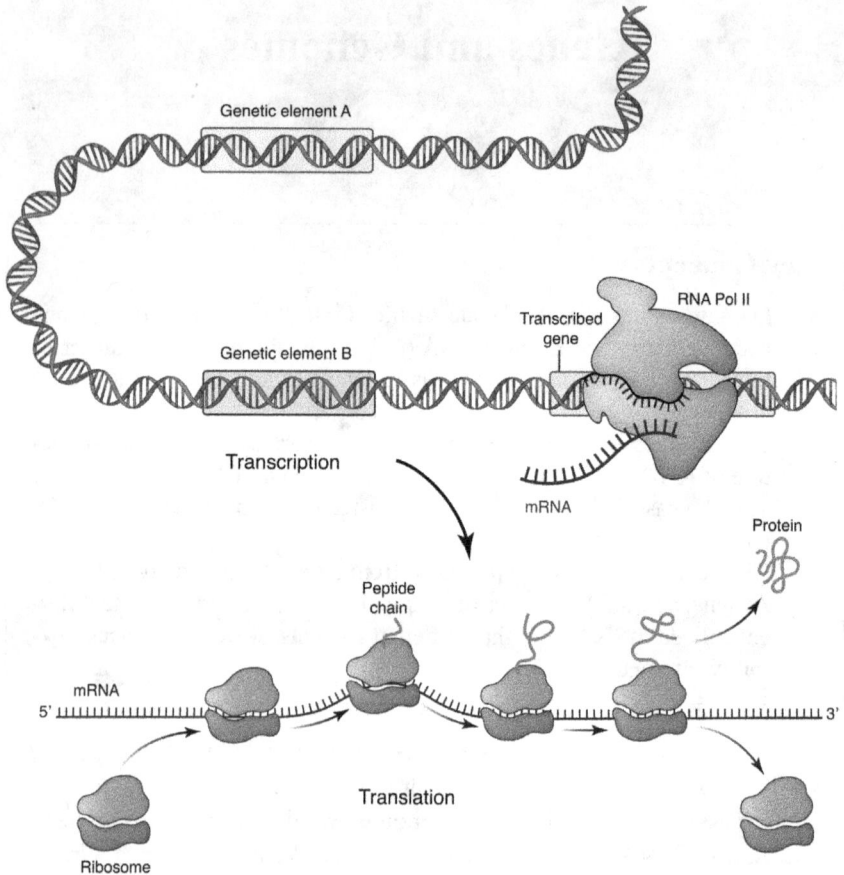

Fig. 2.1. Diagram illustrating the process of transcription, translation, and gene expression depicting how genes encode the instructions for constructing proteins, which in turn control the expression of characteristics and biological activities. It shows the transfer of genetic information from DNA to RNA to protein.

Source: Reproduced from Hameed, H. *et al.* (2024) *Functional and Integrative Genomics*, 24:177, with permission.

Another difference is that uracil (U) replaces thymine. The mRNA then serves as a template for producing proteins. The way this works is that each three bases of the RNA codes for an amino acid, the building blocks of proteins, through the process of translation. For instance, the sequence AUG.AUC.UCG codes for the amino acid sequence Met.Ile.Ser. The translation of the mRNA nucleic acid code into proteins occurs on a subcellular structure called the ribosome.

While this is the basic process of gene expression in both prokaryotes and eukaryotes, there are important differences between these two types of lifeforms. Such differences are partly due to eukaryotic cells possessing a nucleus. To illustrate what is similar and what is different about gene expression in these two classes of lifeforms, let us look in more detail at this process, from DNA to RNA to protein.

Gene expression is initiated when a protein called RNA polymerase binds to a gene's transcription initiation site. This only occurs when proteins named transcription factors bind to DNA regulatory regions associated with the gene. The most basic regulatory region occurs near the start of a gene and is known as the promoter.

In bacteria, transcription factors are divided into activator and repressor proteins, and as their names imply, they have a positive or negative effect, respectively, on the activity of the RNA polymerase and therefore on the gene whose expression they control. In many ways, the situation in eukaryotic cells is very similar. Thus, in eukaryotes, expression of any particular gene is also controlled by both activator and repressor proteins. However, while in prokaryotes the promoter is tightly associated with the gene that it controls, the situation is quite different in eukaryotes.

Box 2.1.   The Genome and ENCODE Projects

The initial findings of the ENCODE project – an acronym for Encyclopaedia of DNA Elements – which were first published in 2012, were the culmination of almost a decade's research involving 442 scientists from 32 institutions and costing $288 million. While the original Human Genome Project provided the sequence of letters that make up the DNA code, ENCODE appeared to have gone substantially further and told us what all these different letters actually do. Perhaps most exciting was its claim to have solved a major conundrum in biology, namely the fact that protein-coding genes make up only two percent of our DNA, with the other 98 percent having been written off by many as 'junk'. By scanning the whole genome rather than only the genes, ENCODE researchers came to the startling conclusion that, far from being junk, as much as 80 percent of these disregarded parts of the genome were biochemically active. Indeed, for ENCODE researcher Ewan Birney, this was probably an underestimate, since it was 'likely that 80 percent will go to 100 percent. We don't really have any large chunks of redundant DNA.' Perhaps most excitingly, the findings were claimed to cast important new light on the underlying basis of common diseases, such as heart disease, diabetes, and mental disorders like schizophrenia. Not everyone was enamoured with the claims. Dan Graur argued that the researchers had confused activity with functionality, saying that 'just because a piece of DNA has biological activity does not mean it has an important function in a cell.' In contrast, John Mattick argued that the ENCODE claims were, if anything, too conservative and that the findings show 'we have misunderstood the nature of genetic programming for the past 50 years.' The debate about the exact proportion of the genome that is functional should not obscure the importance of a more general shift taking place in our perception of the genome and how it regulates cellular and bodily processes. So, there is increasing recognition that, far from simply being a linear code, the genome only really makes sense as a 3D entity that dynamically changes in response to signals originating both from within and outside the cell. Another new development is the recognition that RNA, DNA's chemical cousin, is far more important than previously thought. In addition, new evidence shows that far from being a fixed DNA 'blueprint', the genome is exquisitely sensitive to signals from the environment, challenging the idea that life is merely a one-way flow of information from DNA to organism.

Eukaryotic genes also typically have a promoter that is close to the gene, which binds 'basal' transcription factors, but in addition they have regulatory regions named enhancers or silencers that can be quite distant from the gene they control.

As the names imply, enhancers bind activator transcription factors, and silencers bind repressor ones. When these regulatory regions were first discovered, at first it was a mystery how they could control the expression of genes that they were so far distant from. However, we now know that the genome within the nucleus of a eukaryotic cell has a complex 3D shape in which regulatory regions that are distant in terms of linear DNA sequence from the genes they control may be quite close in terms of the 3D genome.[18]

Another difference between prokaryotic and eukaryotic genomes is that while in prokaryotes genes are controlled by just a few transcription factors, in eukaryotes each gene can be controlled by many such factors. For instance, the approximately 20,000 protein-coding genes in the human genome are controlled by around four million regulatory regions.

Perhaps one of the most surprising discoveries about the human genome is that less than two percent of it is composed of genes as traditionally defined, that is, sequences of DNA coding for proteins. Part of the remaining genome is made up of regulatory regions of the sort mentioned above, which bind transcription factors and regulate transcription. It is also becoming clear that extensive regions of the non-protein genome are devoted to the production of RNA species that are not destined to be translated into proteins, as is the case for mRNA, but which instead play important roles in the control of gene expression.[19]

The presence of a nucleus in eukaryotic cells is associated with fundamental differences in gene expression in such cells compared to prokaryotic cells. In prokaryotes, as soon as an mRNA transcript begins to form, it can act as a template for protein production. However, in eukaryotes, the mRNA can only be translated once it has left the nucleus, as the ribosomes that carry out translation reside in the cytoplasm.

Because transport out of the nucleus occurs through structures known as nuclear pores, this process is tightly regulated. Conversely, the protein transcription factors generated in the cytoplasm must enter the nucleus to affect gene expression. A common way for transcription factors to become activated is via some change that allows them to enter the nucleus from the cytoplasm. In both eukaryotes and prokaryotes, transcription factors generally need to be modified to become active.

Such modifications are mediated by signalling pathways that are triggered in response to changes in the cell's environment. An example from the human body is the response triggered by the hormone adrenaline in the liver. Adrenaline is produced by the adrenal gland as part of the fright, flight, or fight response. Binding of adrenaline to beta adrenergic receptor proteins on the surface of cells of organs and tissues, including the heart and liver, activates the enzyme adenylyl cyclase, which produces the cellular messenger cyclic AMP (cAMP).[20]

cAMP can next activate protein kinase A (PKA). PKA adds a phosphate group to the transcription factor cAMP-response element-binding protein (CREB), activating it (Fig. 2.2).

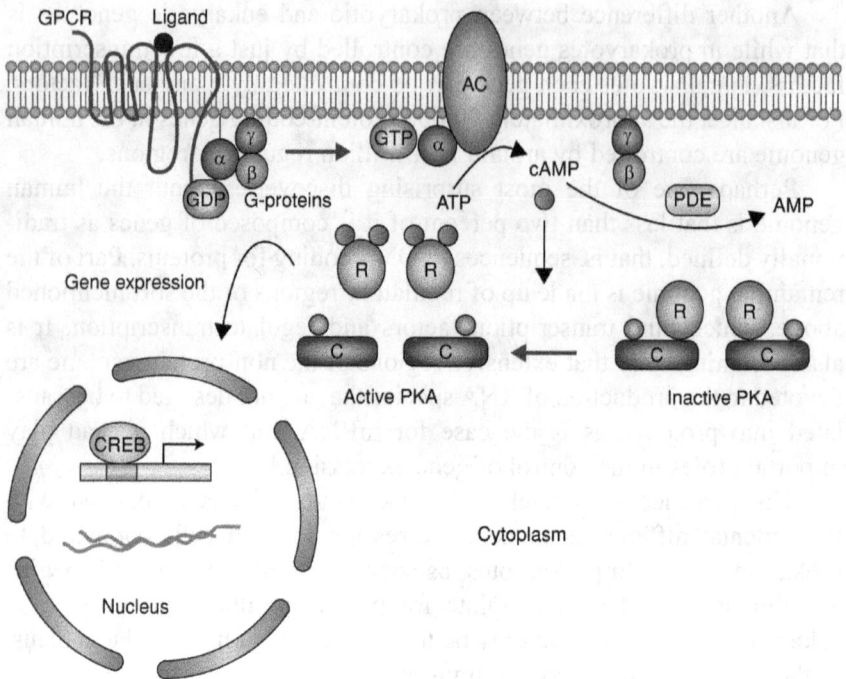

Fig. 2.2. Gsα subunit (G-protein) activates adenylyl cyclase (AC), generating cAMP. Elevated cAMP levels, regulated by PDEs, then activate protein kinase A (PKA). PKA phosphorylates several enzymes and transcription factors downstream (e.g. cAMP-response element-binding protein, CREB).

Source: Reproduced from Hannah-Shmouni, F. *et al.* (2016) *Frontiers in Endocrinology*, 7:111, with permission.

CREB then travels to the nucleus and activates genes involved in the fright, flight, or fight response; it also plays important roles in memory, as we will see later.[21]

Another major difference between prokaryotes and eukaryotes is the way mRNA is produced in the two types of lifeforms. In prokaryotes, the mRNA sequence is a direct copy of the DNA sequence of the gene. The expectation was that this would also be the case for eukaryotes. However, initial comparisons of genes from a variety of complex multicellular organisms, including humans, with the mRNAs coded by such genes, revealed that the mRNA sequence is far shorter than the DNA sequence of the gene. Further studies showed that this apparent contradiction is due to a process called splicing.

Initially, the RNA transcript generated in the nucleus is the same length as the gene's DNA sequence. What happens subsequently is that large sections of the RNA sequence, known as introns, are removed and discarded, leaving only the exons, the protein-coding sequence. At first glance, splicing might seem very wasteful. It does however have an important feature, which is that different exons can be either included in or excluded from the final mRNA sequence.[22] Such alternative splicing means that a single gene can give rise to many different mRNAs and, therefore, proteins that have distinct and sometimes even antagonistic functions, altered stability, or a different subcellular location.

Each mRNA acts as a template for producing proteins through the process of translation, which occurs on ribosomes in the cytoplasm. The ribosome is a complex structure in which ribosomal proteins and RNAs play equally important roles. As we have seen, proteins are assembled from amino acids. The latter are transported to the ribosome by transfer RNAs (tRNAs). Translation can be regulated in various ways. A particularly important recent discovery is that various types of non-protein-coding RNAs play key roles in regulating translation (Fig. 2.3).[23]

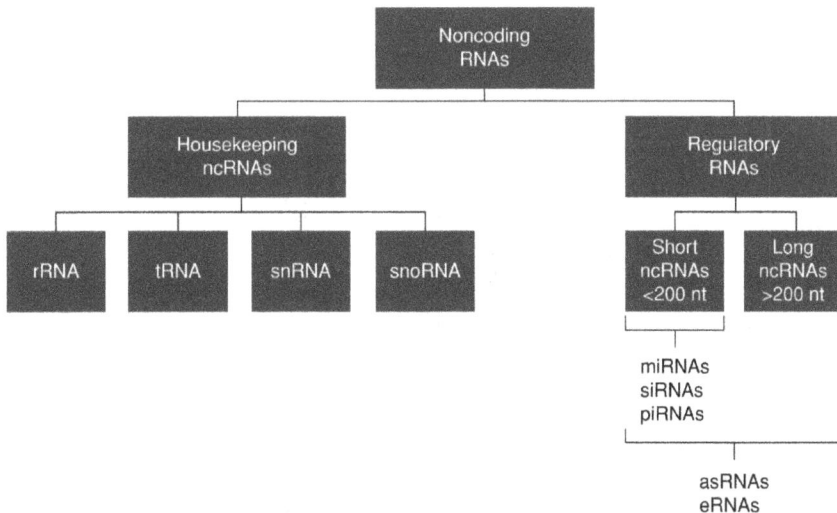

Fig. 2.3. Non-coding RNAs (ncRNAs). Housekeeping ncRNAs include ribosomal (rRNA), transfer (tRNA), small nuclear (snRNA), and small nucleolar RNAs (snoRNAs). Regulatory non-coding RNAs can be short (<200 nucleotides) or long (>200 nucleotides) ncRNAs and include microRNAs (miRNAs), small interfering RNAs (siRNAs), Piwi-associated RNAs (piRNAs), antisense RNAs (asRNAs), and enhancer RNAs (eRNAs).

Source: Reproduced from Losko, M. *et al.* (2016) *Mediators of Inflammation*, 2016:1–12, with permission.

Small interfering RNAs (siRNAs) inhibit translation by destroying the mRNAs they target, rendering them incapable of being translated. Micro RNAs (miRNAs) work differently: by binding to the ends of mRNAs, they prevent translation but in a reversible manner. This is far from the only way that regulatory RNAs regulate gene expression. Another type, named long non-coding RNA (lncRNA), helps to maintain and modify the 3D genome structure mentioned earlier. One important aspect of the varied roles played by regulatory RNAs is that such RNAs not only act outside the nucleus but can also be secreted from cells and travel to other cells in molecular containers called extracellular vesicles (EVs), one important type being known as exosomes (Fig. 2.4).[24]

This means that regulation of gene expression can operate not only outside the nucleus but also outside the cell. Transcription factors and regulatory RNAs control gene expression in different ways. In fact, there are multiple additional mechanisms.

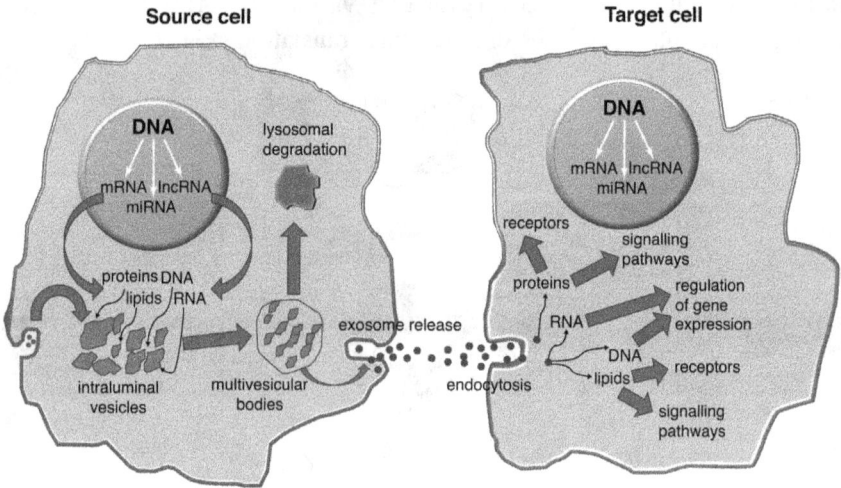

Fig. 2.4. Exosomes form during invagination of the endocytic membrane, resulting in the formation of cytoplasmic vesicles. Nucleic acids, proteins, and lipids are subsequently incorporated into such vesicles. Exosomal cargoes from the source cell can be delivered to target cells, resulting in modulation of target cell signalling, gene expression, and immune response.

Source: Reproduced from Narang, P. *et al.* (2022) *Non-coding RNA Research*, 7:7–15, with permission.

Addition of a methyl group to DNA affects its accessibility to transcription factors. Meanwhile, the 3D structure of the genome is also a key factor in determining which genes are turned on or off within a particular cell. A distinctive feature of eukaryotic cells is that the genomic DNA is associated with proteins called histones.

This association plays a crucial role in how the genome is packaged within the eukaryotic cell. But histones do far more than merely package the DNA. Chemical modifications to these proteins, for instance the addition of acetyl, methyl, or phosphate groups, affect the expression of the genes associated with such modified histones.

Importantly, the activities of transcription factors, regulatory RNAs, DNA methylation, and histone modification enzymes are all highly sensitive to the effects of signalling pathways mediated by receptors on the surface of cells and, thereby, to changes in the cellular and bodily environment. Such environmental effects on the genome and the factors that regulate its activities are known collectively as epigenetic mechanisms.[25] They explain why, although different cell types in the body have the same genomic DNA, the genes that they express and therefore their mRNA and protein content are very different.

For instance, cardiac muscle cells will express genes involved in the contraction of the heart, while neurons will express genes involved in the conduction of electrical impulses in the nervous system and brain. Such differences between cell types are primarily a consequence of the developmental genetic programme that occurs during embryogenesis, the process in which the main tissues, organs, and general bodily form are laid out. But the experiences of an individual during their lifetime can also affect their pattern of gene expression. There is also increasing evidence that epigenetic changes occurring in an individual during their lifetime can also, to some extent, be passed on to their descendants.[26]

Having provided this general outline of gene expression, it is now time to look at the relevance of this for brain function and cognition in complex organisms, including humans. As we will be discussing in more detail shortly, the two main types of cells in the brain are neurons and glial cells. A major step forward in our understanding of brain function was the recognition that neurons are linked together in electrical circuits. This has led to attempts to model brain function, and ultimately consciousness, through artificial computer 'neural networks', in ways that we will explore in more detail later.[27] An assumption underlying such networks is that neurons can be treated as simple on/off switches. But the presence of a complex genome makes each neuron far more than such a binary switch. For instance, the presence of a genome means that each neuron is able to change in terms of its protein components based on the signals that it receives from other neurons, and it does this in ways that are proving to be far more complex even than had been supposed.

As discussed earlier, the phenomenon of alternative splicing means that many different proteins with quite distinct, even opposing, functions can be produced from the same gene. At synapses, different types of neuronal stimulation can generate different alternatively spliced mRNAs and thus different proteins, which introduces functional flexibility into neuronal circuits.[28] This is just one way that this process is important in the brain, and it is a feature of this organ that alternative splicing occurs here much more than in other parts of the body.

A traditional view of gene expression is that the nucleus acts like a kind of cellular command centre via its control of the gene expression process. To some extent, this is true in that signals received by the cell activate the transcription of specific genes in the nucleus, which are then used to produce mRNAs that act as the template for protein production in the cytoplasm. Yet, we have seen that different types of regulatory RNAs act at the point of translation. This has particularly important implications for neurons, as these have a very asymmetric shape, which means that translational control of gene expression can considerably vary in different parts of the neuronal cell, as we will explore in more detail shortly.[29]

We will also see that neurons are not the only cells in the brain. Instead, studies show that cells called neuroglia also play key roles in brain function, and these cell types not only undergo their own types of genomic changes but can also reprogramme gene expression in neurons with which they interact via extracellular entities such as EVs.[30]

We will discuss later how these different facets of gene expression affect cognitive processes in the brain. Before we do that though, we need to consider the brain's cellular components, and to do so, let us go back in evolutionary time to consider how the first neuronal circuits came into existence through sensory and motor processes.

Quiz

Which of these transcription factors plays a role in memory?
A. CREB
B. BREC
C. CERB
D. BERC

Which of these regulatory RNAs plays a key role in modifying the 3D genome?
A. miRNA
B. siRNA
C. piRNA
D. lncRNA

Lipid vesicles that transport regulatory RNAs between cells:
A. Endosome
B. Exosome
C. Regulome
D. Transportome

Chapter 3

Neurons and Glia

Key Concepts

- The simplest neuronal circuit involves a sensory neuron that detects changes in the environment, a motor neuron that triggers movements in muscle cells, and an interneuron that connects these two neuronal types together.
- Neurons have a cell body containing the nucleus, an axon, and dendrites. The dendrites receive incoming signals while outgoing signals are propagated along the axon in the form of an electrical impulse known as an action potential.
- A common view of the brain is that it can be seen as akin to an electrical circuit diagram. While this is one aspect of how the brain works, it does not take into account the contributing role of another very important class of cells: the glial cells.

We have seen how the ability to sense changes in the environment was a feature of the very first unicellular lifeforms on Earth. Today, simple bacteria possess a wide variety of receptors on their surface that allow them to detect a wide variety of chemicals and also light, the latter through the protein rhodopsin, which is the basis for many receptor types in humans. It is not enough, though, for a cell to only detect changes in its environment; for it to survive in a potentially hostile world, it must also possess the means to respond to such changes.

Bacteria do this by changing their metabolism and through their cellular movements. If a bacterium that has been metabolising a source of glucose finds itself in an environment in which glucose is absent, but another sugar, lactose, is present, chemical signals switch off genes that metabolise glucose and turn on ones that can utilise lactose.[31] Sometimes, a physical movement is also required, either to move the bacterium towards a source of food or energy or remove it from danger.

Bacteria are able to move using an ingenious type of molecular motor that employs energy derived from metabolism to power the rotation of a propeller-like protein on the surface of the bacterium.[32] Remarkably, this process has been reversed in order to produce energy by the mitochondria in eukaryotic cells. Recall previously we saw how mitochondria are the descendants of free-living bacteria which became sequestered within the prototype eukaryotic cell. With no further need for a propeller to move them from place to place, this molecular structure instead evolved to work in reverse, with its rotation being used to generate energy. This is further confirmation of the unity of life, but it also shows what a creative process evolution can be in completely transforming life's components.

Multicellular organisms faced a new set of challenges both in terms of detecting changes in the environment and in responding to such changes. Unlike unicellular species, whose environment is the space outside their cell membranes, multicellular organisms have both an external and an internal environment. In a human being, the maintenance of an internal environment conducive to life means keeping the internal temperature and ionic composition of the body cavity at a stable level, ensuring a flow of oxygen to the different organs and tissues, and coordinating interactions between those tissues and organs.

A human being, like other organisms, also needs to be aware of their external surroundings and has the means to respond rapidly to changes in those surroundings. The need to monitor the internal as well as the external environment poses a similar challenge for even the simplest multicellular organisms, and a solution to this challenge in prehistory involved the evolution of the first nervous systems.

Jellyfish represent some of the simplest types of multicellular organisms with a nervous system. They have sensory neurons that detect changes in their surroundings, motor neurons that trigger movements in the muscle cells that power the jellyfish's contractile bell, and interneurons that connect these two neuronal types together.[33] This interconnection allows a jellyfish to coordinate its movements in such a way that,

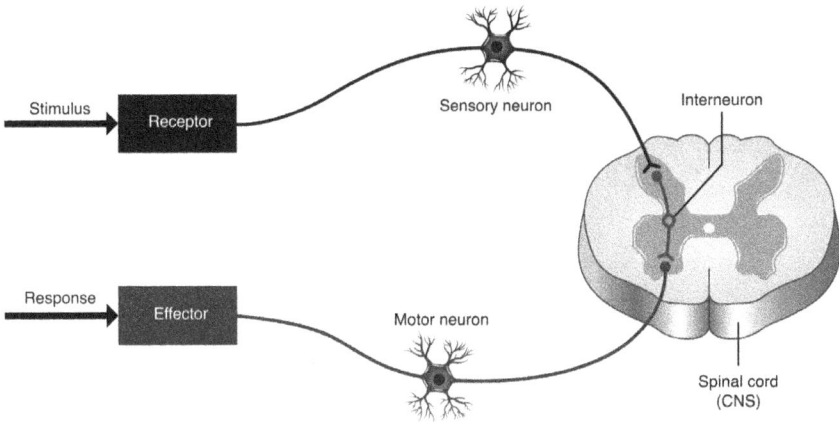

Fig. 3.1. Neuronal reflex arc. It consists of a receptor, a sensory neuron, a reflex centre (spinal cord), a motor neuron, and an effector.

Source: Reproduced from Li, G. *et al.* (2014) *Journal of Bionic Engineering*, 11:389–399, with permission.

for instance, it can swim towards a food source or away from a toxic substance or predator. This simple circuit of sensory neuron/interneuron/ motor neuron is also central to how human beings make a reflex movement in response to a sensory stimulus (Fig. 3.1).

As more complex multicellular organisms began to evolve, the increased complexity of their internal environment and also the increasing sophistication required of them in terms of their behaviour led to an increase not only in the numbers of their sensory and motor neurons but also of their interneurons. As the bodily form evolved, collections of interneurons began to assume the role of coordinators of activities in particular parts of the body. Since much of the sensory apparatus was increasingly concentrated in the head region of the body, this led to a particular concentration of interneurons in this region, and eventually this formed the basis of the first brains.[34] Yet, despite the difference in complexity between a jellyfish and a human nervous system, the neurons of these different lifeforms have the same essential features, and it is these that we will now look at in detail.

Neurons can be found in all shapes and sizes, but they all possess a cell body containing the nucleus, an axon, and dendrites (Fig. 3.2).[35]

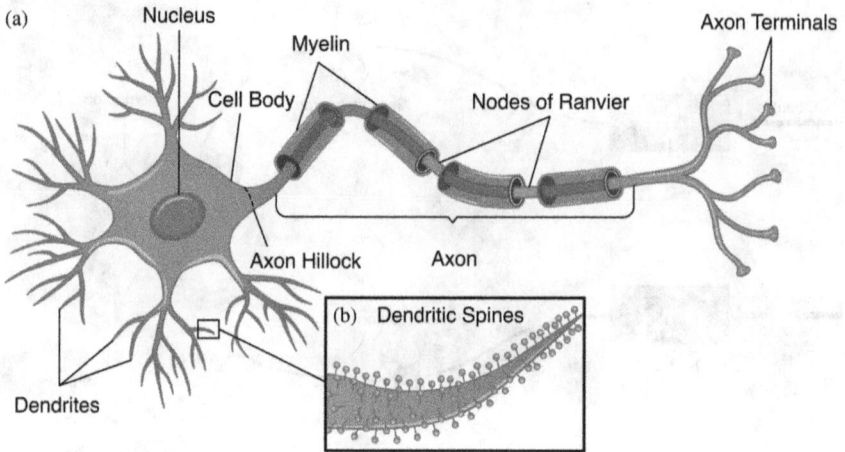

Fig. 3.2. The neuron: the primary cell in the nervous system. (a) General structure of a multipolar neuron containing dendrites, a cell body or soma with a nucleus, the axon hillock, axon, myelin, nodes of Ranvier, and axon terminals. (b) Close-up of dendrite showing structure of dendritic spines.

Source: Reproduced from Prieto, N. and Wroblewski, J. (2022) Neuron, pp. 4655–4659. In: Vonk, J. and Shackelford, T.K. (editors) *Encyclopedia of Animal Cognition and Behavior* (Springer, Cham), with permission.

Box 3.1. The Discovery of the Action Potential

It is a remarkable fact that all of human consciousness, from the most basic thought to the height of artistic creativity, is based on the same phenomenon – electricity – that illuminates a lightbulb or heats an electric oven. This feature of nervous systems, if not brains themselves, was recognised as early as 1780, when Luigi Galvani and his wife, Lucia Galeazzi Galvani, discovered that the muscles of dead frogs' legs twitched when activated by an electrostatic spark. Based on this observation and subsequent experiments, the Galvanis concluded that the motive force in the nervous system was electricity rather than a mystical 'vital force'. A century later, observations of brain tissue under a microscope by Ramon y Cajal, in 1888, suggested how electricity might be transmitted in both the brain and the peripheral nervous system by identifying neurons as the units of transmission and showing that these were linked together in circuits. That still left the question of how neurons transmit electricity. Studies showed that an electrical wave passes along the axon – the action potential – and it was suspected that this was due to changes in the concentration of ions inside the axon. However, the exact details of this ionic change remained a mystery until pioneering experiments by Alan Hodgkin and Andrew Huxley in the 1940s. A major obstacle to directly measuring the ionic changes in a typical neuron was its small size. To get around this obstacle, Hodgkin and Huxley studied the action potential in the giant axon (up to 1 mm in diameter) of the squid. By inserting an electrode into this axon, they were able to measure electrical changes within it during an action potential. They found that the membrane potential of the neuron actually reversed during this event, causing this potential to momentarily become positive. This reversal is the impetus for the generation of the electrical signal underlying the action potential. Importantly, Hodgkin and Huxley also developed an innovative experimental tool that allowed them to determine the contribution of different ions to the change in membrane potential. This device, called a 'voltage clamp', sets the membrane potential of a neuron at a particular voltage and keeps it there. Hodgkin and Huxley used the voltage clamp while also manipulating the concentrations of different ions in the extracellular fluid. In this way, they were able to show that an influx of sodium ions through voltage-gated sodium channels causes a rapid shift in membrane potential, which initiates the action potential. Immediately after this change in membrane potential, however, ion channels open, which allow potassium ions to flow out of the neuron. This helps the membrane potential return to a normal level.

The dendrites receive incoming signals, while outgoing signals are transmitted through the axon. In the human body, axons may be a metre long. Signals are propagated along the axon in the form of electrical activity. This axonal electrical impulse is known as an action potential.[36]

The action potential is a rapid sequence of changes in the voltage across the neuron's outer membrane. The membrane voltage, or potential, is determined at any time by the relative ratio of ions, extracellular to intracellular, and the permeability of each ion.

The rapid rise in potential, depolarisation, is an all-or-nothing event that is initiated by the opening of sodium channels within the neuronal membrane. The subsequent return to resting potential, repolarisation, is mediated by the opening of potassium channels. To re-establish the appropriate balance of ions, a pump (Na/K-ATPase) induces movement of sodium ions out of the cell and that of potassium ions into the cell.

In some neurons the action potential's speed is enhanced by the process of 'myelination'. Myelin is wrapped around the axon apart from at

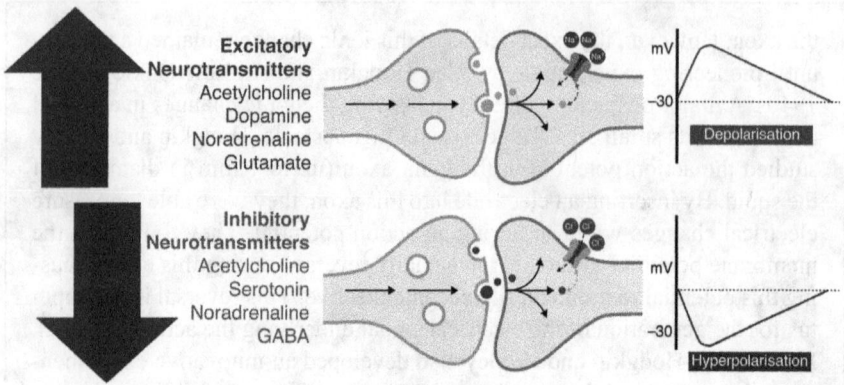

Fig. 3.3. Representation of excitatory and inhibitory synapses. Ionic changes lead to depolarisation or hyperpolarisation in response to excitatory or inhibitory neurotransmitters, respectively.

Source: Reproduced from Chauhan, N. *et al.* (2020) *Process Biochemistry*, 91:241–259, with permission.

regions called nodes of Ranvier. In myelinated neurons, the electrical impulse 'jumps' from one node to the next in a process called saltatory conduction.[37] This greatly speeds up the action potential. Action potentials are triggered within a neuron by inputs entering via the dendrites. Any particular neuron may have hundreds of dendritic inputs. These inputs may be either excitatory or inhibitory (Fig. 3.3). If the inputs are largely excitatory, an action potential will be triggered. But if the inputs are largely inhibitory, they will prevent firing of the action potential. The neuron thus acts like a gauge of incoming influences from other neurons.

Sensory neurons are stimulated by some kind of sensory signal. This may be a chemical, as in taste or smell, or light, sound, or touch; later, we will look at these sensory processes in more detail. For now though, let us consider how a particular scent triggers a response in the human nose. We saw earlier how a class of receptors called GPCRs play particularly important roles in sensory and many other physiological processes in humans. GPCRs are a family of proteins that vary in subtly different ways, and one type of GPCR, called olfactory receptors, mediates the smell response in the nose.[38]

When a molecule of a particular scent binds to its target olfactory receptor, this triggers a signalling pathway that induces an action potential in the olfactory neuron. Other sensory stimuli will trigger electrical impulses in other types of sensory neurons. As we have seen, in a simple organism like a jellyfish, the sensory response to a chemical substance involves a simple three-cell circuit composed of the sensory neuron, an interneuron, and a motor neuron. Such a circuit may trigger, for instance, a movement of the jellyfish away from a noxious chemical response. However, in a human being, the scent response is far more complex, involving a structure called the olfactory bulb located in the forebrain, another region of the forebrain known as the olfactory cortex, and also other brain regions that include the hippocampus, the amygdala, and the prefrontal cortex.[39]

Yet, despite the huge difference in complexity between a jellyfish and a human being in their physiological response to a novel chemical in their environment, what their nervous systems have in common is that in each case, circuits of neurons are connected together by cellular junctions. Such junctions are called synapses.[40] Communication across a synapse is not electrical but chemical. What happens is that when an action potential reaches the end of an axon, this triggers the fusion of vesicles containing a neurotransmitter chemical into the synaptic cleft between the end of the axon and a dendrite from another neuron.

The neurochemical then diffuses across the space between the axon and dendrite and binds to receptors on the dendrite, which, depending on the excitatory or inhibitory inputs entering through other dendrites, may then trigger an action potential in the neuron (Fig. 3.4).

Because neurotransmitter left remaining in the synaptic cleft could continue to stimulate the dendrite, such neurotransmitter is either destroyed or transported back into vesicles within the end of the axon.

The importance of the latter process is shown by the fact that a class of drugs often prescribed to treat depression, selective serotonin reuptake inhibitors (SSRIs) – whose clinical applications we will look at in more detail later – work by inhibiting uptake of serotonin into axons in the brain.[41] This prolongs the effects of the serotonin response, which may be defective in depressed individuals' brains.

While neurons need to connect with other neurons in the nervous system, motor neurons must connect to muscle cells to fulfil their action. They do this via a cellular junction with many similarities to a synapse, which is known as the neuromuscular junction (NMJ).[42] As with a synapse, at the end of the axon of the motor neuron, a neurotransmitter, in this case one named acetylcholine (ACh), is released into the NMJ cleft.

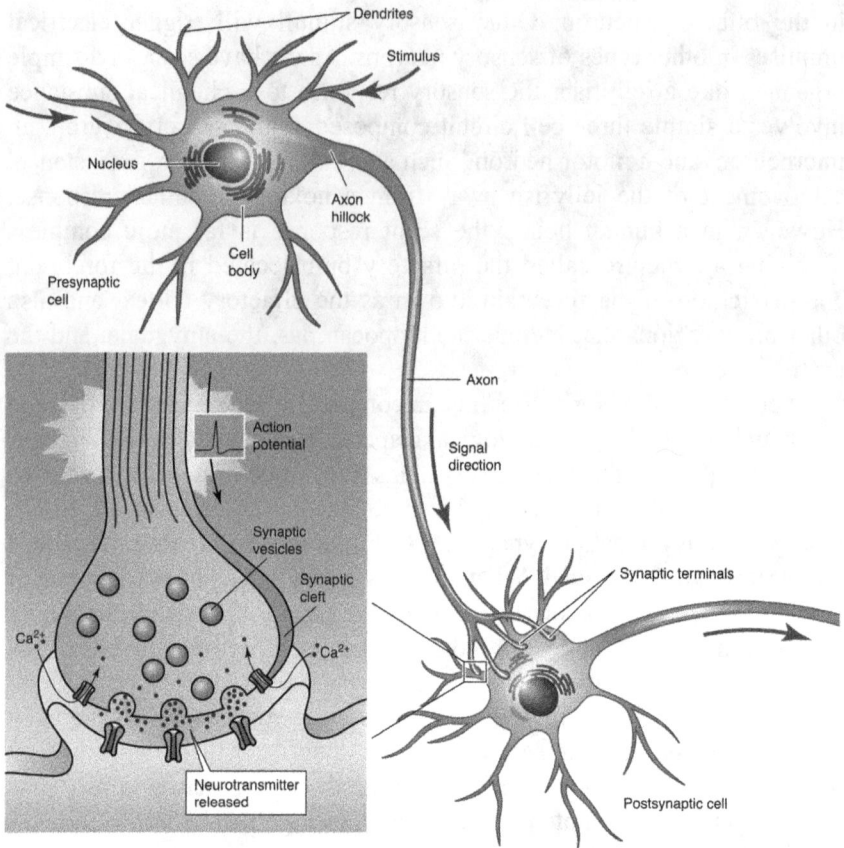

Fig. 3.4. The synapse connects the axon terminal of the presynaptic neurons and the dendrite of the postsynaptic neuron. Calcium ion influx causes the release of neurotransmitters from synaptic vesicles, and when they reach the synaptic cleft, they bind with receptors in the postsynaptic neuron, leading to ion channels opening or closing, causing a change in the ionic potential of the postsynaptic neuron.

Source: Reproduced from Tang, J. (2019) *Advanced Materials*, 31:1902761, with permission.

ACh then diffuses across this cleft and, by binding to receptors on the muscle cell membrane, activates muscle contraction. The response is terminated by an enzyme, acetylcholinesterase, which degrades ACh, preventing it from causing further contraction.

While we have so far classified neurons into three primary classes: sensory neurons, interneurons, and motor neurons, in practice there are hundreds of different types. Even a glance at some of the names given to neurons in the human brain – cone, climbing fibre, crab-like, medium spiny, pyramidal, chandelier, and tripolar – should give a sense of the great variety of neuronal cell types in the brain. Importantly, this complexity is not confined to neurons, for they are not the only types of cells that make up a human brain.

A common view of the brain is that it can be seen as akin to an electrical circuit diagram. However, while this is undoubtedly one aspect of how the brain works, such a viewpoint does not take into account the contributing role of another very important class of cells in the brain besides the neurons. These are the glial cells.

Glial cells' name derives from Greek for 'glue' and reflects the fact that when these cells were first discovered in the brain, they were assumed to be merely the structural firmament that held the neurons in place. More recently, it has become clear that glial cells play all sorts of important roles in the brain and are as indispensable as neurons.[43]

Just as there are many different types of neuron, there are multiple classes of glial cell. Glial cells called oligodendrocytes make the myelin sheath, which, as we have seen, plays an important role in the rapid conduction of action potentials; it also protects the axon.

Astrocytes are glial cells that perform metabolic, structural, homeostatic, and neuroprotective tasks such as clearing excess neurotransmitters, stabilising and regulating the blood–brain barrier, promoting synapse formation, and regulating the activity of synapses.

A class of glial cells called microglia make up about 10 percent of cells in the human brain. For some years, microglia have been known to be the brain's primary defenders against injury and disease; thus, they identify damaged neurons and destroy them. However, more recently, microglia have also been shown to play a more creative role in the absence of disease, for instance by 'pruning' synapses, much as a gardener prunes plants, in order to regulate the numbers of synapses and therefore the connections in a neuronal circuit.

A fundamental difference between neurons and glial cells is that the latter are not electrical cells joined by synapses. This was one reason why glial cells were not assumed to be as important as neurons as mediators of brain function because it was not clear how they would communicate with neuronal circuits without synapses. However, we now know glial cells can communicate with neurons in various ways.

One is by secreting chemicals that can stimulate neurons. Like the neurotransmitters released by an axon at a synapse, such chemicals bind

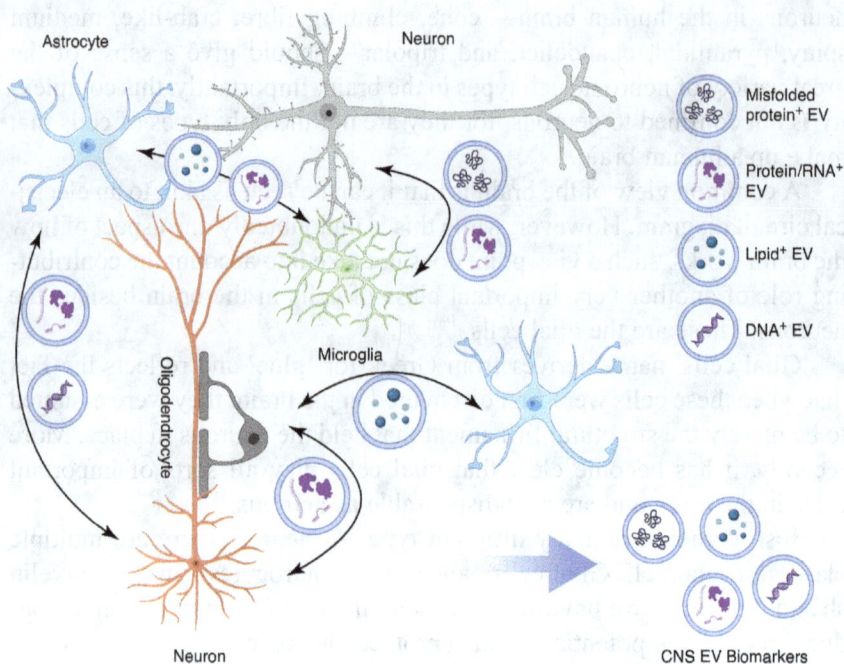

Fig. 3.5.   Communication of neurons and glial cells via extracellular vesicles (EVs). EVs carry lipids, nucleic acids (DNA and RNA), and proteins including misfolded proteins. EV-mediated transfer of proteins and nucleic acids has been shown to occur between neurons and astroglia, microglia and oligodendrocytes, and misfolded proteins between neurons and microglia to neurons. Arrows indicate EV-mediated signalling pathways. The EV cargo is representative of the donor cell and may be detected as a biomarker, assisting the decoding of disease states and mechanisms.

Source: Reproduced from Frühbeis, C. *et al.* (2012) *Frontiers in Physiology*, 3:119, with permission.

to receptors on neurons and influence the electrical activity of the latter. Conversely, glial cells have receptors on their surface that can bind neurotransmitters released by neurons and chemicals released by other glial cells, which make them highly responsive to chemical changes in the brain. As we have seen, recent studies have shown that regulatory RNAs can be secreted from cells in extracellular vesicles (EVs), and there is evidence that such EVs secreted from glial cells can alter neuronal function in key ways (Fig. 3.5).[44]

While we now have a clear idea of how individual neurons are linked with other neurons via synapses and an increasing recognition of how

neurons and glial cells interact, many questions remain about how neuronal circuitry and neuronal–glial cell interaction work at the level of the
whole brain. In order to begin to explore this question, let us now turn to
the question of brain structure and how this relates to its function.

Quiz

Which pair of scientists uncovered the ionic changes that underlie
the action potential?
A. Hodgkin and Huxley
B. Hodgkin and Huntington
C. Huxley and Hedges
D. Hodgkin and Highgate

Type of glial cell that makes the neuron's myelin sheath:
A. Astrocyte
B. Microglia
C. Chandelier cell
D. Oligodendrocyte

The neurotransmitter released at the neuromuscular junction:
A. Dopamine
B. Acetylcholine
C. Noradrenaline
D. Glutamate

Chapter 4

Structure and Function

Key Concepts

- Studies over many years have identified particular roles for specific brain regions, in particular cognitive functions. Yet, there is contrasting evidence that cognition can only properly be understood as a process that is distributed across the brain.
- The human brain is a typical vertebrate brain with three main parts: the forebrain, midbrain, and hindbrain. These three parts are clearly delineated in, say, a fish. In humans, the forebrain has expanded to obscure from view the two other parts.
- A notable characteristic of the human brain is its size, being relatively three times bigger than that of chimpanzees. We are starting to understand the genetic basis of this difference; a gene named NOTCH2NL plays a key role.

To understand how the human brain works, we need to discover not only how its individual components – the different types of neurons and glial cells – function but also how these components interact together within the brain to give rise to cognition. In trying to address this issue, we face a problem. Unlike organs in the body, such as the heart or kidney, whose structures provide important clues about their functions as a pump or filtration device, respectively, there is nothing obvious about the brain's structure that easily betrays how it is likely to work as a unified whole.

Instead, insights into how the human brain functions have tended to come from studying the effects of injury to the human brain, investigations of experimental animals, and, most recently, non-invasive imaging studies, as well as more invasive electrophysiological recordings, of the brains of living human volunteers. Such studies have begun to identify particular roles for specific brain regions, especially cognitive functions. Yet, there is contrasting evidence that cognition can only properly be understood as a process that is distributed across the brain. Let us look, therefore, at this apparent contradiction and how we might find a way to explain these two different facets of brain biology.

The idea that specific aspects of cognition are performed by particular brain regions has a long history. For instance, 19th-century clinical examinations of patients with language defects followed by post-mortem analysis of these individuals' brains identified regions of the brain that appeared to be associated with language.

Thus, Broca's region was found to be damaged in individuals with problems generating intelligible words, while Wernicke's region was damaged in people with trouble comprehending language (Fig. 4.1).[45]

Later, we will look at evidence that a brain region called the hippocampus plays a role in the formation of new memories based on the effects of injury to this region on memory formation in unfortunate individuals.

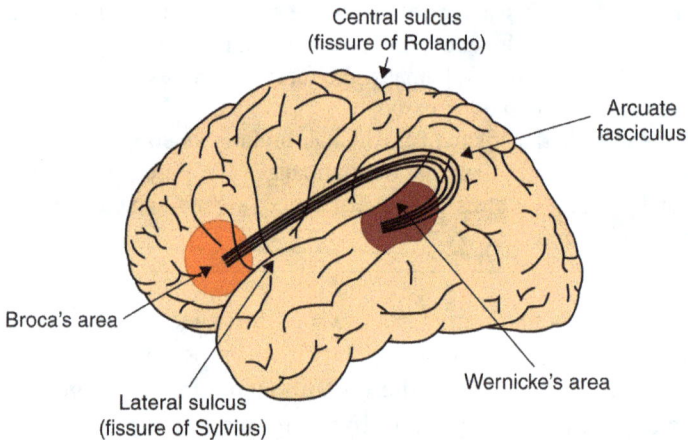

Fig. 4.1.   In this model, Broca's area is crucial for language production, Wernicke's area subserves language comprehension, and information exchange between these areas (such as when reading aloud) occurs via the arcuate fasciculus, a major fibre bundle connecting the language areas in the temporal cortex (Wernicke's area) and frontal cortex (Broca's area). The language areas border a major fissure in the brain, the so-called Sylvian fissure.

Source: Reproduced from Hagoort, P. (2013) *Frontiers in Psychology*, 4:416, with permission.

Further studies of human beings whose brains have been injured through infection or because of traumatic injury or necessary surgery to treat conditions like epilepsy, as well as studies of experimental animals subjected to brain lesions, have identified other brain regions that, when absent or defective, have a specific effect on a particular brain function.

One problem with this approach is that while it might identify a potential role for a brain region in a specific cognitive process, it does not necessarily reveal what sort of role or even how important the contribution of the brain region is to the process. An analogy would be removing a spark plug from a car and concluding that because the car no longer starts, this shows that the spark plug is the master controller of the car's movement, rather than being a necessary, but minor, component.

An opposite kind of approach involves stimulating neurons in the brain and seeing what effect this has upon some facet of behaviour or measuring the activity of a neuron in a particular brain region in response to some sensory stimulus, for instance a visual one. Since this involves exposing some part of the brain, it is not surprising that such an approach is primarily conducted in experimental animals. However, sometimes human patients undergoing necessary therapeutic brain surgery may volunteer to take part in studies in which neurons in their exposed brain are stimulated or their electrical activity monitored.

A third, increasingly used approach records electrical or biochemical activity in the brain in a non-invasive manner using various types of imaging devices. This approach is particularly popular for studies of human brain function since it is non-invasive.

Box 4.1.   Types of Brain Imaging Approaches

Brain imaging is an important tool for both research and clinical purposes. Types of imaging methods used to study human brain function include the following:

Functional magnetic resonance imaging (fMRI) detects changes in blood flow and oxygen levels that result from the brain's activity. It uses the magnetic field of the scanner to affect the magnetic nuclei of hydrogen atoms, so they can be measured and converted into images. fMRI can be used to assess brain activity, identify brain abnormalities, and create maps of brain activity to guide surgical interventions.

Computerised tomography (CT) creates a series of X-ray images converted into cross-sectional images of the brain. These X-rays are combined to form cross-sectional slices or even a 3D model of the brain. CT scans can identify brain injuries or tumours and reveal structural brain changes in disorders such as schizophrenia.

Positron emission tomography (PET) uses a radioactive tracer to label a metabolite, for instance glucose, and thereby monitor its presence in the bloodstream and metabolism in tissues and organs. Since the brain uses glucose as its primary fuel source, a PET scan can identify areas of high brain activity and also abnormalities in brain activity that may occur in a variety of disorders. PET scans can be used to evaluate seizures, neurodegenerative disorders such as Alzheimer's, and tumours.

Magnetoencephalography (MEG) measures the magnetic field from neuronal-electrical activity. Clinicians use MEG to evaluate both spontaneous brain activity and neuronal responses triggered by stimuli. MEG makes it possible to assess areas of the brain, such as epilepsy sources, motor areas, and sensory areas.

Throughout this book, we will return to these three different types of approach as part of our exploration of different aspects of cognitive function; for now, having introduced them, let us look at what they have revealed about human brain structure and function.

In its general structural plan, the human brain is a typical vertebrate brain with three main parts: the forebrain, midbrain, and hindbrain. These three parts are clearly delineated in, say, a fish. In mammals, particularly in primates and especially so in humans, the forebrain has expanded to obscure from view the other parts of the brain.

In humans, the forebrain includes the cerebrum, which has two hemispheres and a highly folded surface 'cortex', this word being derived from the Latin word for bark, reflecting the way that the cortex is wrapped around the rest of the brain like the bark around a tree (Fig. 4.2).

This is the brain region most associated with planning, reasoning, and problem-solving. But showing how specific brain regions may perform multiple functions, different parts of the cortex are involved in movement, perception, vision, hearing, and speech.

Buried within the forebrain are the various parts of the limbic system, which were the first region of this part of the brain to evolve and are often

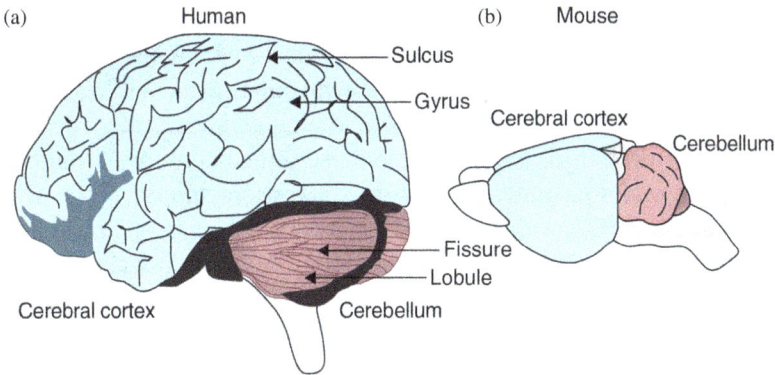

Fig. 4.2. (a) The human cerebral cortex (blue) and cerebellum (pink) both have characteristic folding patterns. The cerebral cortex contains gyri (peaks) interrupted by sulci (valleys). An equivalent architecture is observed in the cerebellum, which comprises lobules and fissures. (b) The mouse cerebellum is folded, whereas the cerebral cortex is not.

Source: Reproduced from Miterko, L. *et al.* (2018) *Frontiers in Neural Circuits*, 12:83, with permission.

called the 'emotional brain' due to their association with the different emotions, or the 'lizard brain' to convey the fact that human beings share these brain regions with 'lower' organisms.[46] The limbic system contains the thalamus which, like a central postal-sorting depot, channels information both into and out of the cortex. The hypothalamus lies underneath the thalamus, as its name implies, and regulates thirst, hunger, sexual desire, reproduction, and the body clock.

The amygdala is a region of the limbic system involved in processing emotions; it is active in responses associated with fear but also with pleasure. Adjacent to it is the hippocampus, named after the Latin word for seahorse, which early researchers thought it resembled. As already mentioned, the hippocampus appears to play roles both in forming memories and in the transition from short- to long-term memory.

The midbrain is involved in vision, hearing, motor control, sleep, alertness, and temperature regulation. The hindbrain includes the cerebellum, which means 'little brain'; it acquired this name because, like the cerebrum, it has two hemispheres and a highly folded surface (Fig. 4.2). This brain region has long been associated with regulation and coordination of movement, posture, and balance; however, there is new evidence that it also plays important roles in 'higher' mental processes, such as imagination and creativity. The hindbrain also contains the pons, which controls wakefulness and sleep, and the medulla, responsible for maintaining vital bodily functions such as breathing and heart rate.

The organisation of the brain into these three main regions and their further division into a number of sub-regions is something that the human brain shares with the brains of other vertebrates. This is one reason why we can learn a lot about human brain function from studies of experimental animal species, which include, but are not restricted to, mammals. But if we want to begin to understand what makes human consciousness different from that of every other species, we need to know what is unique about the human brain, as well as what it has in common with the brains of other species.

A notable characteristic of the human brain is its size, being relatively three times bigger than that of chimpanzees. We are now starting to understand the genetic basis of this difference; thus, a recent study revealed that a gene named NOTCH2NL, which is only found in humans and the proto-human species Neanderthals and Denisovans, may play an important role in the distinctive large size of the human brain.[47]

Neurons are formed during the development of the embryonic brain from neural stem cells. Like other stem cells, the neural version has the ability to divide repeatedly but also to differentiate into more specialised cell types. Studies have shown that NOTCH2NL delays the differentiation of neural stem cells in the human brain, thereby allowing them to divide for longer and produce more neurons. Intriguingly, NOTCH2NL arose in our ancestors' genomes 3–4 million years ago, having developed as an offshoot of another gene named NOTCH2 that is present in many other species; interestingly, it was in this period of prehistory that the brains of proto-humans first began to grow in size.

In fact, NOTCH2NL is likely to be only one of multiple genetic factors that underlie humans' distinctively large brains. Some of the other genomic regions that have been linked to the expansion in the size of the human brain code not for proteins but for regulatory RNAs of the sort mentioned previously.[48] This shows that at a cellular level, the factors that underlie human brain expansion may be quite complex genetically.

The expansion of the human brain compared to those of other species has not been uniform; rather, it has been particularly acute in the frontal lobes and the prefrontal cortex (PFC) region at the front of the brain (Fig. 4.3). The PFC is bigger relative to the rest of the brain in primates compared to other mammals and particularly so in humans.

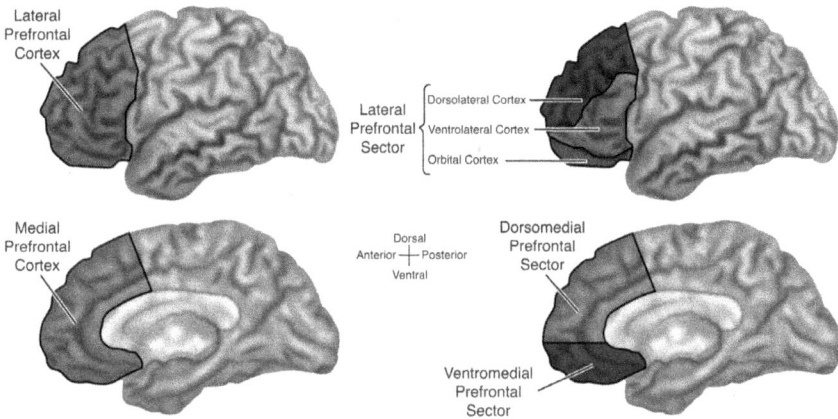

Fig. 4.3. The human prefrontal cortex and its components.

Source: Reproduced from Ramchandran, K. *et al.* (2016) *Adaptive Human Behavior and Physiology* 2:325–343, with permission.

In line with this expansion of the PFC in humans, multiple studies suggest that this brain region plays an important role in 'higher' brain functions such as planning, reasoning, problem-solving, imagination, and creativity. It is common to describe such complex cognitive activities as 'executive functions'. However, this term is problematic if viewed as analogous to a corporate executive managing a company in a top-down manner. For there can be no controlling centre in the brain, as this would only raise the question of what controls this, and so on. Instead, increasingly, the PFC is viewed within neuroscience as merely one part of an interacting whole. According to this viewpoint, the PFC sends out signals that act to coordinate the actions of other regions of the brain, but it is equally a receiver of such signals.[49]

What we still incompletely understand is how the PFC interacts with the rest of the brain, the role of different regions within it, and the precise nature of the signalling pathways that coordinate the actions of different parts of the brain. One obvious way that different brain regions may interact and how areas within such regions might fulfil distinctive functions is through precise neuronal circuitry. To some extent, this seems to be the case. The PFC has a number of sub-regions that include the ventromedial PFC, orbitofrontal PFC, and dorsolateral PFC (Fig. 4.3), all of which appear to play distinctive roles in the higher aspects of human consciousness.

In addition, recent studies suggest that novel neuronal connections between brain regions have evolved in human beings that are not present in even our closest primate relatives.[50] Such changes may have led to the human brain having particularly long-range connections between different regions that could have important implications for the functional connectivity of the human brain and therefore our cognition.[51]

In contrast to such evidence of the importance of precise neuronal circuitry, other studies of the role of the PFC in the process of working memory have shown that far from playing fixed, defined roles, specific neurons in the prefrontal cortex can play multiple roles. What seems to decide which specific role that a particular neuron will play is its grouping within a working ensemble of other neurons. Instead of being fixed, such ensembles come together in a fluid manner, fulfil a function, and then dissipate. This raises the question of what controls the formation and dissipation of such ensembles.

As we will discuss in more detail soon, recent studies have identified an important role of oscillating brain waves of different frequencies as coordinators of such ensembles. It is worth briefly discussing the source of such waves. We saw earlier that the brain contains both excitatory and inhibitory neurons. There is a good evolutionary reason for this. If the brain contained only excitatory neurons, there would be nothing to stop neuronal impulses sweeping across the brain in an uncontrolled manner. Indeed, this is what happens in epilepsy, where it causes convulsive seizures (Fig. 4.4).[52]

Epilepsy is a pathological condition. Normally, the fact that excitatory neurons have inputs from inhibitory neurons as well as excitatory ones prevents uncontrolled spread of neuronal impulses.[53] Another feature of the brain is that any particular neuron will have inputs to its dendrites from the axons of many other neurons. The fact that this relationship is highly dynamic, with the balance between excitation and inhibition constantly changing, means that neurons will typically show regular oscillations in their electrical potential. This then is the basis for brain waves, and the different frequencies of these waves simply reflect the balance between excitation and inhibition in a particular neuron. And recent studies show that brain waves appear to be mediators of interactions between different brain regions that occur during working memory, perception, and indeed cognition as a whole.[54]

The discovery of the importance of brain waves for cognition is linked to an increasing recognition that, although circuitry is essential for

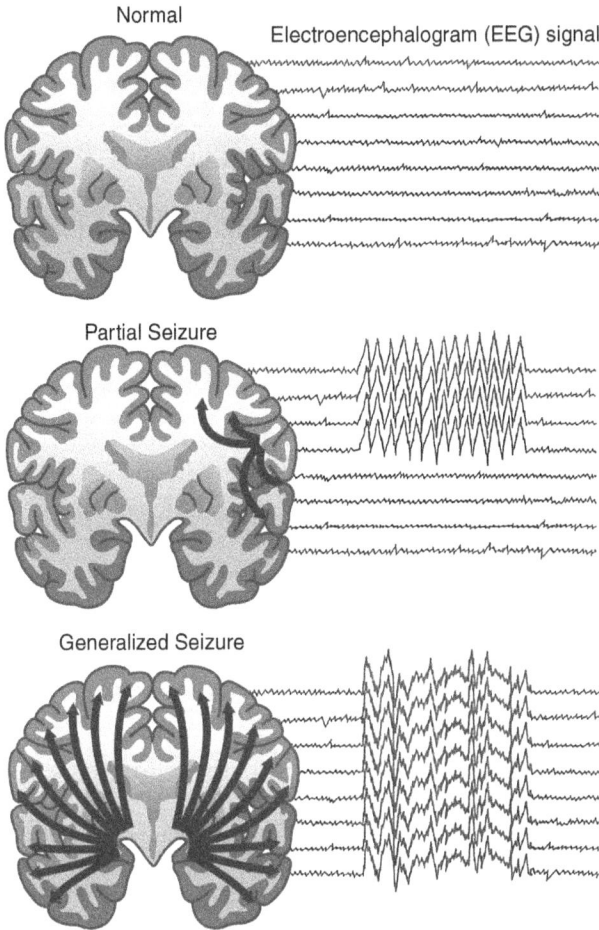

Fig. 4.4. Comparison of the normal brain with partial (focal) seizure and generalised seizure brains and their EEG signals.

Source: Reproduced from Sadiq, M.T. *et al.* (2021) *Journal of Healthcare Engineering*, 2021:1–24, with permission.

brain function, the brain is far more dynamic and fluid than had been previously realised. In the following part of the book, we will look in more detail at the molecular and cellular basis of such dynamism and fluidity and relate it to cognition. This means returning to the question of how changes in the environment are sensed by living organisms, how incoming signals are then transmitted to and interpreted by cells in the brain, and what role cell surface receptors and intracellular signals play in this process.

Quiz

Brain region shown to play a role in language in the 19th century:
A. Broca's region
B. Braca's region
C. Brica's region
D. Breca's region

Brain region that regulates and coordinates movement, posture, and balance:
A. Hippocampus
B. Amygdala
C. Cerebellum
D. Hypothalamus

Brain region particularly associated with emotions:
A. Hippocampus
B. Amygdala
C. Cerebellum
D. Prefrontal cortex

Chapter 5

Receptors and Signals

Key Concepts

- The nature of an odour, the colour of a beam of light, the amplitude and frequency of a sound wave, or the temperature of an object pressed against the skin can be gauged by the receptors these stimuli activate and the degree of activation.
- Receptors on the surface of sensory cells are only the first stage of a signal transduction network that stretches from the sensory organs to the brain. In sensory cells, activation of a particular receptor activates specific intracellular signals.
- Despite the importance of the brain cortex in sensory perception, we are beginning to realise that perception, like other aspects of cognition, is far more complex and far more a property of the whole brain than had been realised.

The ability of lifeforms to survive in what can often be a very challenging world is highly related to the extent to which they can sense changes in the external environment and respond appropriately. As we have seen, even a simple bacterium has a range of sophisticated molecular mechanisms for detecting both negative and positive factors in its environment that allow it, for instance, to swim towards a source of food or away from a noxious stimulus. Such survival mechanisms are equally a feature of complex multicellular organisms, including human beings, as anyone who has been startled by a sudden unexpected noise in, say, a dark alley can testify, for this will invariably trigger the 'fright, flight, or fight' response that is powered by a rapid increase in adrenaline levels in the blood.

Our sensory apparatus is, however, now employed for far more than mere rapid reactions to danger.[55] Our different senses instead allow us to build up a multi-faceted and detailed picture of the world around us to such a degree that this can simply appear to be what exists directly outside our heads. Yet, what we appear to see, hear, smell, taste, and touch is in many ways an illusion, being as much a creation of our brains as a separate reality existing outside us. To see why this is, let us look in more detail at how signals from the outside world are detected by our senses and processed within our brains.

The human senses may be divided into touch, taste, smell, vision, and hearing. Of the bodily regions that mediate our sensory experiences, the skin may be seen as the most ancient from an evolutionary perspective since long before our worm-like ancestors developed eyes, ears, and noses, they could sense the environment through their skin, and this remains a vital part of our senses today.

Our external skin and the other cell layers that line the interior of our body cavity are able to sense a wide range of sensory stimuli that include touch, pressure, vibration, limb position, heat, cold, itch, and pain. We can distinguish such stimuli as distinct entities and also by their intensity due to the presence of different types of cells in our skin and other epithelial layers, joints, and muscles that possess distinct types of cell receptors.[56] For instance, pressure on the skin is detected by a mechanosensitive ion channel called a Piezo receptor, this name being derived from the Greek word for pressure. Pain is sensed by a different set of receptors, known as nociceptors from the Latin word for hurt.

Sensory neurons convey the signals triggered by the different types of receptors to the brain's somatosensory cortex, with different types of sensory neurons associated with each type of sensory stimulus. Studies first performed in 1937, in which the activities of neurons in the somatosensory cortex were recorded in human patients undergoing surgery to treat conditions such as epilepsy, showed that the body surface was represented on the cortex like a kind of map of the body (Fig. 5.1).[57]

Interestingly, the face, mouth, hands, and fingers are grossly overrepresented. This shows that these regions are much more highly innervated than other parts of the body, and this may be due to the importance of our hands for manipulating tools, our mouth's role in speech, and the importance of the face in human social interactions.

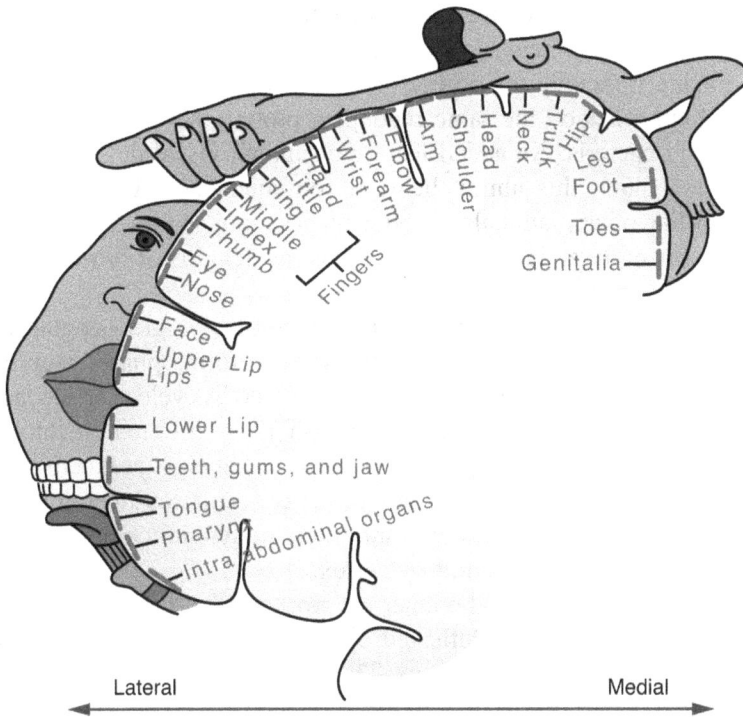

Lateral — Medial

Fig. 5.1. The mapping skeleton of the somatosensory cortex in the brain and the human body. The somatotopic map describes how the reverberatory cortical regions and the responding parts of the human body correspond to each other under tactile stimuli.

Source: Reproduced from Luo, C. *et al.* (2022) *Cognitive Neurodynamics*, 16:1–25, with permission.

The way that we see, hear, smell, and taste involves equally specific types of receptors that have evolved to precisely register these distinct types of sensory input. Take for instance smell. The fact that the human nose is able to distinguish hundreds of distinct scents so precisely remained a mystery until the discovery of the olfactory receptors. These are variants of the G-protein coupled receptors (GPCRs) mentioned previously, and the fact that over a thousand different genes exist that code for olfactory receptor proteins helps explain how we are able to distinguish different scents so precisely.[58]

Our ability to distinguish the five different types of taste stimuli – salt, sour, sweet, bitter, and umami (a Japanese word meaning savoury) – is also based on the action of GPCRs in taste buds present not only in the tongue but also in the pharynx, larynx, and upper oesophagus.

The human eye has long inspired admiration as an illustration of the exquisite connection between natural form and function.[59]

Ultimately though, the ability of most people to visualise the world around them relies on the same rhodopsin protein that is central to light detection in bacteria. An added feature of human visual detection is that we see in colour, this ability being a consequence of the fact that in humans – like other mammals – rhodopsin has mutated into different opsin proteins that preferentially respond to the wavelengths of blue, green, or red light.

The human ear is similarly a masterpiece of biological engineering. Sound waves have four major features: waveform, phase, amplitude (expressed in decibels), and frequency (expressed as cycles per second, or Hertz). The ear has evolved to distinguish these different features by means of the outer ear, which concentrates sound energy and focuses it on the eardrum, and the inner ear, which further concentrates incoming sound waves but also breaks these down into their individual components that are then transmitted to the auditory cortex.

Central to the way that the inner ear works is that hair-like structures called cilia on its cells are deflected by incoming sound waves, and this triggers signals in auditory neurons. The cochlea in the inner ear is structured so that sound waves of different frequencies trigger its cells in an orderly sequence like the keys on a piano.[60]

Whatever the specific nature of the sensory signals collected by the skin and other sensory structures in the body, all go on to stimulate neuronal impulses in the brain. An important issue to consider is how such incoming impulses from the world around us allow us to create a detailed and informative picture of that world in our individual minds.

To some extent, such information is conveyed by the architecture of the sensory organs. The structure of the human eye has evolved to precisely convey a sense of the world around us through a lens that focuses incoming light waves, much as a camera does. Meanwhile, the inner ear has evolved to register features such as the amplitude and frequency of incoming sounds. The particular nature of sensory information is also conveyed by the specific receptors that detect particular sensory signals in the environment.

The precise nature of an odour, the colour of a beam of light, the amplitude and frequency of a sound wave, or the temperature of an object pressed against the skin can all be gauged by the type of receptors these stimuli activate and the degree of activation. This molecular coding of sensory stimuli has relevance for a philosophical debate about whether science will ever be able to explain subjective experiences.

Thus, some philosophers of mind have challenged the idea that even with advances in neuroscience, we will ever be able to provide a scientific explanation of what it feels like to taste a ripe mango for the first time, hear Mozart's *Queen of the Night* aria, or experience the caress of a lover, since these are all highly subjective personal experiences.

Yet, one could argue that the more we uncover the molecular machinery that recognises specific sensory signals, the more we are moving toward a precise scientific understanding of even the most personal sensory experiences. Importantly, genetic analysis is also revealing subtle differences in this machinery between individual human beings.

A well-known example of this is red-green colour blindness.[61] Typically, this is due to changes in genes coding for the opsin proteins that sense this part of the visual spectrum. These genes are present on the X chromosome; therefore, this condition generally only affects men, as they only have one X chromosome and no compensation by the normal version of this gene, unlike the situation in women.

Despite its effect on their vision, individuals with red-green colour blindness often only realise they have this condition when it is identified through a visual test. Until this point, these individuals are unaware of their altered vision because it is what they have grown up with. While this represents a very obvious sensory difference in certain individuals, more subtle genetic variations among the human population that have been identified in the receptor proteins involved in sensory perception mean that subtly different individual subjective reactions to the same phenomenon may, to some extent, have a genetic basis.

Our sensory apparatus may also be shaped in important ways that are not due to individual genetics. For instance, one notable feature of the COVID-19 pandemic was that many people infected by the SARS-CoV-2 virus lost their sense of smell and taste (Fig. 5.2).[62]

Even when this returned after recovery from the infection, some individuals were left with subtle changes in these senses. While disturbing for anyone who suffered such a change, it was particularly a concern for affected individuals who relied on their sense of smell and taste for their job, such as chefs or sommeliers.

Receptors on the surface of sensory cells are only the first stage of a signal transduction network that stretches from the sensory organs to the brain. Within sensory cells, activation of a particular receptor activates

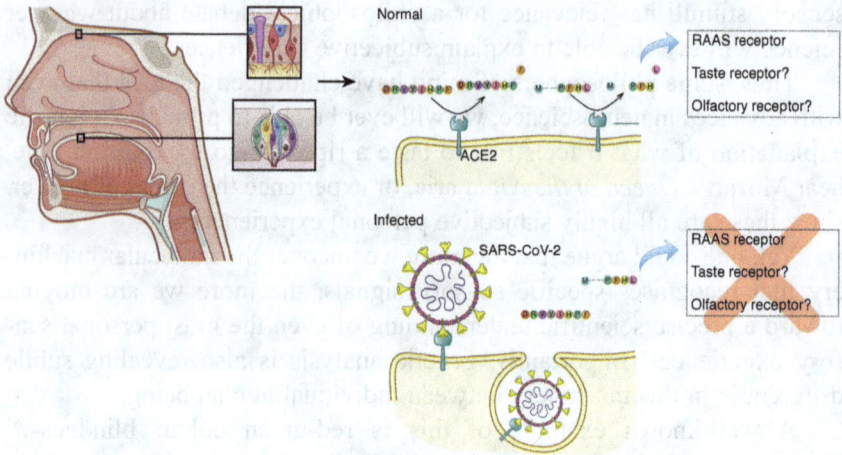

Fig. 5.2. One of the symptoms of SARS-CoV-2 infection is loss of smell and taste. A recent study suggests that such a loss is mediated by a reduction in the renin-angiotensin-aldosterone system (RAAS) peptidase activity.

Source: Reproduced from Luchiari, H.R. *et al.* (2021) *Pharmacogenomics Journal*, 21:109–115, with permission.

a specific type of intracellular signalling pathway. The GPCR class of receptors, which, as we have already noted, play diverse roles in a variety of sensory processes, can trigger a number of different signalling mechanisms. One is the cAMP pathway that activates the PKA enzyme and CREB transcription factor, which we have already mentioned. This pathway is activated by the Gα class of GPCRs. But a different GPCR class, Gq/11, activates the enzyme PLCβ, which generates calcium (Ca^{2+}) signals in cells. These activate a variety of calcium-sensitive enzymes and transcription factors.[63]

Box 5.1.   Signalling and Second Messengers

A major breakthrough in our understanding of cell signalling came with the discovery of 'second messengers' by Earl Sutherland in 1958. Breakdown of glycogen to glucose in the liver in response to adrenaline provides energy for the body as part of the 'fright, flight, or fight' response. Sutherland wanted to know how adrenaline exerts its effects in liver cells, about which nothing was known at the time. Using biochemical analysis methods, he showed that a novel chemical, cyclic AMP (cAMP), is formed in liver cells when they are stimulated by adrenaline, and he described cAMP as a 'second messenger' by analogy with adrenaline's role as the first messenger to the cell. Initially, Sutherland's suggestion that a single small molecule led to the numerous effects of adrenaline was met with disbelief. However, not only was Sutherland correct about the role of cAMP in adrenaline's action, but subsequent studies showed that many other hormones stimulate the production of this molecular messenger. In addition, the concept of a second messenger was shown to have general relevance, as many other such messengers have been identified, and these include small molecules, such as cyclic GMP (cGMP), diacyl glycerol (DAG), and inositol trisphosphate (IP$_3$), but also ions, such as calcium (Ca^{2+}), and even a gas, nitric oxide (NO).

These are only two of the many different types of signalling pathways that operate in human cells. Typically, such pathways rely on the action of intracellular 'messengers' that can be small molecules, such as cAMP, but also an ion, such as Ca^{2+}, or even a gas like nitric oxide.[64] Signalling pathways also have components acting in sequence, each component activating the next in the chain. Because a sensory cell can have many different types of receptors on its surface, the precise molecular character of signalling pathways is an important way that the cell delineates the effects of the stimulation of different receptors. Signalling pathways activate neurons that transmit sensory information to the brain. A major target of neurons in the optic nerve is the dorsolateral geniculate nucleus in the thalamus brain region (Fig. 5.3).[65]

The thalamus works like a relay station on the way to the visual cortex. But demonstrating the neuronal complexity of the visual process, neurons in the optic nerve also connect to a part of the hypothalamus that is involved in regulating the day-night cycle, as well as the superior colliculus region in the midbrain, which is involved in coordinating head and eye movements to visual and other targets.

A key next stage in vision is what happens in the brain cortex. In the 1950s, electrical recordings of the visual cortex in cats exposed to different visual stimuli first showed how such stimuli are registered by the brain. Such studies showed that individual visual cortex neurons respond not to complex shapes as such but to simple lines and edges.[66] Since some neurons respond to vertical lines or edges, others to horizontal ones, and others to ones at angles in between, the combination of these different neurons allows us to see complex shapes.

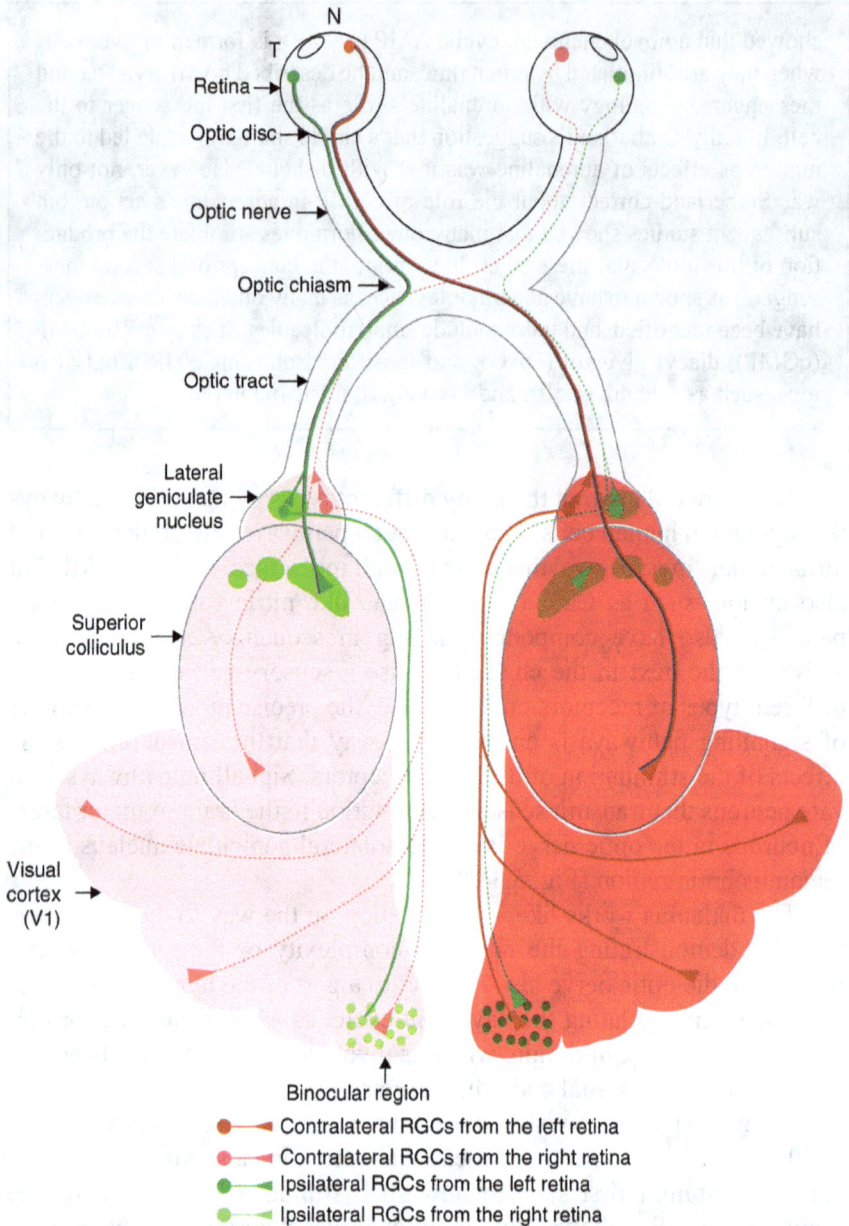

Fig. 5.3. Schematic representation of the visual pathway in the mouse. RGC axons transverse the eye to exit at the optic disc. The axons then travel via the optic nerves to the optic chiasm, where they cross or avoid the midline to project ipsilaterally or contralaterally in the optic tracts to the main visual targets: the LGN in the thalamus or the superior colliculus.

Source: Reproduced from Erskine, L. and Herrera, E. (2014) *ASN Neuro*, 6:6, with permission.

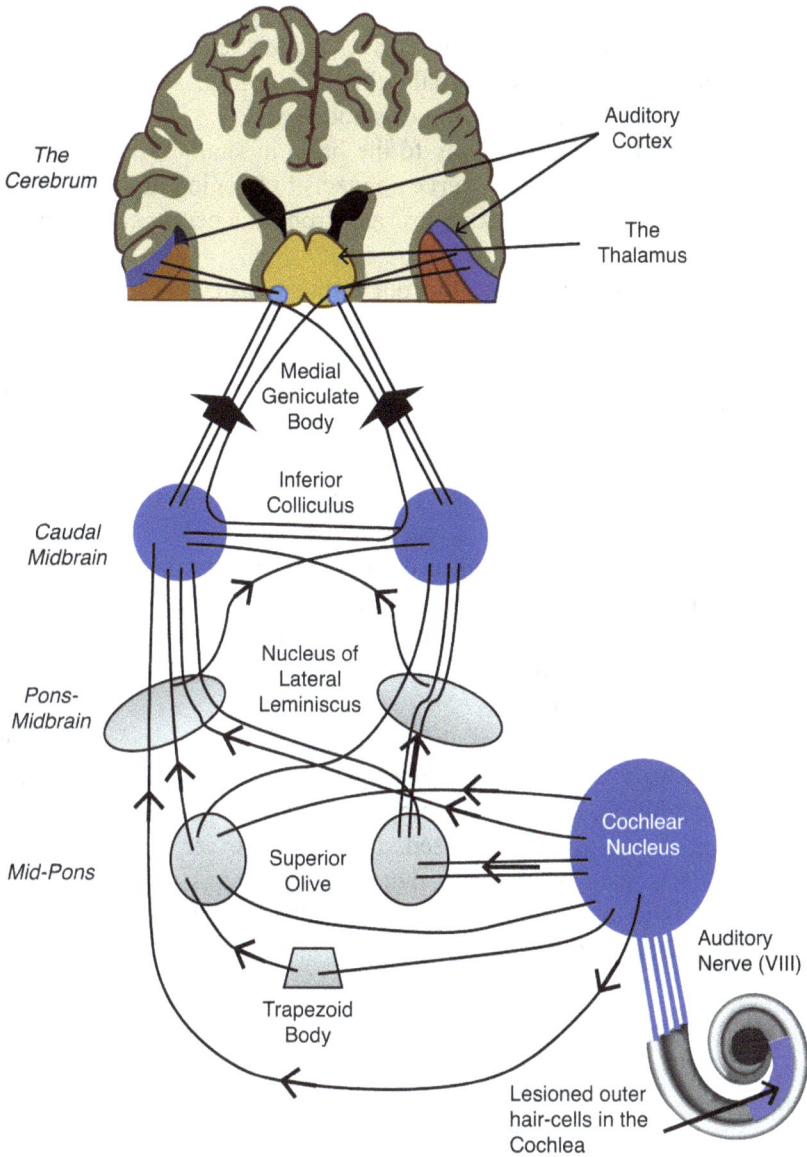

Fig. 5.4. The primary auditory pathway starts from the cochlear nuclei in the brainstem. Subsequently, auditory signals are transmitted to the superior olivary complex and then to the inferior colliculus in the midbrain and continue to the median geniculate body in the thalamus, before terminating in the auditory cortex.

Source: Reproduced from Adjamian, E.D. *et al.* (2014) *Neuroscience and Biobehavioral Reviews*, 45:119–133, with permission.

In fact, this is only one aspect of how the visual cortex works. So, while one part of this brain region receives signals relating to an object's shape, another area receives signals about its colour, and another one about whether the object is moving or stationary.

Sound signals make their way to the brain in similar ways to visual ones. In this case, the auditory nerve connects to a region in the thalamus called the medial geniculate complex, and from this neuronal signals are transmitted to the auditory cortex (Fig. 5.4).[67]

But while evidence suggests that our auditory fields are mapped out on the auditory cortex similarly to how the visual field is mapped on the visual cortex and sensations to skin are represented in a map-like form on the somatosensory cortex, we know much less about the specific ways in which the auditory cortex is structured, compared to the visual cortical areas.

Much also remains unclear about how our perception of odours is processed in the brain. In this case, incoming signals from the nose carrying information about scent first reach the olfactory bulb, and from here neuronal signals are transmitted to the pyriform cortex, as well as other brain regions. Intriguingly, unlike the situation with other sensory inputs, these include the amygdala, the brain region that plays a major role in regulating emotions.[68] This may explain why smells in particular can have such a powerful effect on us.

Despite the importance of the brain cortex in sensory perception, increasingly, we are beginning to understand that perception, like other aspects of cognition, is far more complex and far more a property of the whole brain than had been realised. However, we are also starting to understand how such whole-brain dynamics operate. As a step to doing so, it is now time to consider the circuitry of the brain as well as the role of oscillating brain waves.

Quiz

Type of receptor involved in sensing pressure:
A. Nociceptor
B. Piezo receptor
C. Ryanodine receptor
D. Purinergic receptor

Chromosome associated with red-green colour blindness:
A. X chromosome
B. Y chromosome
C. Chromosome 1
D. Chromosome 21

Brain region that acts like a relay station for neuronal signals:
A. Cerebellum
B. Amygdala
C. Thalamus
D. Hypothalamus

Chapter 6

Circuits and Waves

Key Concepts

- Such is the centrality of neuronal circuits to brain function that some neuroscientists have proposed that if we could map the circuitry of a human brain, we would understand human consciousness. However, there are flaws in this viewpoint.
- Recently, there has also been a radical change in views about how brains operate, and this has major relevance for the quest to understand human consciousness. In particular, the new viewpoint stresses the key role of oscillating brain waves.
- Brain waves occur at different frequencies. Recent studies suggest that gamma waves coordinate neurons carrying 'bottom-up' information, while beta waves coordinate neurons that convey 'top-down' information, such as prior knowledge and goals.

A central aspect of how the brain works is that neurons are cells that conduct electrical impulses and are joined together in circuits. To recap, electricity is conveyed down the axon of a neuron in the form of an action potential. When this reaches the end of the axon, it triggers the release of a neurotransmitter into the synaptic cleft, separating the axon from the dendrite of a subsequent neuron in the circuit, which is known as the post-synaptic neuron. The neurotransmitter diffuses across the cleft, and when it binds to receptors on the dendrite, this can trigger a new action potential in the postsynaptic neuron.

Neurons may have hundreds of dendrites, all receiving inputs from presynaptic neurons, and these can be either excitatory or inhibitory. Thus, what determines whether an action potential will be triggered in a post-synaptic neuron depends on the sum effect of the incoming inputs and whether they lead to the stimulation or inhibition of the neuron.

Such is the centrality of neuronal circuits to brain function that some neuroscientists have proposed that if we could only map the circuitry of a typical human brain, then we would effectively understand human consciousness. Indeed, with the announcement of the start of the Human Connectome Project, this approach is already underway. Analogous to the Human Genome Project, the aim of this project is to precisely map all neuronal connections in the human brain and relate them to the functional activity of the brain.[69]

The connectome approach is likely to generate much useful data about brain anatomy. It is associated, though, with a number of potential problems. One is the sheer scale of the undertaking. To give a sense of this, recently, the findings were published of a study that mapped the interconnections of 75,000 neurons in the mouse brain.[70] While a phenomenal piece of science, this represents only one-thousandth of the neurons in the whole brain. Moreover, the human brain, containing around 86 billion neurons, is a thousandfold larger still. Thus, it is unclear how easily it will be to bridge this gap technologically.

Another potential problem with the idea that mapping all the brain's neurons and their connections will reveal the material and mechanistic basis of human consciousness is that neurons are not the only cell type in the brain. Instead, as we have seen, the human brain also contains different types of glial cells, which number around 85 billion, approximately the same number of neurons. Far from being merely the 'glue' that holds neurons in place, as was formerly thought, glial cells are now recognised as major players in brain function; therefore, their positions in the brain also need to be mapped. The mouse connectome project, mentioned previously, did include glial cells in its analysis. But the need to include them is a further challenge for this type of project.

A final problem is one that specifically affects the Human Connectome Project. A key feature of the recent mouse connectome study was that neuronal positions and connections were recorded after extensive electro-physiological recordings had been made from the neurons of the mouse while it was still alive and taking part in activities designed to stimulate different aspects of brain function. Only after these recordings were completed was the mouse killed and its brain analysed. Obviously, this type of approach would be impossible in humans. Instead, the Human Connectome Project must rely on brains donated by volunteers after their death, and there is no possibility of coupling functional analysis with neuronal mapping, as is the case with mice.

Given the logistical challenges of mapping the human brain connectome, coupled with the difficulties in performing parallel functional analysis and neuronal mapping, it remains to be seen how soon we can expect a complete human connectome analysis, or even if this is achievable. However, there are other ways to study human brain circuitry that may help identify unique aspects of that circuitry.

One such approach involves searching for differences between the circuitry of the human brain and that of the brains of other species, including those of our closest primate relatives. Intriguingly, such analysis has shown that a class of glial cells called astrocytes are much larger and grow to a much greater length in the human brain compared to other species.[71] Since astrocytes play important roles in synapse formation and regulation of synaptic function, such expanded versions of these glial cells might result in greater connectivity of the human brain. This finding also shows the importance of not only focusing on neurons in the quest to understand what underlies the unique aspects of human consciousness.

Alongside increased appreciation of the importance of non-neuronal cells in the brain, there is also growing awareness that regions of the human brain that had not previously been thought to be involved in 'higher' cognitive processes are in fact important mediators of such processes and may have a particularly enhanced role in human beings.

One such brain region is the cerebellum (Fig. 6.1).

This hindbrain region has long been associated with movement regulation and balance control; it plays a vital role in learning repetitive actions, such as playing the piano, learning to ride a bike, or throwing a ball in a hoop.[72] But recent studies suggest that the cerebellum is also an important mediator of processes such as imagination and creativity, in ways that may be specifically linked to its evolution in humans.[73]

As we have seen, discussions about the material basis of the unique aspects of human consciousness have tended to focus on the expanded nature of the human cerebrum, particularly the frontal lobes and the prefrontal cortex, which is much bigger in primates compared to other animal groups and particularly so in human beings. Yet, recent anatomical studies of the cerebellum and comparisons of this structure with those of other

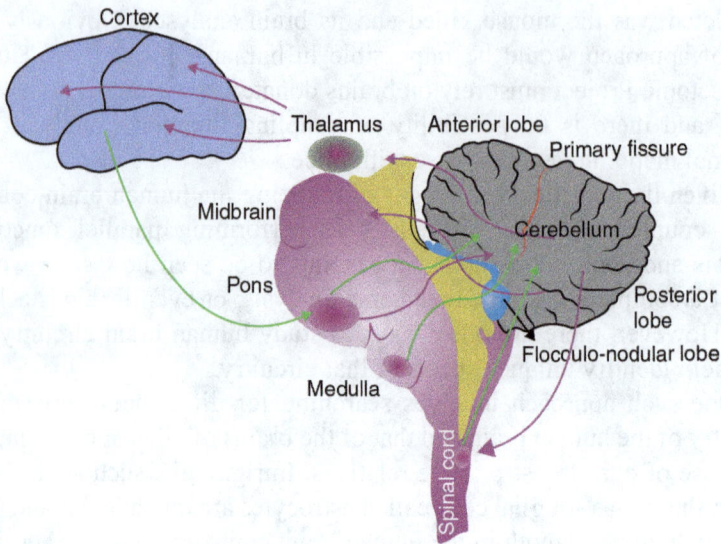

Fig. 6.1.   Scheme of circuits connecting the cerebellum with other brain areas. Afferent connections are represented in green, efferent connections in violet.

Source: Reproduced from Farini, D. *et al.* (2021) *Cellular and Molecular Life Sciences*, 78:6431–6451, with permission.

species have shown that it too has greatly expanded in human beings. Indeed, a recent study that compared the human cerebellum with that of a monkey found that this structure has actually expanded relatively even more than the cerebral cortex in our species.[74]

Other evidence is emerging of enhanced connectivity between the cerebellum and cerebrum in primates compared to non-primate species, and this connectivity appears to be enhanced further still in humans. Later in this book, we will discuss in more detail the evidence of a role for the cerebellum in 'higher' aspects of cognition, such as imagination and creativity, and how the enhanced size of the cerebellum and greater connectivity with the frontal lobes and other parts of the brain in humans have allowed it to fulfil this role.

Undoubtedly, there will be many more examples of changes in neuronal circuitry underlying the unique characteristics of the human brain and the consciousness that flows from it that will be discovered in future. But recently, there has also been a radical change in views about how brains – both of humans and other complex organisms – operate, and this has major relevance for the quest to uncover the material basis of human consciousness. In particular, the new viewpoint stresses the key role of oscillating brain waves.

That waves of different oscillatory frequencies exist in the brain has been known for over a century; such waves can be recorded in a non-invasive fashion by placing electrodes on the skull. Brain waves were first detected in animals in the late 19th century and in humans in the early 20th century; they are now routinely recorded clinically. Such a recording is known as an electroencephalogram (EEG).[75]

The studies of EEG patterns in animals first showed that such brain waves existed in multiple frequencies and that the particular pattern observed in an animal was related to whether it was asleep or awake and its state of mental excitation. Later studies showed that this was also true of EEG patterns in humans and that abnormal patterns were altered by injuries to the brain.

Box 6.1. Invention of the Electroencephalogram

In 1875, Richard Caton showed that electrical activity within the brain could be recorded by the simple measure of attaching electrodes to the skull of a rabbit or monkey. Caton noted that there were distinct types of brain 'waves', each with a distinct frequency. However, such was the scepticism about the validity of Caton's findings that they were almost totally ignored by the scientific community. When Hans Berger, one of the few people who took Caton's discovery seriously, followed it up by recording brain waves in a human being in 1925, he was so doubtful about his own findings that he did not publish them for a further five years, and there was considerable scepticism about the findings for a further decade. Eventually though, the importance of the findings was recognised, and today the electroencephalo-gram (EEG) is a commonly employed approach in clinical psychiatry.

Such studies have shown that alpha waves (8–12 Hz) are associated with a relaxed state of mind, beta waves (12–30 Hz) with an alert state, gamma waves (30–80 Hz) with problem-solving and concentration, theta waves (4–8 Hz) with deep relaxation, and delta waves (1.5–4 Hz) with deep, dreamless sleep (Fig. 6.2).

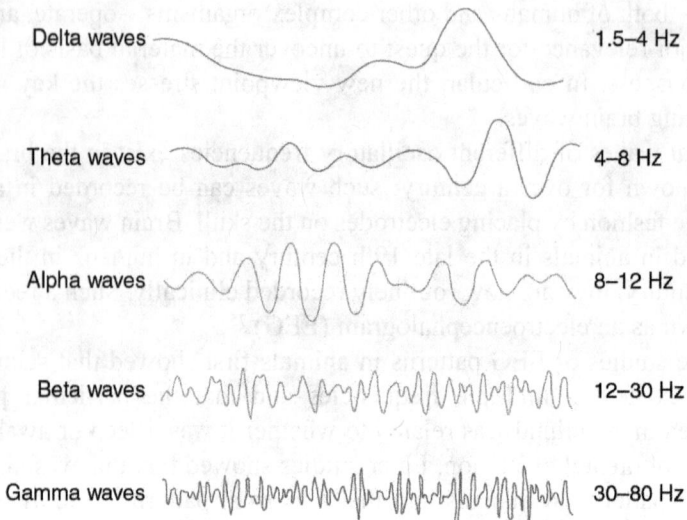

Fig. 6.2.   Human brain waves at different stages during sleep.

Source: Reproduced from Gao, G. and Su, J. (2021) *Journal of Healthcare Engineering*, 2021:1–10, with permission.

Abnormal EEG patterns have also been found in psychiatric patients.[76] Yet, despite these indications of a link between brain waves and mental state, they have tended to be viewed by many neuroscientists as an epiphenomenon, a reflection of mental state but in no way a fundamental contributor to it.

That viewpoint, however, has begun to change significantly in recent years. For the new studies suggest that brain waves play fundamental, and frequency-specific, roles as regulators of a number of important mental processes and may be key to understanding how the brain as a whole operates. One particular mental process in which brain waves appear to play a fundamental role is working memory.

Working memory is the phenomenon whereby a number of pieces of information relevant to a particular task are processed in the mind simultaneously.[77] Working memory is required in situations such as one in which an individual is remembering directions received from a friend about how to reach their new house, or they are in a shop selling different mobile phone brands and weighing up their positive and negative features before buying one. But these are only two examples; the general relevance of working memory for everyday life is why it has been referred to as the 'sketchpad of conscious thought'.[78]

Given its proposed primary role in 'executive' or controlling aspects of consciousness, the prefrontal cortex should be a key mediator of working memory, and it must do so by coordinating the behaviour of other parts of the brain: memory, as well as visual and other sensory inputs, and brain regions responsible for motivation. An unexpected outcome of studies of the role of the prefrontal cortex in working memory performed at the turn of the millennium was that around 30–40 percent of neurons in the prefrontal cortex showed task-related activity.[79] At first, this seemed to make little sense, for a common view of how the brain worked at that time saw each neuron as having one specific task. Yet, if almost half of the neurons in the prefrontal cortex were engaged in one task, surely that would mean this brain region would only be capable of performing two or three tasks – something clearly not the case. This led to the realisation that, rather than each neuron having a dedicated, specific role, instead neurons in this region must be able to multitask.

A potential problem with the idea of multitasking neurons in the prefrontal cortex was how it would be possible for their activity to be distinguished within this brain region and for mental tasks to remain separate. The answer came with the recognition that neuronal activity can become synchronised when neurons become sensitised to oscillating electrical waves of the same, specific frequency.[54] With regard to the working memory, studies found that this process involves the coordination of different ensembles of neurons by brain waves of different frequencies that fulfil different roles in such coordination.[80]

The studies have shown that higher-frequency gamma waves coordinate ensembles of neurons that carry signals relating to the incoming data about a memory of an object or a number. In contrast, lower-frequency beta waves coordinate neuronal ensembles that carry signals from the prefrontal cortex that can not only both stimulate and select such signals but also suppress them when a shift in direction is required. This suggests that gamma waves coordinate neurons carrying 'bottom-up' information, and beta waves coordinate neurons that convey 'top-down' information, such as prior knowledge and goals.[81] In line with this, gamma waves were detected in the uppermost layers of the brain cortex, where incoming sensory neurons are located, and beta waves were detected in deeper layers, where neurons carrying signals from the prefrontal cortex to the rest of the brain are to be found.

Another key finding was that ensembles differed in having distinct frequencies in the beta or gamma range compared to other ensembles in that range. This could allow discrete 'packets' of memorised information to be held separately by gamma labelling, and different aspects of executive control distinguished by beta labels.

Importantly, other studies have provided evidence for a similar role of brain waves in mental processes as diverse as vision, hearing, attention, and movement in species ranging from cats to monkeys to humans.[82] As well as confirming the role of gamma waves as coordinators of sensory input and beta waves as 'top-down' regulators of such input by 'higher' brain regions, these studies have also shown that theta waves seem to play a particular role in shifting attention, the process by which our minds stop focusing on one feature of the world and begin focusing on a different feature instead.

The discovery of such a fundamental role of brain waves of different frequencies, as mediators of diverse mental processes, does not mean that neuronal circuitry is not important. The new findings introduce a new dynamic element to brain function, but precision in neuronal circuitry remains central to how the brain works. Moreover, abnormalities in such circuitry – but also in the ways that neuronal circuits and brain waves interact – are likely to play key roles in psychiatric and personality disorders, as well as in those that affect learning.

We will be looking in more detail at a variety of psychiatric conditions, personality disorders, and other conditions that affect the brain later in this book. What is becoming clear about many such disorders is that, even if their effects only become apparent in adulthood, the changes in neuronal circuits and brain processes that underlie them may occur much earlier in life. To understand why this is so, we need to look at how the brain and nervous system develop, both in terms of evolution and during the formation of an individual human being.

Quiz

Approximate number of neurons in the human brain:
A. 86 thousand
B. 86 million
C. 86 billion
D. 86 trillion

Type of glial cells that play important roles in synapse formation:
A. Astrocyte
B. Microglia
C. Ganglia
D. Oligodendrocyte

Brain waves that coordinate neurons carrying 'bottom-up' information in the brain:
A. Alpha waves
B. Beta waves
C. Gamma waves
D. Delta waves

Chapter 7

Development and Plasticity

Key Concepts

- An embryonic structure called the notochord is of key importance for the development of the nervous system. It induces the development of a structure called the neural tube. This subsequently gives rise to the brain and nervous system.
- Neuronal growth, differentiation, and synapse formation are highly dependent on sensory signals entering the developing brain. For instance, early visual inputs are critical to the development of a connection between eye and brain.
- A child's brain is particularly sensitive to interactions with caregivers and other individuals they encounter at this life stage. Stress caused by trauma or neglect in this period can greatly influence an individual's brain development.

One of the most remarkable processes in nature is the development of a single cell – a fertilised egg – into a complex multicellular organism. In the case of human development, this involves the repeated division of the fertilised egg to give rise to the 37 trillion cells that make up a typical adult human being. But embryo development involves far more than mere cell division; also critical to this process is the formation of the different tissues and organs. Moreover, all of this embryo development is primed to occur in a precise and ordered fashion. If abnormalities occur in this process, this can either lead to the death of the embryo *in utero* or to defects that can have grave consequences for health later in life.

The human brain, with its 86 billion neurons and hundred trillion connections joining these together, as well as an almost equal number of glial cells, is the most complex object in the known Universe. Yet, despite its complexity, the brain is the product of the same type of developmental processes that give rise to other tissues and organs.[83]

A crucial event in early development is gastrulation, during which the embryo acquires the three cell layers that will later give rise to different organs and tissues. These three layers are the ectoderm, mesoderm, and endoderm.

A structure called the notochord, a cylinder of mesodermal cells that forms at the midline of the gastrulating embryo, is of key importance for the development of the nervous system. Although the notochord itself is a transient entity, it sends signals to the ectodermal cells that lie above it, which induce these cells to begin developing into a structure called the neural tube (Fig. 7.1).[84] The multipotent neural stem cells within this tube subsequently give rise to the entire brain and spinal cord, as well as most of the peripheral nervous system.

Soon after the neural tube forms, the precursors of the forebrain, midbrain, and hindbrain develop; these are the prosencephalon, mesencephalon, and rhombencephalon, respectively. The patterned expression of transcription factors coded by the homeotic genes initiates this process of brain region formation. However, subsequent differentiation of cells in these regions into the appropriate classes of neurons and glial cells is regulated by molecular signals that come from cells and tissues adjacent to the neural tube.[85] These send out molecular signalling agents that include retinoic acid, fibroblast growth factor, bone morphogenetic proteins, Noggin, Chordin, Wnt, and Sonic hedgehog proteins. These factors induce the expression of transcription factors which regulate the differentiation of neural stem cells into the different types of motor and sensory neurons, interneurons, and glial cells.

There is interest in the molecular mechanisms underlying early brain development not only to further our basic understanding of this process but also because abnormalities in these molecular mechanisms can cause birth defects.[86] These include spina bifida (failure of the posterior neural tube to close properly), anencephaly (failure of the anterior neural tube to close at all), and holoprosencephaly (disrupted regional differentiation of the forebrain) (Fig. 7.2). Abnormalities in the formation of the embryonic and foetal brain can be caused by mutations of the genes that regulate this process. Mutations in the Sonic hedgehog signalling protein-coding genes

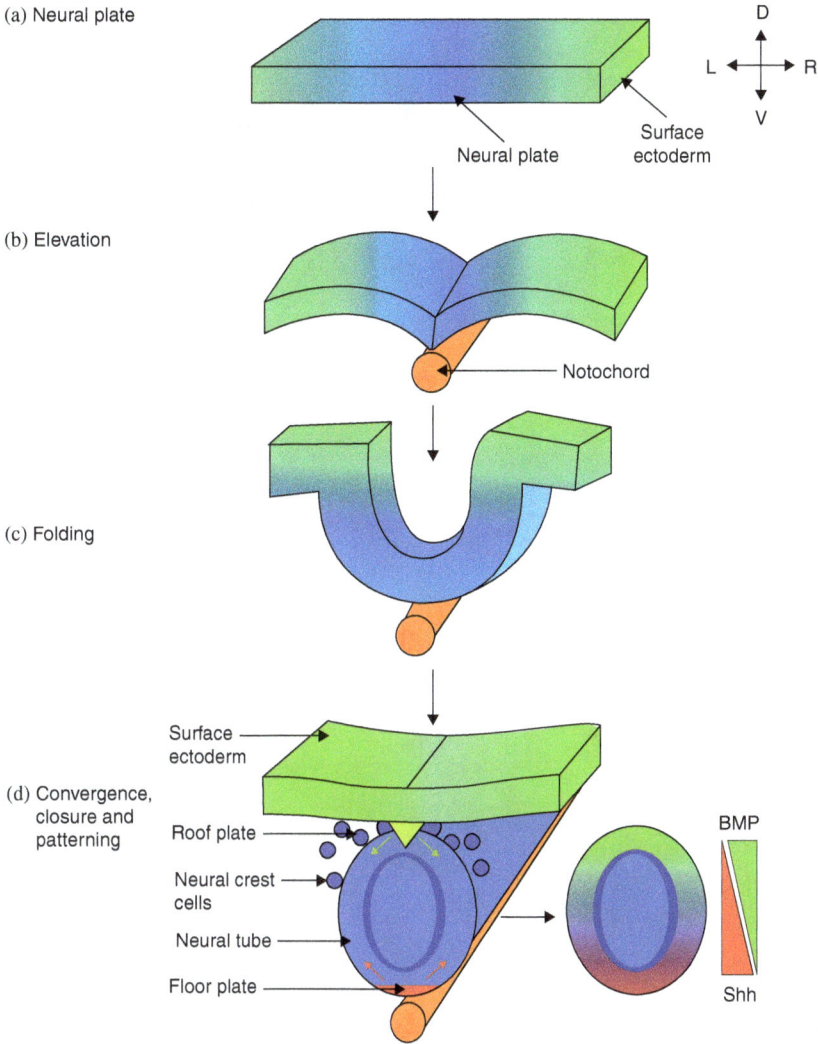

Fig. 7.1. (a) The pseudostratified columnar epithelium of the neural plate forms. The lateral edges of the neural plate then (b) elevate and (c) fold before (d) converging at the midline and closing. Shh (red arrows) and BMP inhibitors secreted from the floor plate, and BMP4/7 (green arrows) secreted from the roof plate pattern the neural tube along its ventro-dorsal axis, giving rise to the layers of the spinal cord.

Source: Reproduced from Shparberg, R. *et al.* (2019) *Frontiers in Physiology*, 10:705, with permission.

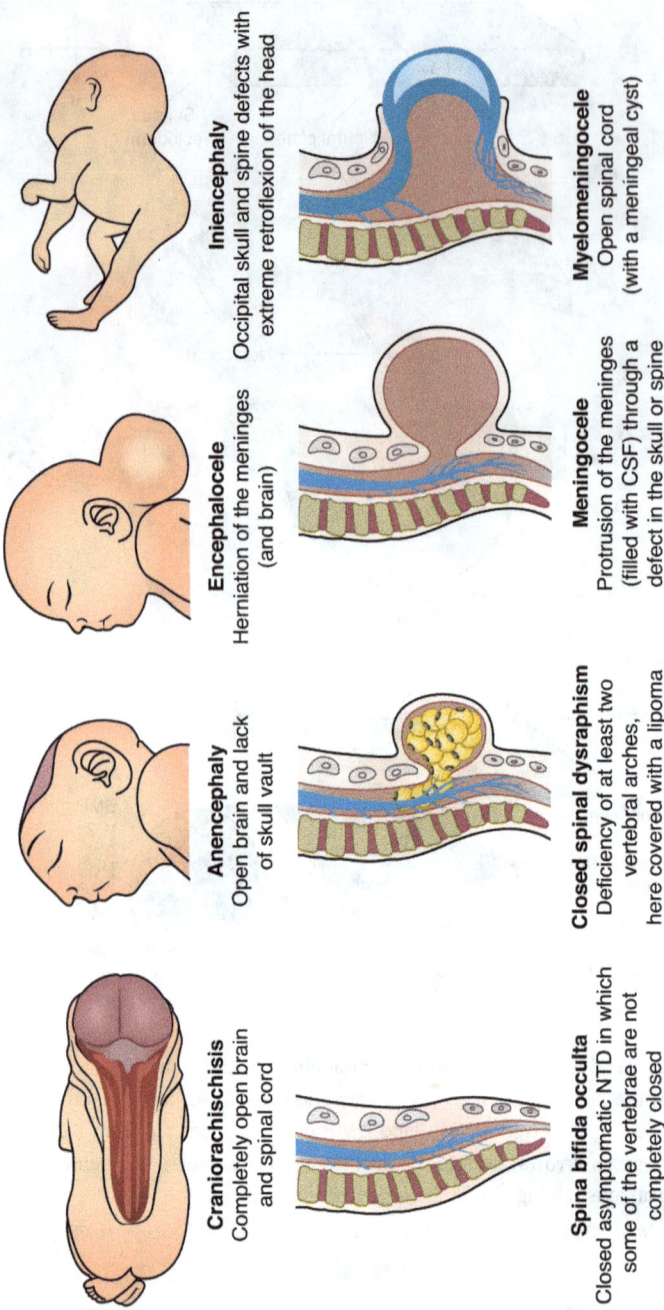

Craniorachischisis
Completely open brain
and spinal cord

Anencephaly
Open brain and lack
of skull vault

Encephalocele
Herniation of the meninges
(and brain)

Iniencephaly
Occipital skull and spine defects with
extreme retroflexion of the head

Spina bifida occulta
Closed asymptomatic NTD in which
some of the vertebrae are not
completely closed

Closed spinal dysraphism
Deficiency of at least two
vertebral arches,
here covered with a lipoma

Meningocele
Protrusion of the meninges
(filled with CSF) through a
defect in the skull or spine

Myelomeningocele
Open spinal cord
(with a meningeal cyst)

Fig. 7.2.   Schematic representation of several neural tube defects (NTDs). Spina bifida occulta is found in up to 10 percent of people and usually occurs in the low spinal region. Closed spinal dysraphism has many variants, including lipomyelomeningocele, low-lying conus, and thickened filum terminale. CSF, cerebrospinal fluid.

Source: Reproduced from Copp, A. *et al.* (2015) *Nature Reviews Disease Primers,* 1:15007, with permission.

are also associated with the most common type of childhood brain tumour, medulloblastoma.[87]

Not only gene mutations but also environmental insults can disrupt the signalling pathways involved in embryonic neural induction. For instance, because of the important role of retinoic acid in this process, pregnant women should avoid excessive consumption of vitamin A – the metabolic precursor of this molecule – as this can impede neural tube closure and disrupt later aspects of neuronal differentiation.[88] Other agents that can affect normal differentiation of the embryonic nervous system include alcohol and the drug thalidomide.

The peripheral nervous system is formed in the embryo by neural crest cells that migrate from the neural tube. These cells begin their migratory journey by undergoing the epithelial-to-mesenchymal transition (EMT), which is mediated by genes such as Snail1 and Snail2 that repress expression of intercellular junction and epithelial adhesion proteins.[89] Since cell migration is a feature of tumour metastasis, Snail genes can mutate to become oncogenes in later life and cause cancer. The neural crest cells encounter signals generated by non-neural peripheral structures. Depending on which signals they encounter, the neural crest cells can differentiate into sensory, sympathetic, parasympathetic, or enteric neurons.

Neuronal migration is important not only for the formation of the peripheral nervous system but also for the subsequent differentiation of specific neuronal cell types within the brain and the formation of specialised patterns of synaptic connections. Such migration of neuronal precursor cells within the developing brain is heavily influenced by glial cells, which act like a scaffolding to support these migratory activities.[90]

Once neurons have been generated, they need to become connected to form the circuits that regulate brain function. The first step in this process is the formation of dendrites and an axon; the neuron's cytoskeleton plays an important role in this process. Subsequently, the axon grows to reach the dendrites of a target neurons, which can be local or distant. The directed growth of an axon depends on the behaviour of a growth cone, a dynamic structure at the axon's tip (Fig. 7.3).[91]

Growth cones are highly motile and explore the extracellular environment, determine the pattern of growth, and guide the extension of the neuron in that direction, the cytoskeleton also playing a key role in this process. The growing axon must eventually find an appropriate target while avoiding inappropriate ones. This occurs through a process of chemoattraction, as well as chemorepulsion.[92] Among the first chemoattractant

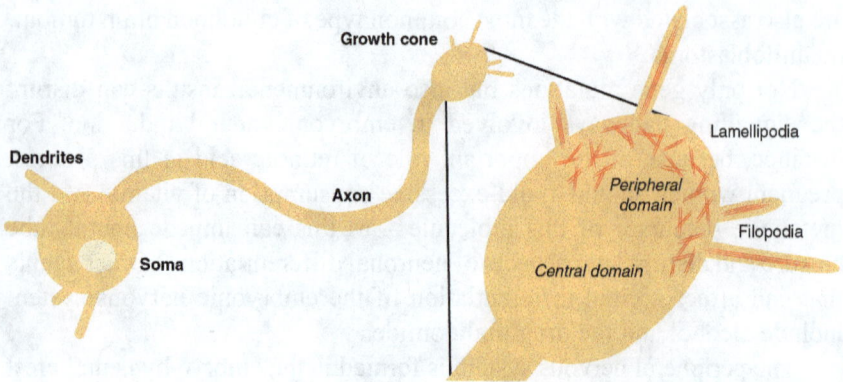

Fig. 7.3.   The growth cone forms at the tip of developing axons to guide their extension and is divisible into a central and peripheral domain, with the peripheral domain containing structures rich in actin that help regulate motility. The lamellipodia is a network of branched actin filaments (red) that is remodelled during growth cone advance. Regulated bundling of actin filaments drives protrusion of filopodia, which sense the environment ahead of the growth cone.

Source: Reproduced from Davis-Lunn, M. *et al.* (2023) *Biology*, 12:954, with permission.

molecules to be identified were the netrins, derived from the Sanskrit word for guide. Chemorepellents include the semaphorins; these cause growth cones to collapse and axon extension to cease.

Developing dendrites are also highly dynamic structures and grow using similar molecular mechanisms to axons. They also undergo a process called 'dendritic tiling', in which developing dendrites are prevented from growing too near to other dendrites so that a sufficient space is created in which axons can form synapses with the dendrites.[93]

Once an axon has located its dendritic target, the process of synaptogenesis can begin.[94] Neuroregulin is an important regulator of this process; it induces the synthesis and insertion of neurotransmitter receptors at a nascent postsynaptic site. Other proteins involved in synaptogenesis include the neurexins and neuroligins. These proteins form interactions with each other that promote the association of pre- and postsynaptic membranes. In addition, neurexins help create the molecular structures in the presynaptic membrane that will release the neurotransmitter. Interestingly, changes in the genes coding for these three types of signalling molecules have been linked to certain types of autism.[95]

A central feature of brain development is that neuronal growth, differentiation, and synapse formation are highly dependent on sensory signals entering the developing brain. This was demonstrated by studies of the developing cat visual system.[96] In such studies, one of the eyes of a newborn kitten was sewn shut at birth. The kitten was allowed to interact with its environment, and the eye only reopened after a certain period that could vary. Remarkably, kittens deprived of vision in one eye for only the first three months remained blind in that eye for the rest of their lives. This shows that early visual inputs are critical to the development of a functional connection between eye and brain.

In further studies, newborn kittens were placed in enclosures whose walls were painted with either only vertical or only horizontal lines. Kittens exposed solely to horizontal lines only developed to see horizontal objects, so they could jump onto the seat of a chair but kept on banging into the chair's legs, as these were invisible to them. The kittens exposed only to vertical lines could detect the chair legs but were incapable of identifying the horizontal seat as a place to sit. These studies showed that not only the light coming from the eye but also the spatial information about objects in the outside world was critical to the development of vision. Recall that earlier studies showed that the shapes of external objects are detected by individual neurons not in their entirety but as isolated lines and edges. Presumably, in the kittens exposed only to one direction of line, neurons in the visual cortex did not develop a recognition of other directions, and this was irreversible.

Further demonstration of the importance of environmental input in shaping the sensory cortex has come from observations of people with deficits in different senses; these indicate that the brain is highly plastic in responding to such deficits. Thus, people born blind or who become blind early in life have more nuanced hearing, especially when listening to music and tracking moving objects in space (Fig. 7.4).[97]

To explore this issue further, a recent study used fMRI to compare the brains of blind versus seeing individuals and found that the auditory cortex of blind people showed narrower neuronal 'tuning' than sighted individuals in discerning small differences in sound frequency.[98] Conversely, another fMRI study found that the brains of deaf individuals have enhanced capacity in other senses.[99]

Neuroplasticity, also known as neuronal plasticity or brain plasticity, is the term used to describe the brain and nervous system's ability to change through growth and reorganisation.[100] We have already discussed the dramatic changes that occur in the developing brains of embryos and foetuses; such changes continue after birth.

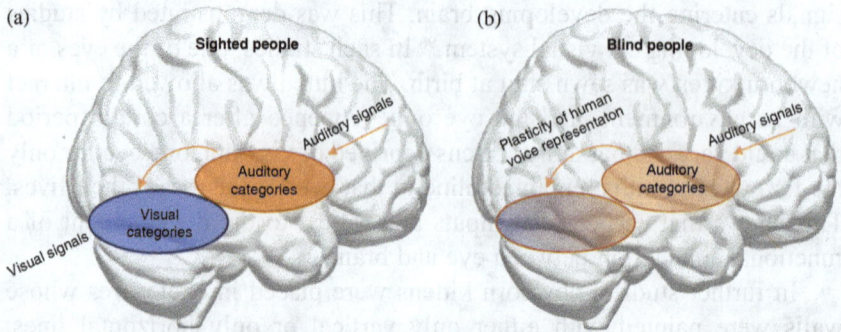

Fig. 7.4. (a) In sighted people, high-level visual areas in the ventral occipitotemporal cortex (VOTC) sort incoming visual signals into categories (blue), and high-level auditory areas in the superior temporal cortex do the same with incoming sounds (orange). The high-level visual and auditory areas also communicate with each other. (b) In blind participants, the high-level auditory areas are less involved in sorting sounds into human and non-human sounds than in sighted participants. In addition, VOTC regions primarily associated with visual processing in sighted people have become involved in sorting incoming sounds into these two categories.

Source: Reproduced from Bola, L. (2022) *eLife*, 11:e82747, with permission.

A newborn human baby's brain is like a sponge, soaking up all kinds of environmental information, particularly from parents or caregivers. In their first year, babies can learn any language, but that ability quickly narrows based on the sounds or signs to which the baby is exposed. The ability then decreases during childhood, which is why it is much more difficult to learn new languages later in life, particularly those very different from an individual's native language.

The great receptiveness of a baby's brain to new environmental input is partly based on the large number of new synapses that are formed during the first few years of life.

Many of these new connections are excitatory; thus, this offers a huge amount of learning potential. But there are many other important cellular and genetic processes that occur at this stage of life. While most neurons are already present at birth, other types of brain cells, such as neuroglia, are developing and maturing rapidly in the first years of life.

From about 18 months to two years old, toddlers are learning all sorts of novel aspects of the world around them, and in the brain this involves both the strengthening of important connections and weakening ones not being used. To help the brain prioritise certain experiences, more inhibitory connections, which act as brakes for information processing, develop across neuronal circuits. To reduce unwanted connections, the toddler's brain loses about half of the synapses that had previously been formed in a process known as synaptic pruning. To strengthen connections, myelination, the process by which neurons are insulated, rapidly increases throughout childhood and beyond.

With so much connection building and strengthening, the child's brain is particularly sensitive to interactions with caregivers and other individuals they encounter at this life stage. Stress caused by trauma or neglect in this period can thus have profound effects on an individual's brain development that can affect them for the rest of their lives.

From the age of 10 through the teenage years, young people must navigate a diverse range of friendships and other social interactions outside the home, particularly at school and also via extracurricular activities, at the same time as major changes are taking place in their bodies, emotional state, and sexual awareness. The hypothalamus plays a central role in stimulating the sex hormones at this stage of life, and these in turn influence brain development (Fig. 7.5).[101] Teenagers' heightened sensitivity to the social environment is accompanied by further widespread synaptic pruning and myelination, particularly in neuronal circuits underlying emotion and reward processing.

Recent studies have identified interesting differences between human beings and even our closest animal relatives, the great apes, in terms of the stage of life at which myelination of neurons in the brain is complete. While in chimpanzees this occurs at the end of puberty, in humans myelination is only complete in the late 20s.[102] This process begins at the back of the brain and moves forward; thus, neurons in the frontal lobe areas most associated with planning, reasoning, and problem-solving are last to be myelinated. This is one reason why young adults can be highly imaginative and creative but are more likely to act in ways that can seem irrational and impetuous to older people.

While brain plasticity is a recognised feature of youth, such plasticity has not been thought to be true of the middle-aged human brain. One reason why the mid-to-late 20s were thought of as the peak of brain development is that the volume of white matter, which is linked to neural connections and the speed of neural processing, reaches a high level at these ages. This is because neuronal networks are continually being modified and adjusted into young adulthood, especially those involved in rational thought and considering future consequences.

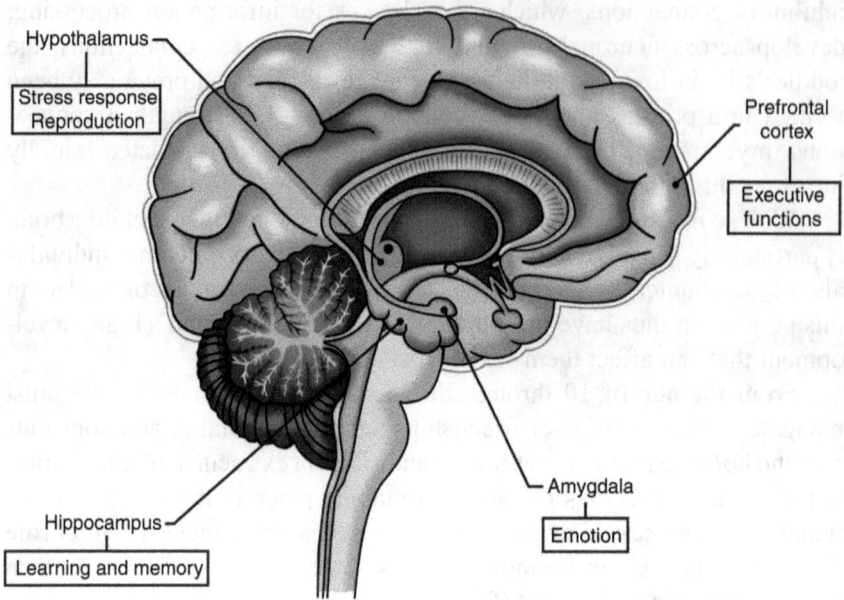

Fig. 7.5. Effects of the sex hormones on different brain areas. Besides influencing reproductive behaviour, gonadal hormones are also assumed to have an influence on many cerebral functions.

Source: Reproduced from Pompili, A. *et al.* (2020) *Acta Neurobiologiae Experimentalis*, 80:117–128, with permission.

Yet, recent studies indicate that brain development is far from complete at this stage of life. Instead, as our brains develop in our 30s and 40s, brain plasticity, as defined by the ability for connections to be strengthened or weakened in response to changes in the activity of different brain regions, is reprioritised rather than diminished.

Challenging the assumption that the brains of middle-aged people have much less plasticity than those of young people is the discovery of new roles for 'silent' synapses.[103] First identified in the brains of young mice, these are immature connections between neurons that remain inactive until some mental process recruits them to become active. During early development, these synapses are believed to help the brain acquire the massive amounts of information that babies need to learn about their environment and how to interact with it.

In mice, these synapses were initially thought to have disappeared by about 12 days of age, equivalent to the first months of human life. But a recent study has shown that they are present in adult mice brains, accounting for 30 percent of all synapses.

It still remains to be shown what roles these silent synapses might be playing in the adult brain and what sort of stimuli might activate them. Recent studies in mice suggest that they allow the mature brain to form new memories and learn new things without having to modify existing conventional synapses. Such findings support the idea that a wide range of different brain plasticity mechanisms may exist that could explain how brains can both efficiently learn new things and retain them in long-term memory. To allow this to occur, some synapses must be established or modified easily to form new memories, while others must remain in a more stable state to preserve long-term memories.

While the discovery of silent synapses and understanding of the ways in which they work in the mature adult brain have come from studies of mice, because of the many similarities between rodent and human brains at the level of basic structure and function, it is likely that silent synapses exist to a similar degree in the brains of mature adult humans. Studies are now underway to identify and study such synapses in the human brain.

Findings like these have challenged the idea that brain plasticity is only a feature of young brains. But how does all of this relate to human cognition? A place to start will be to connect what we have learned about brain plasticity to a key cognitive function – memory.

Quiz

Embryonic precursor of the forebrain:
A. Prosencephalon
B. Mesencephalon
C. Rhombencephalon
D. Tevacephalon

Molecular signalling agent involved in brain region formation:
A. Sonic scooter
B. Sonic screwdriver
C. Sonic frontier
D. Sonic hedgehog

Age at which myelination in the human brain is complete:
A. Mid teens
B. Early 20s
C. Late 20s
D. Late 30s

Chapter 8

Learning and Memory

Key Concepts

- In the sea slug's learning response, the enzyme PKA activates enhanced glutamate release at the synapse and the production of proteins in the synapses of the neuronal circuit, modifying its functional behaviour over a longer time period.
- Long-term potentiation (LTP) is a key part of learning in mammals because it strengthens synaptic connections in neuronal circuits that have been recently stimulated. Long-term depression (LTD) has the opposite effect.
- An important role for the hippocampus in the human memory process has been shown by studies of individuals who have suffered damage to this brain region through injury, disease, or via the unintended consequences of surgery to treat epilepsy.

The importance of learning and memory for human existence is reflected in the fact that there has been speculation about their physical basis since the time of the ancient Greeks. The philosopher Plato speculated almost 2,400 years ago that the process of human memory formation is similar to a scribe making impressions on a wax tablet.[104] In modern times, the first insights into the molecular basis of learning and memory came not from studies of human beings but from investigations in a much simpler organism: the sea slug, Aplysia.

If the Aplysia gill is repeatedly touched with no obvious ill effects to the creature, eventually this organism will cease reacting in this way, showing that it has learned to ignore a harmless stimulus; in other words, it has become 'habituated' to the stimulus. Conversely, if an Aplysia that has become used to having its gill touched is given a noxious stimulus – for instance an electric shock – at the same time that its gill is stimulated, it becomes super-sensitised to having the gill touched. Demonstrating that the habituation and sensitisation responses are simple forms of memory, these can persist for several weeks.

Studies showed that these learned responses in Aplysia are accompanied by changes in synapses in the neuronal circuits involved in this stimulus-response mechanism.[105] During habituation, transmission at the glutaminergic synapse that connects the sensory and motor neurons is depressed. In contrast, during sensitisation, transmission is enhanced.

Such studies showed that the sensitisation response involves production of the intracellular messenger cAMP, which, as we saw in humans, is involved in the fright, flight, or fight response that is mediated by the hormone adrenaline. In Aplysia's learning response, cAMP stimulates the enzyme PKA. In the short term, this stimulates enhanced glutamate release at the synapse (Fig. 8.1). In addition, by activating the transcription factor CREB, PKA switches on specific genes that lead to the production of new proteins in the synapses of the neuronal circuit, modifying its functional behaviour over a longer time period.

The importance of cAMP in learning and memory at the level of the whole brain has been confirmed by studies in another experimental organism, the fruit fly. The advantage of this organism is that it is possible to create mutant fruit flies on a mass scale. By screening such mutants to select flies with defects in learning and memory and then identifying which genes were altered in these mutant flies, three genes were identified, which were named dunce, rutabaga (inspired by the name of a kind of turnip), and amnesiac.[106] Such studies showed that dunce codes for the phosphodiesterase enzyme, which degrades cAMP and thus negatively regulates its concentration; rutabaga for the adenylyl cyclase enzyme, which creates cAMP from ATP; and amnesiac for a peptide transmitter that stimulates adenyl cyclase.

Our understanding of the molecular and cellular basis of memory in mammals received a boost from a study performed in 1968 on the rabbit hippocampus. As mentioned earlier, it has been known for some time that the hippocampus is crucial for the formation of new memories based on the effects of injury to this region on memory formation in human individuals. In the experimental study, neurons in the rabbit hippocampus

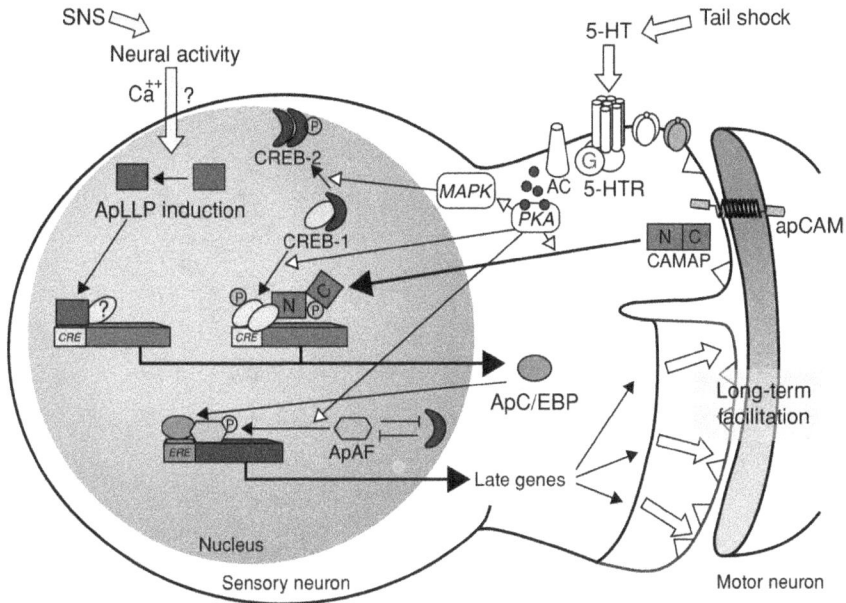

Fig. 8.1. Schematic model of signalling pathways underlying long-term facilitation in an Aplysia sensory neuron. Neurotransmitter 5-HT stimulates adenylyl cyclase, which in turn activates PKA. MAPK is also activated and translocates into the nucleus, where it phosphorylates CREB2, which represses CREB1 and ApAF in the absence of 5-HT. Once freed from repression, CREB1 activates ApC/EBP. This interacts with ApAF to form a core downstream effector of CREB1. ApC/EBP-ApAF induces late genes critical for maintenance of LTF. Robust neural activity activates ApLLP in the nucleus in a calcium-dependent manner.

Source: Reproduced from Lee, Y.-S. *et al.* (2008) *Molecular Brain*, 1:3, with permission.

were subjected to stimulation to study their electrical characteristics. A surprising by-product of this study was the discovery that only a few seconds of high-frequency electrical stimulation can enhance synaptic transmission by hippocampal neurons for considerable periods of time.

This phenomenon, named long-term potentiation (LTP), is a key part of the learning process in mammals because it leads to a strengthening of synaptic connections in neuronal circuits that have been recently stimulated (Fig. 8.2).[107]

If LTP were the only process involved in learning and memory, this would create a problem, namely that synapses could only be strengthened, not weakened, and if allowed to continue increasing in strength, synapses

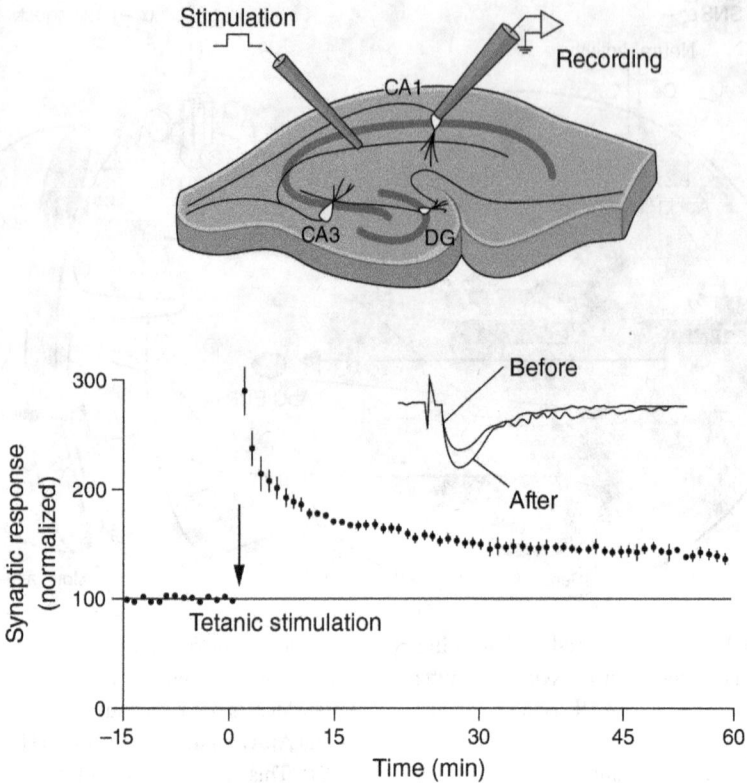

Fig. 8.2. A typical experiment of LTP recording from a hippocampal slice. A brief strong stimulation, e.g. tetanic stimulation at 100 Hz for one second, potentiates the subsequent synaptic transmission for the long term. In slice, it lasts a few hours. *In vivo*, it can last days.

Source: Reproduced from Hayashi, Y. (2022) *Neuroscience Research*, 175:3–15, with permission.

would ultimately reach a ceiling level of efficiency, which would inhibit the encoding of new information. In fact, not long after the discovery of LTP, another process, long-term depression (LTD), was identified that works to weaken synaptic connections and thus acts to oppose the effects of LTP.[108]

Studies over the past few decades have revealed the molecular and cellular mechanisms that underlie both LPT and LTD. A key discovery was that the induction of LTP is dependent on the binding of the excitatory neurotransmitter glutamate to NMDA receptors.

These are ion channels that are permeable to sodium, potassium, and calcium, but the central pore that allows these through is blocked by magnesium. Under normal circumstances, the NMDA receptors are closed by this block, and glutamate is released from the presynaptic neuron by two other receptor types, the AMPA and kainate receptors. But high-frequency stimulation of the type that induces LTP increases the amount of glutamate released, and this overcomes the magnesium block, activating the NMDA receptors.

NMDA receptors are well suited to their role in LTP; the magnesium block means they are only activated in response to high-frequency stimulation from the presynaptic neuron, and the calcium that flows through them stimulates enzymes that catalyse lasting changes in the postsynaptic neuron. LTP mobilises AMPA receptors, which become highly concentrated at the synapse but not in other parts of the dendrite. There is also evidence that LTP can activate silent synapses by stimulating insertion into them of AMPA receptors, which such synapses normally lack. Alongside such changes in the postsynaptic neuron, there are also long-lasting ones in the presynaptic neuron. These are induced by the postsynaptic neuron in a retrograde manner by the gaseous neurotransmitter nitric oxide.

LTD, which is induced by repetitive low-frequency stimulation of a presynaptic neuron in the absence of a postsynaptic response, largely involves the reversal of such changes; thus, AMPA receptors are removed from the membrane of the postsynaptic neuron (Fig. 8.3).

While much of our understanding of the molecular mechanisms underlying LTP and LTD has come from studies of brain slices, there is evidence of the importance of these processes for learning and memory in the intact, living brain. For instance, treating mice with drugs that block the NMDA receptor prevents them learning new tasks. Ultimately though, if we want to understand how learning and memory work at the level of the whole brain, we need to consider how different brain regions are involved in these processes, both in terms of the particular contribution of such regions to this process and how they interact.

Our knowledge of which brain regions play important, and distinctive, roles in the memory process has come partly from studies of experiments on animals but also through investigations of the effects of the loss of specific brain regions in unfortunate human individuals that were the result of accidental damage through surgery or infection. Before we look in detail at what we have learned from such individuals, it is worth

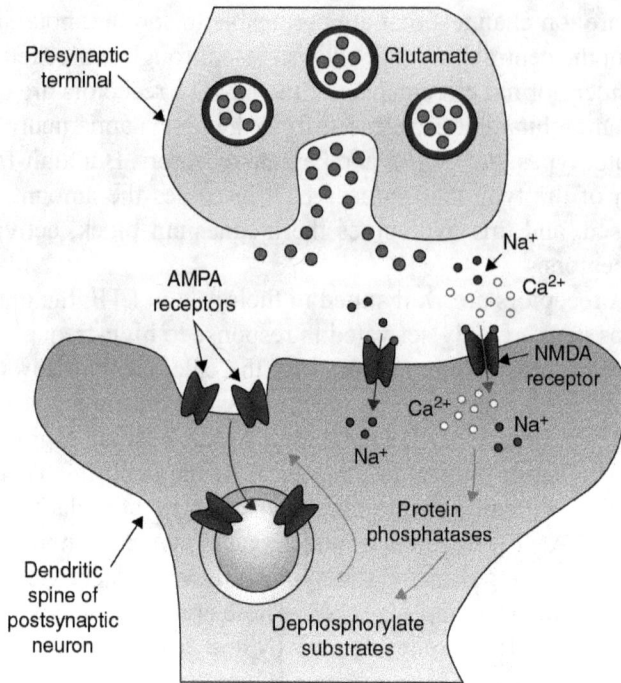

Fig. 8.3. LTD mechanism: (a) Ca²⁺ ions enter via NMDA receptors. (b) Activation of protein phosphatases. (c) Dephosphorylation of AMPA receptors leads to endocytosis of AMPA.

Source: Reproduced from Atluri, V. *et al.* (2015) *Neural Plasticity*, 2015:138979, with permission.

defining the terms used to describe the different types of memory that exist in human beings.[109]

Humans have various ways of storing information. Declarative memory is the storage and retrieval of material that is available to consciousness and can be expressed by language, that is, it can be declared. Examples include the ability to remember a phone number, the words of a song, or a past event. In contrast, non-declarative memory, also known as procedural memory, is not available to consciousness, at least not in any detail. Memories of this type involve skills and associations generally acquired and retrieved at an unconscious level. Examples include remembering how to ride a bike, play the piano, or hit a ball with a bat. It can be difficult to explain to others exactly how we do such things, and thinking about it can even impede performance.

Box 8.1.   Henry Molaison and the Hippocampus

The first recognition that the hippocampus has a role in memory came in the 1950s because of the unfortunate consequences of an operation on a young US man called Henry Molaison. He suffered from epileptic seizures that were so frequent and violent that, in 1953, a neurosurgeon called William Scoville proposed to drill into Molaison's skull, insert a metal tube, and suck out the hippocampal region from which his seizures seemed to originate. At that time, almost nothing was known about the functional role of the hippocampus, and the operation was given the go-ahead. Initially, the operation was judged a success since the seizures were greatly reduced. But it soon became clear that Molaison had been left without the ability to store or recall any experiences after his operation. While a personal tragedy for Molaison, his condition was a revelation for scientists seeking to understand the biological basis of memory. Until this point, it was assumed that memory was a property of the whole brain. But only Molaison's capacity to store and recall new memories appeared defective. In contrast, his memories of life before the operation seemed to have been retained but only in a general fashion. Thus, Molaison could remember that his father was born in Louisiana and that he had accompanied his parents on holidays in Massachusetts. But if asked about specific episodes in such holidays, he had no idea. This led to the proposal that different parts of the brain play distinct roles in memory formation, with the hippocampus being the place where new memories are formed, while long-term memory storage takes place in other brain regions. Molaison's memory defects suggested that the hippocampus knits together our experiences – which can encompass sights, sounds, smells, emotions, and every other aspect of a given moment, each processed in a different brain region – into a single remembered event that can be recalled in the future. This type of memory is called 'episodic', to distinguish it from 'semantic' memory, which is concerned with general facts. That Molaison remembered such general facts suggested that the hippocampus plays little role in this type of memory. Another type of remembering is called 'procedural' memory. A classic example of this is learning to ride a bike – once learned, you do it without thinking. Interestingly, Molaison could learn new practical skills. For instance, in one study, he was told to trace the image of a star on a piece of paper while looking only at the image of his hand in a mirror. Such a task is difficult at first but gets easier with practice. Molaison improved with each time that he carried out the task, even though he had no conscious memory of having tried it before. This suggests that procedural memory is less dependent on the hippocampus, and we now recognise the cerebellum as a key brain region involved in this type of memory.

These are not the only ways of categorising memories. Within declarative memory, we can also talk about general versus episodic memory. Episodic memory is the type that allows us to remember a specific event that took place in our individual lives. In contrast, general memory underlies our knowledge of an important historical event like World War II. Meanwhile, if we categorise memory according to the time over which it is effective, we can distinguish between immediate memory, short-term memory, and long-term memory.

Immediate memory is the ability of the brain to hold on to ongoing experience for a second or so. This type of memory allows us to briefly picture a scene we have just seen if we shut our eyes at some random moment. Short-term memory is the ability to hold and manipulate information in the mind for seconds to minutes while it is being used to achieve a particular goal; it is also known as 'working' memory, and we have already mentioned how recent studies have identified the role of brain waves of different frequencies as modulators of this process. Short-term memory allows us to keep a phone number or password in our heads as we key it in but is also vital to navigating many aspects of everyday life; as such, it influences and is influenced by many aspects of brain function.

Long-term memory allows us to retain memories for days, weeks, or even a lifetime. The transfer of information to long-term memories can occur through unconscious brain mechanisms but also by conscious rehearsal or practice. Initial memory traces that have become encoded in a more long-term form are said to be 'consolidated'.

If these are the different forms of memory that occur in humans, what is their basis in terms of brain structure and function? An important role for the hippocampus in the human memory process has been shown by studies of unfortunate individuals who have suffered damage to this brain region either through the unintended consequences of surgery to treat epilepsy or because of the effects of infection.[110] From the point at which such individuals lose their hippocampal function, they become incapable of remembering any new experience for more than a few minutes. However, such individuals can remember, albeit only in general terms, things that happened to them before the injury. Interestingly, affected individuals can learn new tasks but cannot remember doing so.

These types of observations suggest that the hippocampus is involved in the process of episodic memory and in the transformation of short-term into long-term memory. Further evidence of such a role has come from studies of experimental animals that have had their hippocampus removed

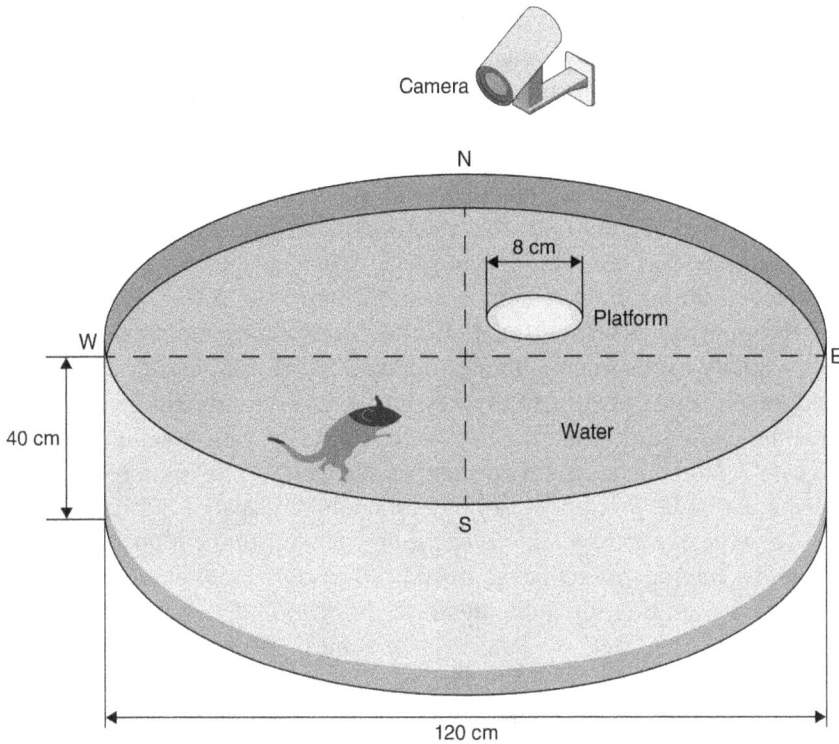

Fig. 8.4. A Morris water maze.

Source: Reproduced from Wen, J. *et al.* (2023) *Oxidative Medicine and Cellular Longevity*, 2023:4822767, with permission.

surgically. Both rats and monkeys with such lesions seem to have lost their ability to store new memories. For instance, rats treated this way are incapable of learning how to negotiate a water maze: a circular tank of milky water in which is an underwater platform, concealed from view by the liquid's opaqueness (Fig. 8.4).[111]

On the walls of the experimental room are visual cues, for instance, a window, a door, and a wall clock. The rats are tested to see how long it takes them to locate the underwater platform. On its first attempts a normal rat only finds the platform by trial and error but soon becomes able to immediately locate the platform. This shows that the rat has memorised the position of the platform by referencing the visual clues in the experimental room. However, rats with hippocampal lesions never learn this step. Studies of monkeys with similar lesions show that they too can no longer perform delayed response tasks.

A different sort of evidence of a role for the hippocampus in specific types of memory processes has come from brain imaging studies of volunteers asked to look at a list of items that was then removed and the volunteers asked to remember what they could from the list. Such studies showed that not only does the task trigger increased activity in the hippocampus, but the activity is particularly enhanced for items that volunteers subsequently remembered compared to ones they later forgot.

Intriguingly, in line with the effect that the environment can have on the plasticity of the human brain, London's 'black-cab' taxi drivers, who traditionally must memorise the key street networks within 25 miles of Charing Cross station in London, were shown by one imaging study to have an enlarged posterior hippocampus, the part of this brain region that plays a particularly important role in remembering spatial information.[112]

The type of condition that is caused by damage to the hippocampus is known as anterograde amnesia, in contrast to retrograde amnesia, which refers to a condition in which memories prior to injury can no longer be remembered.[113] In fact, this latter type of amnesia is much more common, being associated with severe head trauma and also with neurodegenerative disorders such as Alzheimer's disease that cause generalised damage to many different brain regions. This is in line with other evidence that long-term memory is associated with many different parts of the brain cortex and not with one specific region.

The idea that long-term memories are distributed across the brain cortex has a long history. In studies performed in the 1920s, lesions were made in different cortical regions of rats, and their subsequent ability to learn to find their way in a water maze was assessed.

The study showed that the lesions' locations did not seem to have much effect on the ability to develop long-term memories. What did begin to have an impact was the extent of cortical damage, with performance only declining after widespread damage to multiple regions.

Other studies have assessed human beings with injuries to different regions of the cortex. Such people have memory defects linked to the functions of the cortical areas in which the injuries have occurred. For instance, injuries to Wernicke's area, which has been linked to language comprehension and which we will discuss in more detail later, lead to an inability to remember the meaning of words. In contrast, damage to cortical regions involved in facial recognition typically gives rise to an inability to remember faces.

Brain imaging studies of healthy human volunteers are also providing insights into the mechanisms underlying long-term memory formation and recall. In one study, volunteers first examined words paired with either pictures or sounds. Their brains were then imaged while the volunteers were asked to recall whether each word was associated with either a picture or a sound. The study showed that cortical areas that became active when a volunteer was exposed to a specific picture or sound were reactivated when that individual was asked to recall it. Other studies have revealed a surprising specificity in the neuronal circuitry that underlies memories of specific objects encountered in the past.

One study was performed in people undergoing surgery to treat their epilepsy. Such individuals typically receive a local anaesthetic; their brains are exposed while they are still conscious, and recording electrodes are then inserted into specific neurons. The idea is to try and determine the source of the epileptic seizures so that this might be surgically removed with as little damage to surrounding brain regions as possible. But this also offers an opportunity, namely to record the activity of particular neurons in the hippocampus when volunteers undergoing such surgery were shown specific photographic images.

An unexpected outcome of this study was that some neurons only became activated in response to a specific image.[114] Thus, one neuron was only activated when a volunteer was shown a photograph of former US President Bill Clinton. In another individual, a neuron only became activated by an image of actor Jennifer Aniston. Other neurons responded to images of famous landmarks. A dynamical aspect to the responses was shown by the fact that when the volunteer whose neuron had responded to the Jennifer Aniston image was shown a picture of the actor alongside an image of the Eiffel Tower, the neuron soon began to respond to pictures of the landmark shown on its own.

Another intriguing discovery of the study was that there seem to be more abstract aspects to visual memory than simply image recognition. This was shown by the fact that in one volunteer, a neuron was activated by a photo of the actor Halle Berry, but also by her wearing a mask while playing the movie character 'Catwoman', and even by an image bearing just the words 'Halle Berry'. This suggests that this neuron's response is not merely to the facial features of the actor but also to the 'concept, the abstract entity, of Halle Berry', in the words of the neuroscientist who led the study. But this suggests that the neuronal memory in this case is linking a visual representation of another human being with a linguistic representation of that individual. So, how might this work in terms of neuronal and brain mechanisms? To investigate this issue further, let us now look at what we are beginning to learn about the mechanisms underlying complex thought processes.

Quiz

Studies of this organism played a key role in determining the molecular basis of memory:
A. Aplysia
B. Placidia
C. Chlamydia
D. Procidia

Which of these genes is NOT involved in learning and memory in the fruit fly?
A. Dunce
B. Rutabaga
C. Forgetful
D. Amnesiac

Receptor that plays a key role in long-term potentiation:
A. DAMN receptor
B. MDAN receptor
C. NDMA receptor
D. NMDA receptor

Chapter 9

Thoughts and Actions

Key Concepts

- The ability to evaluate has been linked to a part of the prefrontal region named the orbitofrontal cortex (OFC). This receives input from all the senses, giving it access to a variety of information that can help in making a choice.
- The ability to make decisions is associated with the dorsolateral prefrontal cortex (DLPFC). This communicates with brain regions linked to reward, such as the OFC and other brain regions involved in attention, that is, the ability to focus.
- An important aspect of flexible behaviour is a capacity for acting in a different way if this seems more appropriate to the situation. The ventrolateral prefrontal cortex (VLPFC) appears to play an important role in this aspect of cognition.

What is the material basis of human thought, and how can we link this to brain function? There are a number of ways to begin to tackle this question scientifically. One is the fact that although human thoughts are likely to have unique attributes compared to those of other species, at the level of basic molecular and cellular mechanisms and even in terms of how the brain works as a whole, there must be lots in common between the human thought process and the thought processes taking place in animal brains, which we can investigate.

One obvious problem in studying the material basis of thought in an animal is the inability of non-human species to tell us what they are thinking while being analysed. For this reason, neuroscientists studying brain function in experimental animals typically set such animals tasks that have relevance to aspects of human cognition, such as reasoning, planning, and making decisions, and then study brain activities while animals undergo such tasks. Lesions may also be made in the brains of experimental animals to see how this affects their ability to perform problem-solving tasks and qualitatively how this is affected.

The second major way that the material basis of different aspects of human cognition can be studied is through imaging the brains of human volunteers and sometimes even performing electrophysiological analysis of the neurons of volunteers undergoing therapeutic brain surgery while they are engaged in different mental activities.

These twin approaches have provided many important insights into the molecular and cellular mechanisms and also brain regions that underlie aspects of human cognitive functions, such as reasoning, planning, and decision-making. So, what are these insights?

One insight concerns the brain regions involved in what are sometimes called the 'higher' aspects of cognition, or 'executive' brain functions. One problem with such terminology is that it can convey the idea that, analogous to a CEO in charge of a commercial company or other organisation, there is a 'higher' part of the brain that is also ultimately in charge. One particular brain region that is often thought to personify such executive control is the prefrontal cortex. Yet, as we have pointed out previously, this begs the question of what controls the controlling region, and so on. Instead, recent studies suggest that although the prefrontal cortex does seem to play an enhanced role in human cognition, in line with its relatively greater size in our species compared even to our closest primate cousins, it only does so as part of a complex, interactive network with many other brain regions, receiving as many inputs from such regions as it sends out to them.

A second insight is that new findings about the role of brain waves of different frequencies and their involvement in creating transient ensembles of functionally linked neurons have introduced a more dynamic element to our view of how the brain works. Such a view does not disregard the importance of neuronal circuitry in brain function, but it does see connections between different parts of the brain as being far more fluid than had been realised. And this means that brain plasticity may involve far more than just changes in synaptic connections, with brain waves also playing important roles in this process.

A third insight is linked to what we are learning about the role of glial cells in the brain. As we have seen, previous views of glial cells as playing an essentially passive, supporting role in the brain compared to neurons are being challenged by new findings. Such findings have shown that glial cells play a variety of vital roles in the brain, for instance in the formation and maintenance of synapses as well as 'pruning' unwanted connections. While glial cells do not form electrical circuits like neurons, they do release chemicals and also respond to such chemicals via receptors on their surface. So, it is likely that to fully understand the material basis of 'higher' cognitive functions, we need to consider not only the neuronal circuitry that underlies such functions but also the potential role of glial cells.

A fourth insight is that however sophisticated and unique we may feel our ability to reason, plan, and make complex decisions is compared to the cognitive capacities of other species, our evolutionary origins in the animal kingdom mean that even the 'higher' human cognitive functions must ultimately be related to processes occurring in the brains of other species. Having said this, we should also then consider how such processes may have become transformed materially at both molecular and cellular levels during human evolution.

With all this in mind, let us now look at what we have learned from the approaches mentioned above about the material basis of the complex cognitive functions that both human beings and some other experimental animal species seem to have in common.

One cognitive function that is very important both in terms of animal survival and reproduction in the wild, and in human society, is the ability to evaluate. Evaluation involves estimating the value of an object or activity based on both past and present information. For instance, a monkey may decide to avoid an attractive-looking berry because of a prior experience of food poisoning after eating such a berry, and a human being might also decide to avoid certain foods because they were associated with negative after-effects. But evaluation is also taking place when someone is using an online booking service to search for a good hotel to stay in during a forthcoming holiday and using reviews by previous guests about the quality of their experience as a guide to choosing the best hotel.

The ability to evaluate has been linked to a part of the prefrontal region named the orbitofrontal cortex (OFC) (Fig. 9.1).[115]

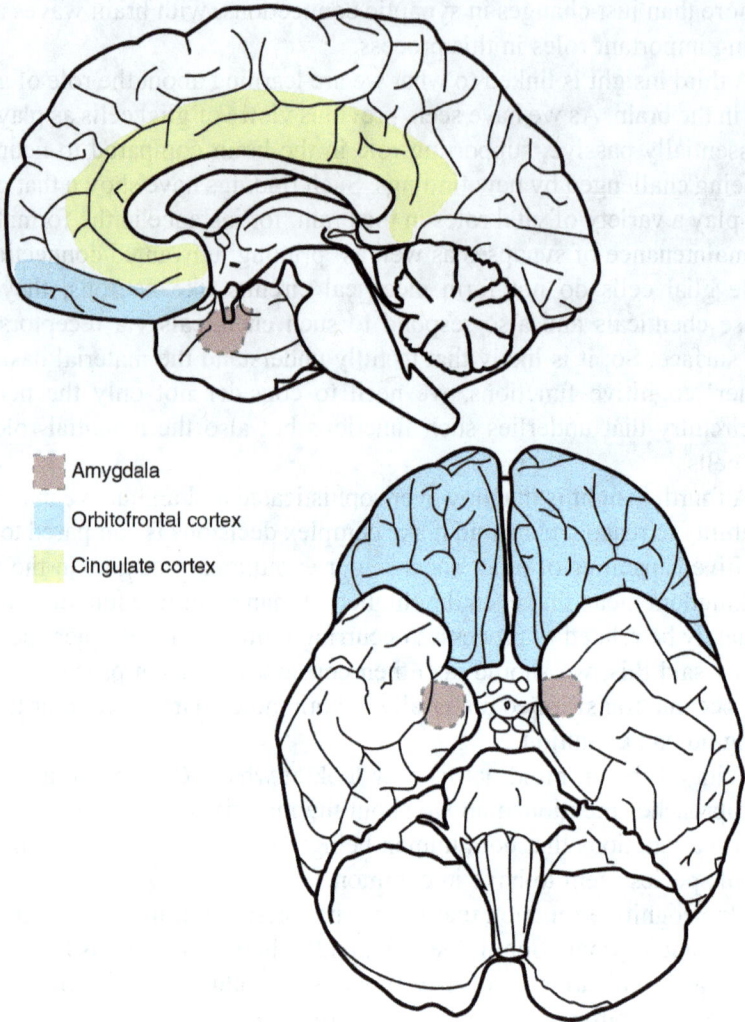

Fig. 9.1. Some of the key brain structures implicated in emotion. The positions of the amygdala, orbitofrontal cortex, and cingulate cortex are shown on a midsagittal view (top) and on a ventral view (bottom) of the human brain.

Source: Reproduced from Kringelbach, M.L. and Rolls, E.T. (2004) *Progress in Neurobiology*, 72:341–372, with permission.

Box 9.1. The Prefrontal Cortex and Executive Functions

A historical example often used to support the idea that the prefrontal cortex plays a dominant coordinating role in human consciousness is that of a man called Phineas Gage. In September 1848, Gage, a 25-year-old construction foreman, was in charge of men building a railway in Vermont, US. The team employed explosives to clear a route for the railway, and at one point, Gage was using an iron rod to compact gunpowder in a borehole. Unfortunately, the iron produced a spark that prematurely ignited the explosive, and the resulting blast propelled the rod – which measured 3.5 feet long and 1.25 inches wide – straight through his head. Remarkably, Gage survived and made what initially appeared to be a full recovery. Subsequently though, he was said to have undergone dramatic changes in personality. Previously described as efficient, well-balanced, shrewd, and energetic, Gage now apparently became 'fitful, irreverent, indulging at times in the grossest profanity, impatient of restraint or advice when it conflicts with his desires, obstinate, devising many plans of operation which are no sooner arranged than they are abandoned'. In 1860, Gage began having epileptic convulsions of increasing severity, and he died that year. Postmortem examination of his brain showed that the rod had destroyed much of Gage's left frontal lobe and prefrontal cortex. This, and the reported changes in his personality after the accident, has been used to support the idea that the prefrontal cortex plays an organising role in the 'higher' brain functions that distinguish us from 'lower' species. Yet, recent reconsideration of this case and new evidence about how the human brain functions have challenged established ideas about the role of the prefrontal cortex. One problem with the standard account of Gage's accident and subsequent life is that he maintained several jobs in the years after his injury, working first in a stables in Hanover, New Hampshire, later as a long-distance coach driver on the Valparaiso-Santiago route in Chile, and finally on a small farm in Santa Clara, California. This raises questions about whether the accident's effect on Gage's personality was as far-reaching as has been claimed. Second, the claims made about his personality suggest possible effects of the injury on Gage's ability to handle his emotions but do not necessarily indicate an all-important executive function for the prefrontal cortex. Indeed, recent studies have challenged the idea that the prefrontal cortex is the master coordinator of consciousness, arguing instead for a more distributed role for many different brain regions in mediating higher mental functions.

This brain region receives input from all the senses, giving it access to a variety of information from the external world that can help in making a choice, but unlike other prefrontal regions, it has few motor connections, consistent with the idea that it provides inputs to other parts of the brain that select and execute different behaviours. The OFC also receives inputs from the hippocampus and adjacent areas involved in memory storage and retrieval, which provide a link with past experience. The final set of inputs the OFC receives is from brain regions linked to reward that are located in the midbrain, which are particularly associated with the neurotransmitter dopamine.

Evidence of the important role that the OFC plays in evaluation comes from a number of sources. One is that when experimental monkeys are offered a range of different foods, particular neurons in the OFC show activity linked to an individual monkey's preferences for a foodstuff. Interestingly, when a monkey that likes peanuts is fed with them to satiety, this leads to a reduction in activity of neurons that had previously responded strongly to this foodstuff. This suggests that the OFC neurons are providing a measure not only of an object in the outside world's sensory properties but also of its subjective value.

Another piece of evidence comes from brain imaging studies of human volunteers, which showed that their OFC had enhanced activity when they were making decisions. For instance, in one such study, volunteers were asked to rank samples of wine in terms of taste preference.[116] Previous studies have shown that other factors besides taste can influence people's perception of how good a particular wine is. Indeed, in this study, although the volunteers were given identical samples of wine but with different labels that also included the price of the wine, they ranked most highly the supposedly more expensive wines, and this choice was accompanied by increased activity in the OFC region.

Let us consider another type of decision-making. Imagine you are cycling or driving to work along a familiar route and encounter some roadworks blocking your way. Faced with this obstacle, it will be necessary to find an alternative route. The ability to make such an alternative choice and act upon it is an important aspect of not only human cognition but that of a range of other complex organisms. For instance such flexibility in behaviour is also a feature of other mammalian species with relatively large brains, like primates and carnivores, and also in some cetaceans. This capacity appears to be particularly associated with the dorsolateral prefrontal cortex (DLPFC) (Fig. 9.2).[117]

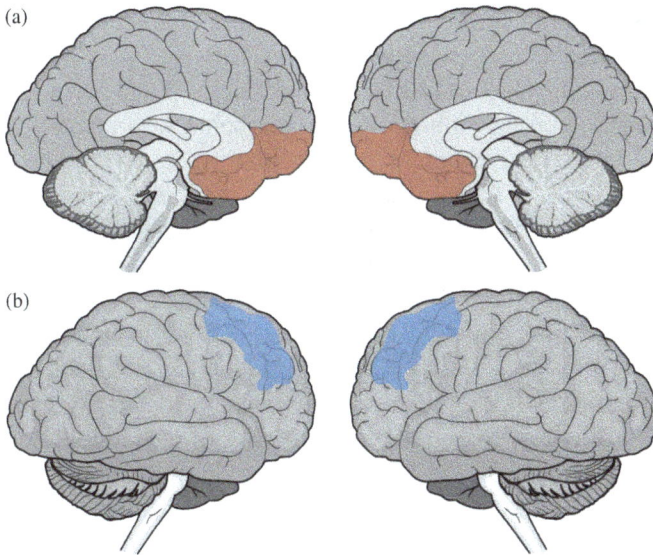

Fig. 9.2. (a) Depiction of vmPFC (in red) in midline views of each hemisphere. (b) Depiction of dlPFC (in blue) in lateral views of each hemisphere.

Source: Reproduced from Koenigs, M. and Grafman, J. (2010) *Behavioral Brain Research*, 201: 239–243, with permission.

The DLPFC communicates with brain regions linked to reward, such as the OFC, and other areas of the brain that are involved in attention, that is, the ability to focus on an issue. One view of how the DLFPC works is that it acts a bit like a switch in a railway track, which reroutes connections between different tracks to send trains to different destinations. In a similar fashion, the DLFPC has been proposed to control the responses of other brain regions, making them more or less responsive to different inputs, thus producing different responses relevant to the particular situation in which an organism finds itself.

The ability to weigh up a situation and make alternative choices relevant to that situation in a flexible manner is connected to another cognitive process that we have already mentioned – working memory. In fact, as we noted then, although this process is connected to particularly short-term forms of memory, it is far from merely an act of memory. The fact that working memory has also been referred to as the 'sketchpad of conscious thought' gives a sense of how fundamental this process is to our everyday consciousness.

We also mentioned previously a new view of working memory that sees this as an interaction between many different parts of the brain, regulated by brain waves of different frequencies. Such a viewpoint sees transient functional ensembles of neurons being key to how the brain works and introduces an important dynamic aspect to cognition. But it would be a mistake to believe that this means that neuronal circuitry is not important. Rather, both circuitry and the ability for neurons to take part in dynamic ensembles are both likely to be important aspects of not only working memory but also other aspects of cognition.

Evidence of an important role for the DLPFC in working memory comes from multiple sources. One is that monkeys trained to perform tasks that involve working memory show enhanced activity in this brain region.[117] Further evidence comes from studies of human individuals who have suffered damage to the DLPFC, which show that these individuals typically have defects in short-term memory capacity and duration.[118] In their everyday lives, human beings with a damaged DLPFC tend to become stuck in behavioural routines and are less able to adapt to changing circumstances.

The capacity to respond appropriately to changing situations in both people and some animals is based not only on an ability to be flexible but also on a capacity for learning from experience. Such a capacity involves being able to evaluate the outcomes of decisions that have been made based on monitoring what effect such decisions have upon the organism. A brain region that is believed to play an important role in such monitoring is the anterior cingulate cortex (ACC) (Fig. 9.3).[119] In line with this role, the ACC receives inputs from brain regions involved in processes such as perception, emotion, attention, and memory.

The activity of neurons in the ACC is affected not so much by the type of options available but by the consequences of choosing them. Thus, in experimental studies, ACC neurons are activated by errors that reduce rewards, which in everyday life would correspond to disappointment in not achieving a goal. Importantly, this seems to involve not only being able to sense when a chosen behaviour has had a positive outcome but also to compare the outcome of a particular behaviour with the likely outcome had a different type of behaviour been chosen. The ACC also seems to be particularly sensitive to unexpected or surprising outcomes and those that provide new information about a situation, thus promoting learning. The ACC can also be seen as complementary to the DLPFC,

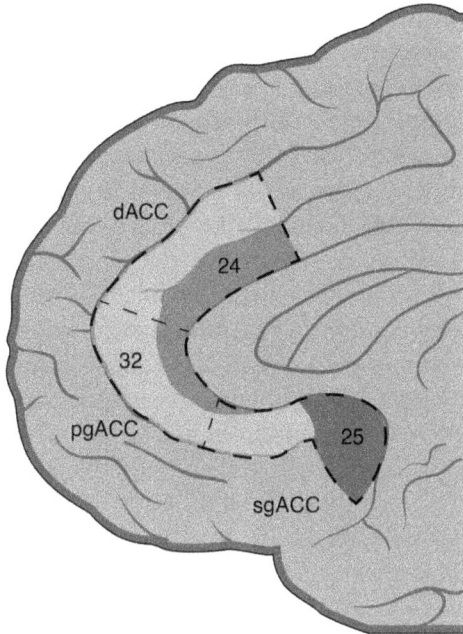

Fig. 9.3.   The anterior cingulate cortex (ACC) consists of subgenual (sgACC), perigenual (pgACC), and dorsal (dACC) portions.

Source: Reproduced from Alexander, L. *et al.* (2021) *Neuroscience and Biobehavioral Reviews*, 127:531–554, with permission.

with the ACC detecting the need to change behaviour and the DLPFC implementing that change.

Having decided to act in a particular way, an important aspect of flexible behaviour is a capacity for changing one's mind and acting in a different way if this seems more appropriate to the situation. The ventrolateral prefrontal cortex (VLPFC) appears to play an important role in this aspect of cognition.[120]

People with a damaged VLPFC respond more rapidly but less accurately in timed experimental tasks, and in their everyday lives, these individuals tend to make poor decisions; thus, they may reach out and touch or even grab things that come into view or say the first thing that comes into their mind, even if it is inappropriate. They typically also continue to make bad choices even when they recognise that such choices have led to unwelcome outcomes. In line with this, there is evidence that clinical disorders associated with an inability to suppress unwanted actions and thoughts, such as Tourette's syndrome, obsessive-compulsive disorder (OCD), and types of depression involving constant negative thoughts, are linked to abnormalities in VLPFC function.

Being able to detect what is happening in the external environment and react appropriately is crucial for survival in nature and also plays a vital role in human society. Of equal importance is an ability to sense what is going on in the internal environment – that is, within our bodies – and to respond with behaviours that rectify imbalances within us. Sensations that can include hunger, thirst, temperature, pain, fatigue, and heart rate, which may be sometimes only sensed at an unconscious level, can none-theless affect our behaviour in important ways, and a brain region that plays an important role in monitoring and responding to such sensory inputs from inside the body, the so-called 'visceral inputs', is the anterior insula.[121] While not part of the prefrontal cortex, this brain region is highly relevant to any discussion about the link between thought and behaviour. The anterior insula cortex (AIC) receives inputs from other parts of the brain, including the ACC, the OFC, the amygdala, and the hippocampus. It seems to play a role in cognitive functions as diverse as attention, time perception, romantic and parental love, mood, speech, and music – maybe because all are to some extent influenced by our bodily state and awareness of this.

Another brain region that is not part of the prefrontal cortex but which seems to play a distinctive role in the link between thought and behaviour is the posterior cingulate cortex (PCC).[122] One of the initially puzzling features of the PCC was that neurons within it show little response to sensory stimuli, and imaging studies of human volunteers showed that this brain region actually showed reduced activity during performance of experimental tasks. Instead, the PCC became active when volunteers were not thinking about a task and was at its highest level of activity when such volunteers were distracted or daydreaming.

What kind of cognitive process might be regulated by the PCC? A clue has come from the discovery that it becomes particularly active when human volunteers are thinking about themselves in the future and also considering themselves in relation to other individuals. This suggests that the PCC may be involved in representations of how an individual sees themself in relation to other individuals and perhaps to the environment as a whole.

Of course, in humans, the concept of self is a complex one, involving a distinction in the mind between self and other that is part of a more general conceptual understanding of the world as an entity and of one's place as an individual person in the world. In this respect, a major difference between humans and other species is our unique ability to describe ourselves and the world around us through the use of language. Another highly distinctive feature of human beings is the way that tools and technologies are central to the way we interact with the world and each other. In the following chapter, we will look more closely at both these unique human characteristics and their connection to thought.

Quiz

Damage to the prefrontal cortex of which of these individuals revealed its executive role?
A. Phineas Fogg
B. Phineas Gage
C. Phineas Flynn
D. Phineas Black

Brain region that plays a key role in evaluation:
A. Dorsolateral prefrontal cortex
B. Orbitofrontal cortex
C. Anterior cingulate cortex
D. Posterior cingulate cortex

Brain region thought to play a role in representations of how an individual sees themselves:
A. Dorsolateral prefrontal cortex
B. Orbitofrontal cortex
C. Anterior cingulate cortex
D. Posterior cingulate cortex

Chapter 10

Tools and Symbols

Key Concepts
Key Concepts • During human evolution, an increased capacity for both tool development and language created challenges for the brain that eventually led to a change in the size, structure, and overall biology of this organ compared to other species. • Understanding the meaning of specific tools and how they are used involves the left middle and inferior regions of the temporal lobe. • The failure to identify dedicated 'language genes' is in line with recent studies that have challenged the idea that the processes that underlie human language capacity are localised only to specific parts of the brain.

Human beings today occupy a unique position on Earth. Alone among other species on our planet, both existing and extinct, only *Homo sapiens* have been able to transcend our biological origins and create our great cities, transport and communication systems, and agricultural and medical advances, as well as our amazing cultural achievements in music, art, and literature. Indeed, such is the technological prowess of humanity that we have recently begun sending our technologies beyond the Earth in the form of spaceships and probes that have reached the Moon, the other planets that orbit the Sun, and even outside the Solar System.

Such advances are based on a remarkable transformation of the human brain that led to a type of consciousness that is qualitatively different from that of other species. Yet, humans remain biological beings, and if we want to understand what makes us different from other species, as well as what we have in common with them, a good starting point is to look at how our ancestors first began to diverge from other species.

The prominence of human intellect compared to that of other species is one reason why human beings tend to focus on our large brains as our main distinguishing feature. Yet, a study of the fossil record shows that while the development of a relatively large brain became a key aspect of how human beings began to diverge from other species, it was only the culmination of a process that began much earlier in evolutionary time, when our ancestors first began to stand primarily on two feet, that is, become bipedal. We do not fully understand exactly what precipitated this bipedalism, but it may have been linked to climatic changes in areas of Africa, where our ape-like ancestors lived, that forced them from forested areas into more open, savannah-like terrain where being able to stand on two feet and thus survey the surrounding area from a vantage point might have been an advantage.

Whatever the exact reason for the change to a bipedal stance, this change created unique opportunities, for it led to our ancestors finding new uses for the forelimbs that had previously been used mainly for locomotion. In particular, our ancestors, who were still essentially ape-like in terms of brain size, began for the first time in Earth's history to systemically design and use tools to transform the world around them.[123]

At this point, it is worth acknowledging that some other species, particularly non-human primates and some types of birds, such as crows, do use natural objects to interact with the world. However, it is the systematic way that humans use tools in practically all aspects of our lives that distinguishes our species, and this was a tendency that developed dramatically during our evolution.[124]

A second distinguishing feature of human beings is that only our species has a form of communication based on a system of abstract symbols that are linked together in a particular order by grammatical rules. This peculiarity of human language is the foundation for our unique human capacity to express ourselves conceptually.[125] Such concepts include notions of past, present, and future, distance and location, quantity and quality, shape, texture, and colour, and all the other complex ways we describe the world around us and our place within it.

These unique features of human language are worth stressing because, although we are far from the only species on Earth that communicate via sounds, it is the abstract symbolism of our communication linked by grammar that only we humans possess.

In trying to trace the evolution of human language, we face a challenge. For unlike the prehistoric tools of our ancestors, which have been preserved as fossils that can be studied and linked to adjacent fossilised skeletons of extinct proto-human species, our ancestors' language abilities cannot be studied directly, only inferred in a very indirect manner from the effects that the development of the larynx and other parts of the vocal apparatus, as well as regions of the brain that have been linked to language, might have had upon the skull. Because of this, we can only speculate about the prehistorical period when human language arose. We can also only make guesses about how exactly the development of both tool use and language might have stimulated the extraordinary growth in the size of the human brain.

One potential pitfall in trying to understand these different evolving capabilities would be to assume that it would be possible to study them as separate entities or as evolutionary changes that occur in series. In fact, it seems far more likely that the evolutionary relationship between tool use, language, and the development of the human brain is better viewed as a complex three-way interaction.

According to this scenario, once our ape-like ancestors began to use and design tools to interact with the world in a far more systematic fashion than any other species had previously, this led to new social forms of social interactions, as our ancestors had new types of experiences to communicate to each other.[126] And it was this that led to the development of the first truly conceptual language as a way to express the complexity of that new type of social experience for our ancestors.

Meanwhile, such increased capacity for both tool development and language, by increasing the potential ways in which our ancestors could interact both with the natural environment and with each other, created challenges for the brain that eventually led to a change in the size, structure, and overall biology of this organ compared to other species. Moreover, as our ancestors' brains began to change in this way, so must have their capacities for tool use and design as well as language. In fact, the emerging evidence shows that this was not a simple, linear process but rather one in which different proto-human species, technically known as 'hominins', emerged and also became extinct, so that although we can view the end result as *Homo sapiens*, in fact there were many evolutionary blind alleys.[127]

Trying to reconstruct the exact ways in which our ancestors' growing capacities for tool design and use and language skills intersected and how this in turn stimulated the development of the human brain will always be somewhat speculative. Nonetheless, it is possible to put forward hypotheses about this evolutionary process and then see how such hypotheses are supported by what can be uncovered about brain structure and function. One hypothesis put forward recently is the idea that the development of our technological and language skills was directly connected and that this connection is reflected in the fact that similar brain regions mediate these twin capacities.[128]

This hypothesis builds on the fact that the more complex stone tools that our hominin ancestors first began to produce 1.8 million years ago (Fig. 10.1) are made in a sequential way that has features in common with the ways in which sentences are constructed in human language.

According to the hypothesis, this is not a coincidence, for the development of such more complex forms of tool-making led to the requirement for ways to pass down such skills, and initially this was done via gestures. Exactly what then led from a gestural form of communication to a verbal one in our evolution is not clear, but it could have been the extra range of communicative possibilities offered by verbal sounds or the advantages of a communication system that left the hands free for tool use and design.

The findings of a recent study support the idea that the evolution of language and tool design may have been interconnected.[129] In this study, volunteers were taught to make sophisticated stone tools and, at a different time, to explain the meaning of sentences with a complex syntax while their brain activity was imaged. The study showed that the left inferior frontal gyrus brain region became active during both the tool design and language comprehension exercises. However, some brain regions only became active during synaptic processing, or alternatively during tool design. This suggests that even if there was a direct link in human evolution between the development of a capacity for tool use and design and that of language, the relationship today between these two capacities is likely to be a complex one in terms of brain regions involved and their interrelationship.

Imaging is not the only approach used to identify brain regions that are involved in our twin human capacities for language and technology.

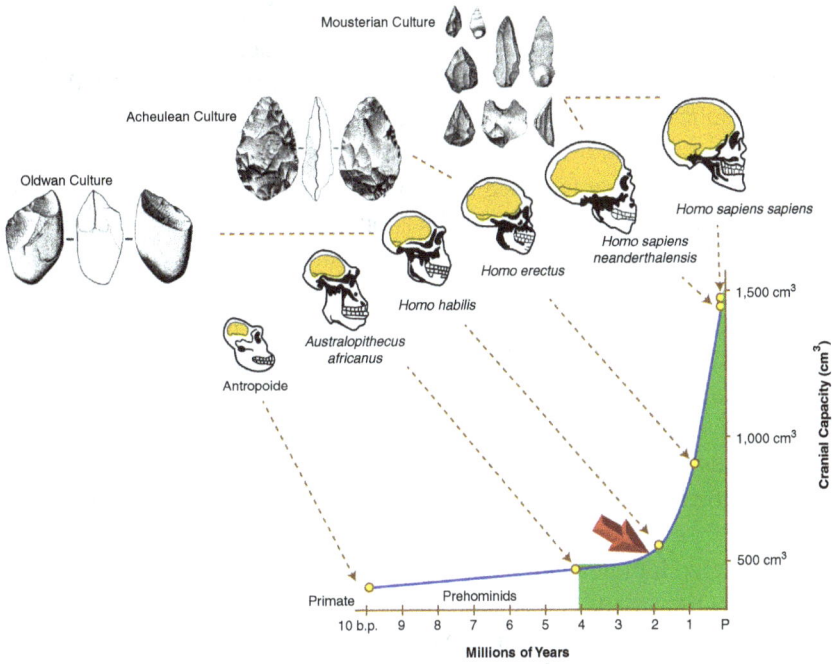

Fig. 10.1. Transition of cranial capacity (ordinate) along the evolutionary process of various ancestral prehominids and hominids (abscissa). Inset illustrations of a skull and brain depict representative hominids plotted on the graph. Brain expansion suddenly accelerated when *Homo habilis* started manufacturing and using stone tools (oblique red arrow). Insets of stone tools (top left) depict the development level of stone tools in each culture.

Source: Reproduced from Bretas, R. *et al.* (2019) *Neuroscience Research*, 161:1–7, with permission.

Another is to study the effect of injuries to specific brain regions or of rare genetic mutations upon these capacities.

We have already seen that in the 19th century, studies of people with the inability to make sense linguistically, or comprehend language, and then the discovery of lesions in the brains of such individuals after their deaths led to the identification of Broca's and Wernicke's brain regions, respectively. While initially this was thought to mean that Broca's region was the part of the brain involved in language production and Wernicke's the region involved in the comprehension of language, more recent studies have challenged this viewpoint, with multiple brain regions now being implicated in both aspects of language.[130]

One insight that has emerged from studies of the effect of lesions on different parts of the brain is that language capacity is to some extent lateralised, that is, distributed unequally between the right and left cerebral hemispheres. The most notable expression of such lateralisation is in 'split-brain' individuals.[131] These individuals suffered from such severe forms of epilepsy characterised by rapid flows of electrical activity across the brain that, in the 1960s, the decision was made to cut their corpus callosum, the bundle of nerve fibres connecting the two cerebral hemispheres. This operation did have some beneficial effects in reducing the epileptic seizures, but it also had some very unusual psychological consequences in the individuals who had been treated in this way.

A curious feature of humans, like many other complex species, is that the sensory and motion functions of the body are connected to the cerebral hemispheres such that the right hemisphere is linked to the left side of the body and the left hemisphere to the right side. Studies of language capacity in split-brain patients made use of this fact by asking patients to look at an image with their right or left eye covered, or while blindfolded, hold an object in their right or left hand and describe what they had seen or felt (Fig. 10.2). These studies found that only when an object was viewed by the right eye or held with the right hand could individuals precisely describe the object's appearance or feel.

In contrast, when the object was viewed or held in the left hand, individuals were incapable of describing what they had seen or felt. However, if later shown the object with both eyes, they could pick it out from a selection of other objects. They also often showed emotional responses to an object that they could not describe; for instance, they blushed or giggled at an image of a nude person. These findings led to the idea that the left hemisphere is involved in processing verbal and symbolic material important in language, whereas the right hemisphere is more specialised for visuospatial and emotional processing.

Studies of people with head injuries have also led to insights about the brain regions involved in our ability to use, manipulate, and understand tools.[132] For instance, some individuals after injury to particular parts of the brain develop an inability to reason about the physical properties of tools, resulting in difficulties in understanding how existing tools might be used in new situations, or conversely, how new tools might be created for existing situations.

Intriguingly, other types of brain injuries leave an affected individual with the ability to understand the physical properties of tools and the

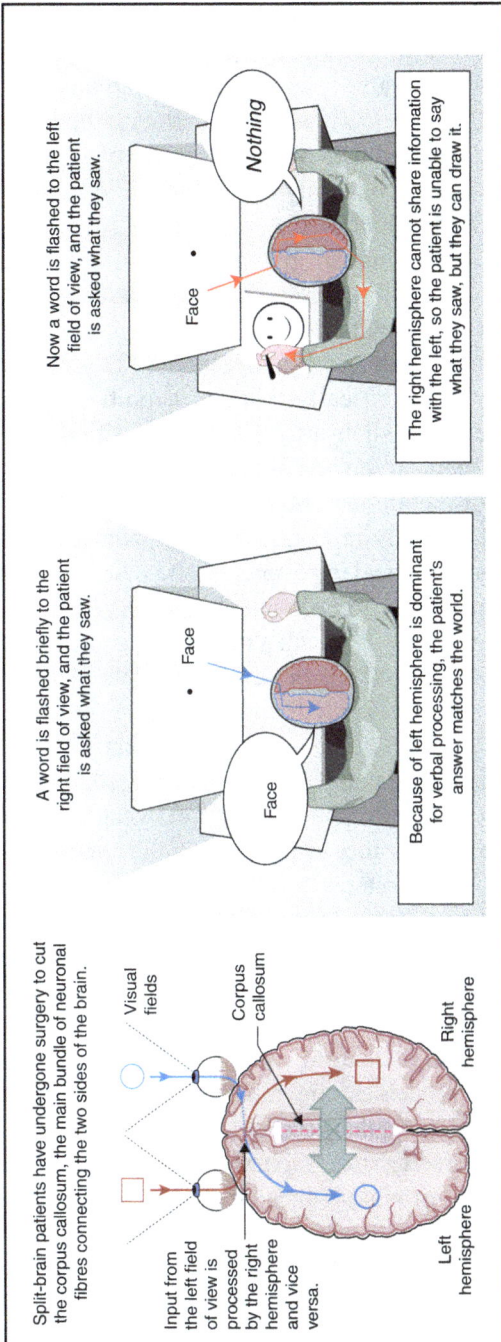

Fig. 10.2. Experiments with split-brain patients have illuminated the lateralised nature of brain function.

Source: Reproduced from Wolman, D. (2012) *Nature*, 483:260–263, with permission.

capacity to use tools effectively but no conception of the functions associated with such tools. Analysis of the brain lesions associated with these conditions suggests that the ability to understand the physical properties of tools and employ them correctly is associated with the inferior parietal cortex. In contrast, understanding of the meaning of specific tools and how they are used seems to be mainly located in the left middle and inferior regions of the temporal lobe.

The sequencing of the human genome and those of other species, including our closest living animal relatives, chimpanzees and gorillas, as well as the genomes of extinct hominin species such as Neanderthals, raised hopes that a comparison of such genomes might reveal genetic differences underlying specifically human cognitive characteristics. Notably, as we have seen, such analysis has identified genes such as NOTCH2NL, which seems to be one of the genetic factors underlying the unusually large size of the human brain.

The discovery of a family in London that contained individuals with major linguistic and grammatical impairments, and the subsequent mapping of this defect to a mutation in a gene named FoxP2, initially led to claims that this was a 'language gene'.[133] Such a possibility gained further support from the fact that although FoxP2 is present in multiple species, the variant present in the human genome is only found in human beings, Neanderthals, and Denisovans. Subsequent studies have shown that FoxP2 is a master controller of the expression of many other genes (Fig. 10.3) and that defects in it in mice are associated with abnormalities in synapse formation in the striatum region of the brain, which is involved in the control of movement, including the production of sounds.

Such findings suggest that despite its initial link to language, FoxP2 is likely to play a variety of roles in the brain, not only in humans but also in other species. In many ways, this should not come as a surprise. Despite our unique characteristics, human beings are the product of biological evolution via the process of natural selection, and this process tends to commandeer existing processes and refashion them, rather than create something totally new. As such, we should expect to find that even the most unique human characteristics, such as the system of abstract symbols that constitutes language or our advanced technological capacities, will be rooted in molecular and cellular processes that we share with other species, and this includes the genes that regulate these processes.

The failure to identify dedicated 'language genes' is also in line with recent studies that have challenged the idea that the processes that

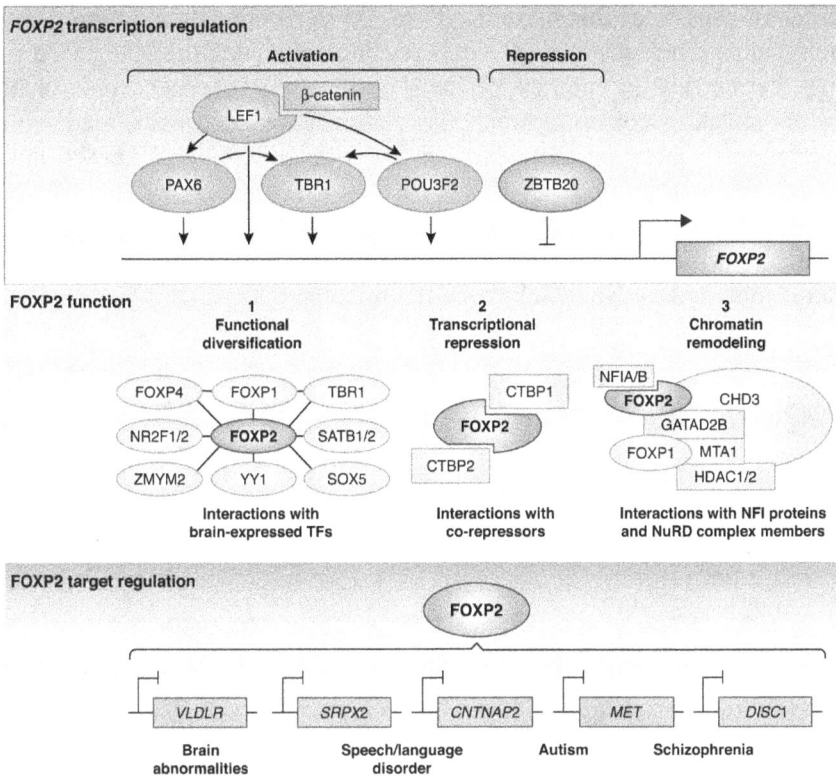

Fig. 10.3. Overview of FOXP2 molecular networks in the brain at the levels of transcription regulation, function, and target regulation. This overview represents results from a selection of separate studies using different types of model systems. TFs: transcription factors.

Source: Reproduced from den Hoed, J. *et al.* (2021) *EMBO Reports*, 22:e52803, with permission.

underlie human language capacity are localised only to specific parts of the brain. We have already mentioned the link between Broca's and Wernicke's areas of the brain and language production and comprehension, respectively. Other studies have identified roles for other cortical regions in language. For instance, the angular gyrus and insular cortex regions appear to work with Wernicke's area to process words and phrases to determine language context and meaning.[134]

In addition, regions other than the cortex, the part of the brain traditionally associated with language, have been shown to play a role in different aspects of this capacity. Thus, the cerebellum was found to be involved in processes related to the meaning of language and the processing of sounds.[135] In contrast, phonetic patterns that transcend individual words and also convey emotional meaning have been associated with activation in the right amygdala, in line with this region's known link to the emotions.[136]

Such findings reflect the fact that language has many different elements. Maybe the biggest unsolved question is how language relates to thought, an issue to which we will now turn.

Quiz

Which of these distinctive human attributes is thought to have evolved first?
A. Growth of the brain
B. Bipedalism
C. Tool use
D. Language

The bundle of nerve fibres that connects the two cerebral hemispheres:
A. Corpus callosum
B. Corpus luteum
C. Corpus spongiosum
D. Corpus cavernosum

Defects in this gene are associated with language impairments in humans:
A. BoxP2
B. SoxP2
C. FoxP2
D. PoxP2

Chapter 11

Language and Cognition

Key Concepts

- A key feature of human language is that abstract symbols – words – are linked together by grammar in ways that allow us to express ourselves conceptually. Only language makes possible concepts such as past, present, and future, distance and location, self versus other, and even more complex ones.
- Ultimately, our thoughts must be based on the same molecular and cellular processes that occur in the brains of many other species, but in humans there is the added input of language. This means that central to human thought is 'inner speech'.
- Inner speech is likely to have much greater fluidity and ambiguity than the external form. This reflects the fact that the dialogue taking place in our minds has a contradictory character that comes from the complexity of human society.

Human beings' sense of ourselves as unified individuals with thought processes that only we can truly know and understand, even while we might reveal aspects of these to other people through our verbal exchanges with them, is one of the most central and apparently indisputable aspects of being human. It is this feeling that led the 17th-century philosopher René Descartes to state that if there is one thing we can be sure of about our own individual consciousness, it is that 'I think, therefore I am.'[137] But where do such thoughts come from, and what relationship do they have to the capacities we have argued are unique to human beings, that is, our language and technological capacities?

One way of beginning to look at this question is to think again about what we seem to have in common with other species, particularly the great apes that are our closest biological cousins. Our knowledge in this area comes from experimental studies as well as observations in the wild of such species. An obvious problem with such studies is that we cannot ask these great apes what they are thinking. Nonetheless, we can draw inferences about the intellectual capabilities of, say, non-human primate species such as chimpanzees or gorillas by both studying their behaviour and setting them experimental tasks.

Such studies have shown that great apes show some impressive levels of sophistication in their ability to manipulate natural objects as tools, communicate in complex ways via gestures and sounds, and recognise and respond to other individuals of their species.[138] So, it seems fair to say that a certain amount of how human beings react and respond to the natural world and to members of our own and other species will be rooted in brain mechanisms that are shared with other species, particularly with the 'higher' non-human primates. Indeed, we have already mentioned studies that have identified some of the brain regions and molecular and cellular mechanisms involved in these types of cognitive responses.

At the same time, it needs to be reiterated just how unique are some human capabilities. For despite repeated attempts to teach gorillas or chimps sign language since the 1960s when such studies became particularly popular, while individuals of such species can learn to associate a large number of symbols with objects and even emotions, there is no evidence that they can learn and understand the complex grammatical rules that lie at the heart of human language.[139] This surely places a fundamental limit on the complexity of the ways that non-human primates can both interpret the world and explain it to others.

Similarly, while some other species, mainly non-human primates but also some crows, may use natural objects like twigs as tools in sophisticated ways, there is no evidence that any of these species design and develop tools in a cumulative fashion in the way that human beings do, with an accelerating pace with each new generation in the modern age.[140] Combined, these differences are the reason why only human beings have shown an ability to transcend our biological roots and for our society to evolve in a way that is primarily social, not biological, because only we understand our unique place in the world and have the capacity to explain this to other humans. And ultimately, this must be based on unique changes in the human brain, both in its unusually expanded size and in its structure.

If the above stands as a reaffirmation of the unique differences between human beings and other species, what can we say about how this relates to human thoughts? In particular, what can we uncover about the link between thought and language?

One view of this relationship is that thoughts have their own unique character and speech is simply a vehicle allowing us to express such thoughts in ways that others can understand. A problem with this view-point is the difficulty it faces in explaining the cognitive differences between human beings and other species. In particular, it does not explain how the structure of human thought is related to the symbolic nature of human language.

To recap, a key feature of human language is that abstract symbols – words – are linked together by grammar in ways that allow us to express ourselves conceptually (Fig. 11.1).

Only language makes possible concepts such as past, present, and future, distance and location, self versus other, as well as more complex ones like Einstein's theory of relativity. But this way of describing the world is not only central to how we express our thoughts to others but also lies at the heart of how we view the world. So, how can this be possible if

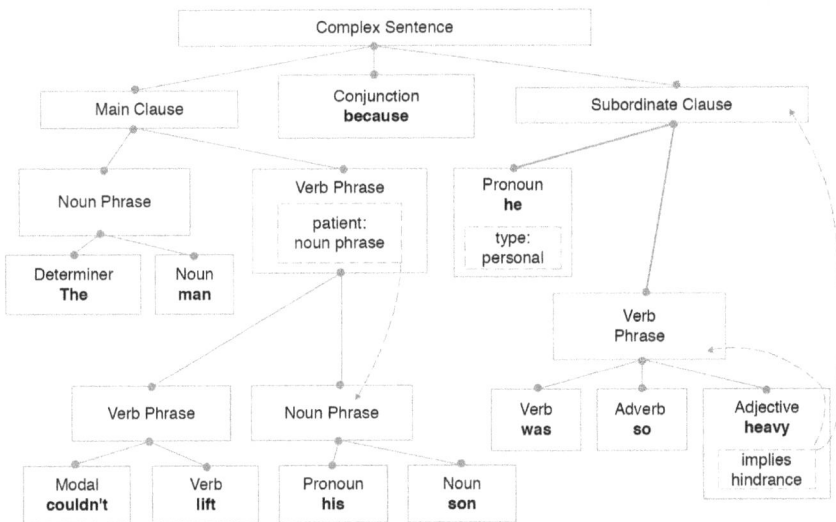

Fig. 11.1. A schematic diagram showing a sentence network of constructions.

Source: Reproduced from Kiselev, D. (2021) *International Journal of Cognitive Informatics and Natural Intelligence*, 15:34–48, with permission.

thought is something different to the words we use when communicating with others?

One response to this conundrum is to argue that thoughts also have a conceptual framework but one that is different from spoken language. But this begs the question of how complex concepts could form in the absence of words. One would have to conceive of a material basis for human thought that was similar to words in providing a framework for complex meaning yet different from words in its form.

A more satisfactory explanation for the way that human thought works is that, although ultimately our thoughts must be based on the same molecular and cellular processes that occur in the brains of many other species, in humans there is the added input of language. And this means that central to human thought is 'inner speech', or more generally, inner symbols.[141] The reason for the broader distinction is that there is evidence that the inner thoughts of people who were born deaf are not the spoken word but rather signs of the sort that deaf people use to communicate with each other using sign language.[142] Moreover, we should also include here other abstract symbols, which could include mathematical symbols as well as the other, many and varied symbolic forms that human beings use to communicate with each other. While these different forms may seem quite different from each other in form, what surely unites them all is the abstract framework based on language.

If anyone doubts this, it is worth considering cartoon imagery. Depending on the skill of the cartoonist, such an image might represent an animal, a celebrity, or a politician, in the most abstract manner, yet be immediately recognisable to the majority of people in the particular group at which the cartoon is aimed. So, what is being recognised in this instance? It is clearly not the exact image of the individual but rather certain conceptual features that we recognise, an abstract version of that individual rather than their apparently more obvious representation in a photograph of that individual. The ability to recognise a cartoon of an individual seems to be a purely human quality, as no studies of other species have shown that they can link a cartoon with its subject. This suggests that even aspects of human thought that may seem distant from language, such as cartoon imagery or mathematical symbols, are nonetheless connected to it.

To some extent, the proposal that language plays a central role in the human thought process may not be very controversial. Anyone rehearsing a speech, trying to keep a set of numbers or a phrase in their minds, or indeed any mental act that involves internally reciting words in some form or other in their minds must surely be engaging in some form of inner speech. However, this might be seen as merely the final stage of a process in which thought that is non-linguistically based is transformed into a verbal form.

More controversial is the claim that all of human thought, from the moment when an only partially formed thought begins to appear in our heads to the point at which we then try and express our thoughts to others, is all to some extent structured by language. An important aspect of such a viewpoint is that there must be different levels of inner speech. While at the uppermost levels of such a phenomenon, thought may be very similar to what eventually surfaces as external speech, at lower levels we may be looking at a very different type of phenomenon. Indeed, a central aspect of the view that language plays a structuring role at all levels of the thought process is that the deeper we go down into consciousness, the further we are likely to get from what is considered 'normal language'. Instead, such lower levels of inner speech must somehow be able to express the great fluidity and ambiguity of human thought, as well as its more imaginative and creative aspects.

A central problem for any attempt to understand the basis of human thought, whatever our hypotheses about this, is the difficulty in observing thoughts directly. William James, who helped to found the field of psychology in the late 19th century, expressed this problem well when he said that trying to understand the basis of our innermost thoughts was like 'trying to turn up the gas quickly enough to see how the darkness looks.'[143] In other words, trying to understand what we might be thinking in verbal terms runs the risk of altering the structure and content of our innermost thoughts as we try and express them.

Despite such problems, there are ways to try and uncover the character of inner speech. One way is to study how inner speech might first develop in a child. An interesting phenomenon in childhood is the so-called 'egocentric speech' – the tendency for young children to talk to themselves while they play or engage in some other solitary activity.[144] Typically occurring between the ages of three and seven, one view of egocentric speech sees it as a sign of children's immaturity, a failure to distinguish private from externally expressed thoughts, and the fact that it ultimately peters out is due to the child realising this. However, another point of view sees egocentric speech as a key stage in development, when

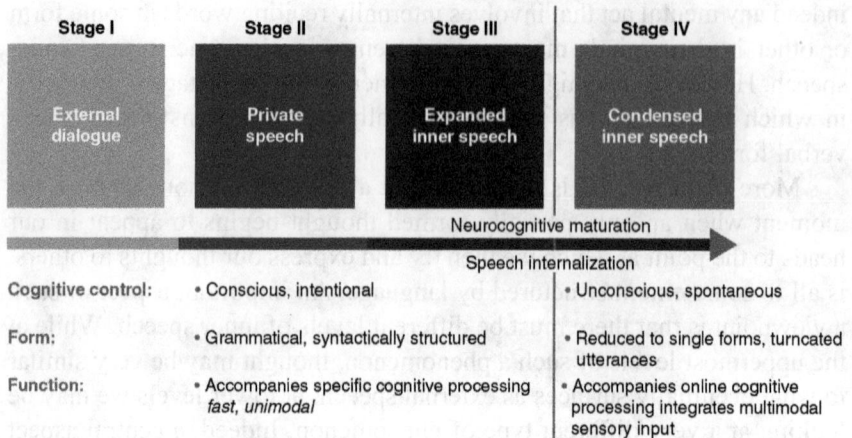

Stage I	Stage II	Stage III	Stage IV
External dialogue	Private speech	Expanded inner speech	Condensed inner speech

Neurocognitive maturation

Speech internalization

Cognitive control:	• Conscious, intentional	• Unconscious, spontaneous
Form:	• Grammatical, syntactically structured	• Reduced to single forms, turncated utterances
Function:	• Accompanies specific cognitive processing *fast, unimodal*	• Accompanies online cognitive processing integrates multimodal sensory input

Fig. 11.2.   Schematic representation of the stages of inner speech development.

Source: Reproduced from Vissers, C.T.V.M. *et al.* (2020) *Frontiers in Psychology*, 11:279, with permission.

the child first begins to use language to guide and coordinate their activities (Fig. 11.2). And far from disappearing, the only reason that children stop talking to themselves is that this speech form goes underground, becoming inner speech. Importantly, this means that by studying egocentric speech, we can learn more about inner speech.

A second approach to understanding inner speech is by introspection. By musing on our inner thoughts, the hope is that we understand more about the character and structure of inner speech.[145] A problem with this approach is one that we have already mentioned, namely that the very act of trying to express the character of our thoughts in external speech runs the risk of altering that character. For this reason, one approach that has recently been pursued by psychologists studying inner speech is to attach to volunteers a device that buzzes at certain intervals during the day and also a recording device. When the buzzer is activated by the psychologist leading the study, at certain intervals during the day, the volunteer must record their inner thoughts exactly as they occur to them at that point in time. The point of this exercise is to try and introduce some spontaneity into the recording process and thereby produce a more accurate record of our inner thoughts.

A final approach to seeking to understand inner speech is to think more about key elements of external speech and how these elements might be the same, or different, in inner speech. A particularly relevant aspect of external speech in this respect is its dialogical character. When we speak, this is typically with a specific listener or listeners in mind. And the responses we receive from others in reply to our utterances not only have us in mind but also set up the next phase of the conversation. Another important quality of external speech is that it tends to follow certain conventions that are linked to the particular social context in which a conversation takes place, the relative status of the participants, and indeed all sorts of other factors related to the particular society to which the participants belong.

Based on these different approaches, what can we surmise about the likely character of inner speech? One important, yet often overlooked, aspect of this phenomenon is its dialogical character.[146] Because external speech typically takes place in response to someone else, the fact that it is a dialogue is obvious. In contrast, inner speech is often assumed to be a monologue because it takes place in the mind of a single individual. Yet, one could argue that because the voices in our heads are drawn from past conversations that we have had during our development from childhood onwards, with past influences including parents, siblings, other relatives, friends, lovers, teachers, colleagues, and so on, inner speech is also a dialogue but with these other assumed voices from the past and present.

An important consequence of such a dialogical character of inner speech is that this means that the contradictions and tensions of our immediate social networks and even wider national and global society have an influence on the character of our inner speech.

Another important aspect of inner speech is that, particularly at the deeper levels of consciousness, it is likely to have a different structure to external speech. Because in this inner dialogue the speaker and listener are both within the mind of the individual, much of the explanatory background that we get in external speech can be left out of inner speech, and as a consequence, the latter is likely to be much more telegraphic than external speech.

Perhaps the most important difference between external and inner speech is that the latter is likely to have much greater fluidity and ambiguity than the external form.[147] This reflects the fact that the dialogue taking place in our minds has a contradictory character that comes from the competing influence of different points of view drawn from our immediate and wider society. This ambiguity and fluidity are likely to extend to the very structure of the deepest form of inner speech. So, opposing word meanings may become joined together in this form of speech, and a single word may express a complex situation. It is also likely to be the case that in our deepest thoughts, words may be linked to images or abstract symbols in ways that only make sense to the inner psyche.

Earlier, we identified humanity's peculiar propensity for designing and using tools as the unique feature, alongside our language capacity, that distinguishes us from other species. In the modern era, the development of new types of tools and technologies has only accelerated, as shown for instance in recent decades by the way that computer technology and the internet have come to assume such a central place in the lives of practically everyone in the developed world and to an increasing degree in the developing world too. A consequence of this is that, increasingly, we are exposed almost 24/7 to news, features, and the messages that we receive from family, friends, and colleagues via the internet in the form of text, images, sounds, videos, and so on. An interesting question then would be to ask how such a bombardment of the senses might affect our inner thoughts.[148]

In fact, it is likely that each new era, bringing with it novel technologies and accompanying new ways in which humans relate to each other, has to some extent challenged our inner thoughts since the dawn of history. Think for instance how human social interactions must have been changed by the inventions of the wheel, writing, the printing press, or the telephone. If inner speech is central to human thought, then it is likely that our inner human consciousness must also have been affected by these inventions.

Similarly, the changes in economic, social, and political relations that accompanied transitions such as that from the ancient slave societies through feudalism to our modern capitalist society must all have had major impacts on human consciousness, and as a key part of such transitions involved changes in the words and symbols human beings used to describe the world around them, so must this have had an impact on inner consciousness.

One view of history is to see the majority of human beings as passive objects at the mercy of the social and political forces around them. But studies of important transitions in history have shown that people are often not passive players but active agents of change. One of the most interesting aspects of seeing language as central to our inner human consciousness is that at times of great social change, the increasingly active roles that some people play at such times must affect the way language structures their inner world. But it is also true that times of social change are also driven by the creativity and imaginations of those involved. This raises the question of where creative and imaginative impulses come from and how these relate to brain mechanisms, which is the subject of the following chapter.

Quiz

One of the founders of the field of psychology:
A. William James
B. Henry James
C. Simon James
D. Paul James

Technical name for the tendency for young children to talk to themselves while they play:
A. Introverted speech
B. Egocentric speech
C. Inner speech
D. Demonstrative speech

Inner speech is thought NOT to be which of the following?
A. Dialogical
B. Unambiguous
C. Telegraphic
D. Rapid

Chapter 12

Creativity and Imagination

Key Concepts

- Many species can respond to novel situations and problems in what seem like creative and innovative ways. However, evidence suggests that human creativity and imagination are qualitatively different from those found in animals.
- One important activity in the development of imagination during childhood is play. Play allows children to reach further than their current stage of development via the role playing that is an important feature of this type of activity.
- Recent studies suggest a role for the cerebellum in creativity. Since this brain region is involved in developing unconscious routines, it may play a role in automatically going through possible solutions to a novel task, aiding the creative process.

The ability to think rationally is an essential feature of being human, but it is likely that we would never have progressed in 30,000 years from scratching a living from the Earth to sending scientific probes to the far reaches of the Solar System if human beings did not also possess great imagination and creativity, for imagination allows us to conceive of much grander situations than currently exist, and our human creativity allows us to work towards such situations.

Do human creativity and imagination have any equivalent in animal consciousness? Recent studies indicate that many species can respond to novel situations and problems in what seem like creative and innovative ways.[149] However, while such findings show that innovation is not a purely human characteristic, there are reasons for thinking that human creativity and imagination are qualitatively different from that found in animals.

Let us consider imagination first. This term is derived from the statues, or 'images', that the ancient Greeks used to adorn their buildings and public squares. In line with this, one view of imagination is that it is the ability to bring to mind an image in the absence of sensations, or as the 19th-century psychologist William James put it, 'fantasy, or imagination, are the names given to the faculty of reproducing copies of originals once felt.'[150]

One problem with this viewpoint is that, as we saw previously, even the perception of actual objects by the visual system is far from a straightforward process. Thus, we should be wary of any view that sees imagined images as simply representations in the mind of actual objects. In addition, an important aspect of imagination is not simply bringing to mind actual objects and situations but rather the ability to imagine completely novel ones. For an important aspect of imagination is an inability to conjure up the unexpected.

Such a capacity may be seen as important for human survival because if our species were only capable of imagining the current state of affairs, it would not equip us very well for circumstances in which that state of affairs changed. In that respect, there are probably aspects of human imagination that are linked to the general flexibility to respond to unexpected circumstances that we have mentioned is a feature of some other types of animals, most notably non-human primates, but also some other mammalian species.[151] Importantly, however, there is likely to be an aspect to human imagination that is unique to our species, linked to the way that language transforms human consciousness.

A key feature of language is the way that particular words can be combined together to make a sentence in an almost limitless manner. Importantly, the very meaning of words is open to change.[152] A particularly striking example of this is the way William Shakespeare created many new meanings for words by using them in unexpected ways or combining them with other words in novel phrases. But it is a feature of language as a whole that it is constantly in a process of flux and evolution, and many different individuals besides those that become famous can play important roles in this redefinition of word meanings.

The fluidity of the possible meaning of language is important for the imaginative process, for it provides a framework in which new possibilities can be expressed, possibly for the first time in history if we are talking about a great writer like Shakespeare, but it is equally true of any one of us that language allows us to imagine new possibilities in our own spheres, and combined, this can cumulatively influence society.

Of course, there is more to imagination than words. To see what I mean by this, try imagining a dolphin holding itself upright in the water during a performance at a zoo. In doing so, it is likely that you will be drawing on previous memories of dolphins that you have seen at a zoo, on a TV screen, or in a picture. Now, try and imagine a dolphin balancing a pineapple on its head. Now, unless you have been to a fairly unusual zoo, it is unlikely that you have ever seen such a thing. Yet, this should not prevent you from imagining it.

What this example shows is not only the ability of the human mind to imagine novel events in the absence of actually having seen such events but also that imagination may involve 'images'. Yet, as we have already seen, even the ability to recognise cartoon images as representations of reality seems to be a peculiar capacity of human beings that is not shared by other species. As such, we should not assume that other species view images in their minds in the same way that we do, even if they presumably have memories of objects in the real world.

In contrast, the highly mediated way in which vision works in terms of brain function, coupled with the role of abstraction in the human mind, means that our imaginations are likely to employ a variety of different forms, ranging from words to images to even more abstract forms of imagination, but all are ultimately linked together by language.

Where does imagination come from? Young children are often viewed as having the most vivid imaginations. This is partially due to the extreme plasticity of the brain at this stage of life, in ways that are linked to neuronal and brain mechanisms already mentioned. Another factor may be that, while in the first years of life children are permitted, and even encouraged, to engage in all sorts of imaginative activity, later in childhood and subsequently through adulthood, ideas that stray too much beyond the bounds of the acceptable, or 'normal', may be discouraged as inappropriate 'daydreaming'.

One important activity in the development of imagination during childhood is play (Fig. 12.1). While it can take many different forms, common features of play are that it involves the creation of an imaginary situation, taking on and acting out specific roles, and following specific rules determined by those roles. An interesting feature of play is that while

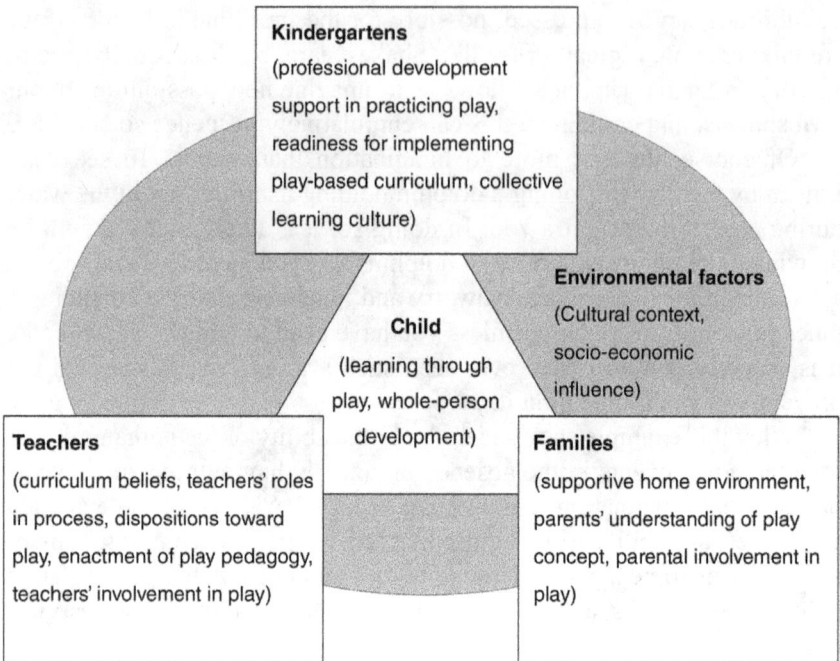

Kindergartens
(professional development support in practicing play, readiness for implementing play-based curriculum, collective learning culture)

Child
(learning through play, whole-person development)

Environmental factors
(Cultural context, socio-economic influence)

Teachers
(curriculum beliefs, teachers' roles in process, dispositions toward play, enactment of play pedagogy, teachers' involvement in play)

Families
(supportive home environment, parents' understanding of play concept, parental involvement in play)

Fig. 12.1.   Triangle of factors in implementing effective play-based learning: a holistic support model.

Source: Reproduced from Keung, C. and Cheung, A. (2019) *Early Childhood Education Journal*, 47:1–14, with permission.

we tend to associate play with 'make-believe', often its activities are grounded in real-life adult activities, as when children play at 'mummies and daddies' or 'doctors and nurses'.

In fact, the apparent contradiction between the 'make-believe' aspect of childhood play and the often socially grounded aspects of such play is much less of a contradiction if we look more closely at the social purpose of play. For one view of play is that it represents an activity in which the child strives to make sense of the adult society that surrounds them; by manipulating the activities and status of individuals represented in the play activity, the child can thereby better understand these and in such a way that they remain in control.[153]

While play allows children to explore the complexities of the world around them in a safe and controlled manner, we should not ignore the more fundamental ways in which play may affect the development of childhood consciousness. The psychologist Lev Vygotsky believed that 'in play a child is always above his average age ... it is as though he was a head taller than himself'.[154] This is because play allows children to reach further than their current stage of development via role-playing, which is an important feature of this type of activity. Given that in some debates about education there have been arguments that young children should spend more time studying and less time playing, this insight provides an important justification for ample amounts of playtime in the school curriculum. It also raises the question of whether more time spent in playful activities could be beneficial for adults.

Studies of hunter-gatherer societies, the type of society that human beings have lived in for the vast majority of the time that we have been on Earth, have shown that there is no real division between work and play.[155] In contrast, in modern society, leisure activities are clearly demarcated from work ones, and it is often the latter that tends to dominate our adult lives. Leisure for many adults also often involves a passive role. To some extent, when we read a work of fiction or watch a film on TV, we might imagine ourselves as one of the characters and thus become 'a head taller than we are' in this way. But taking part in activities outside our normal comfort zone, where we might need to show different aspects of our character than we normally do, or even engage in some form of role-playing, might be more beneficial in terms of developing our imagination. Similarly, the introduction of playful elements into work activities might be one way to help the development of individuals at work and enhance interactions within the workforce.

If these are some of the potentially beneficial aspects of imagination, what can modern neuroscience and psychology tell us about the imaginative and creative process? Traditionally, these aspects of human cognition have been assumed to be a product of the frontal lobes, particularly the prefrontal cortex, in line with the idea that these brain regions are where the 'higher' functions of cognition are based. However, some recent studies have begun to challenge this view. For instance, a study that used fMRI imaging to look at the brains of jazz musicians performing pieces, ranging from a memorised scale to fully improvised music, found that during the improvised pieces the dorsolateral prefrontal cortex (DLPFC) became less active.[156] This brain region has been linked to planning and self-censorship and is inhibited during daydreaming, meditation, and REM sleep.

The finding above could be taken to suggest that far from being the source of creative and imaginative impulses, parts of the prefrontal cortex need to be suppressed for our imaginations to soar. In fact, such a view seems only partially true based on the findings of a follow-up study to the one mentioned above. In this case, jazz pianists were given a photograph of a woman with either a positive or negative expression and then asked to match their improvised musical compositions to the photo's mood.[157] Based on the previous study, it might be expected that activity in the DLPFC would be inhibited in all cases. Yet, the study found that inhibition of the DLPFC was only pronounced in the musicians who had seen the positive face. In addition, those who had seen a negative face were found to have greater activity in brain regions linked to control and reward. This suggests that imagination can involve multiple different brain regions, and depending on the circumstances, emotional responses can have a major impact on the creative process.

The findings of another study support the idea that multiple regions of the brain are involved in the imaginative and creative process. In this study, volunteers were asked to imagine specific shapes and then mentally combine them into more complex figures or dismantle them into their separate parts while their brains were imaged.[158] The study indicated that imagination requires a highly distributed brain network, with 11 different brain regions becoming activated when an individual is asked to take part in creative acts.

Perhaps the biggest surprise from recent studies that have sought to identify brain regions involved in the imaginative and creative process is their demonstration of a role for the cerebellum. As mentioned previously, this brain region has mainly been thought to be involved in the unconscious neuronal routines that develop as a person learns how to play the piano, ride a bike, or throw a ball into a basketball hoop.

One recent study that suggests that the cerebellum can also play an important role in the imaginative and creative process imaged the brains of volunteers who were asked to either draw 'action words' – such as 'vote', 'levitate', 'snore', or 'salute' – or, as a control, a single zigzag line.[159] Drawing a zigzag engages regions of the brain involved in fine movements and attentional focus but does not require more creative aspects of cognition. Later in the study, the drawings were rated by experts for their level of creativity, accuracy, and other cognitive parameters and then compared to the findings from the brain imaging.

The study produced two unexpected findings. The first, in line with another study mentioned previously, was that while more difficult drawing tasks increased activity in the cerebral cortex, higher creativity was associated with reduced activity in this region. The second was that the more creativity an individual displayed, the higher the level of activity in their cerebellum. This raises the question of how the cerebellum might contribute to the creative process, given its other known roles in cognition. Since this brain region is involved in developing unconscious routines, one possibility is that it could play a role in automatically going through possible solutions to a novel task, aiding the creative process.

What the findings do suggest is that deliberate attempts to be creative may not be the best way to optimise a person's creativity. This has important potential implications for educational practice, for it suggests that teaching approaches that are primarily focused on making students consciously 'work' at learning may sometimes prove counterproductive. Instead, it may be better to encourage creativity and imagination in more indirect ways.

One question debated since the time of antiquity is why certain human individuals are especially creative. With no tools other than his imagination, Albert Einstein predicted that massive accelerating cosmic objects would create ripples in the fabric of spacetime – something definitively proven recently with the detection of gravitational waves.

Michelangelo is often held up as an example of an artistic genius because of his creation of some of the most famous artistic works of all time – in a range of different media – that include the statue of David and the frescoes in the Sistine Chapel in the Vatican. So, what makes a genius, and how does this relate to their brain function?

Einstein himself believed that a key part of his own creative process involved unconscious intuition. As he put it, 'a new idea comes suddenly and in a rather intuitive way. That means that it is not reached by conscious logical conclusions. But thinking it through afterwards you can always discover the reasons which have led you unconsciously to your guess and you will find a way to justify it. Intuition is nothing but the outcome of accumulated earlier intellectual experience.'[160]

Einstein's description of the imaginative and creative process is in line with what we have said about the twin roles of the cerebellum and the cerebral cortex in imagination and with the fact that inspiration can arise at unexpected times – in a dream, in the shower, or on a relaxing walk – but also after a period of earlier conscious contemplation of a problem. According to this view of creativity, information arrives consciously, but the problem is processed unconsciously, the resulting solution leaping out when the mind least expects it.

Box 12.1.   Searching for the Secrets of Einstein's Brain

What is it about the mind of a genius that makes them different? The desire to know was so strong on the part of Thomas Harvey, the pathologist who carried out the autopsy of Einstein after the latter's death on 18 April 1955 from a ruptured aorta, that he removed the physicist's brain for scientific study. When Harvey first weighed the brain, he found that, at 1.23 kg, in terms of size, it was actually towards the low end of the normal range for men of Einstein's age. However, over the years, neuroscientists have identified some potentially interesting features about the brain. One was the fact that Einstein seemed to have an unusually high proportion of glial cells compared to neurons. In fact, this difference, observed by Marian Diamond, was only found in one of four of the samples of Einstein's brain that she studied, casting doubt on its general relevance. Further analysis by Britt Anderson has indicated that the number of neurons in Einstein's prefrontal cortex was equivalent to brains in a control group, but they were more tightly packed, suggesting that this might allow faster processing of information. Meanwhile, Sandra Witelson has claimed that the inferior parietal lobule – the brain region responsible for spatial cognition and mathematical thought – is wider than normal and better integrated. Witelson has suggested that this might relate to Einstein's own descriptions of his thinking: 'words do not seem to play any role', but there is an 'associative play' of 'more or less clear images'. Most recently, Dean Falk has studied Einstein's corpus callosum – the bundle of fibres connecting the left and right hemispheres of the brain – and claimed to have found evidence that it was thicker than normal, which he thought might mean that the physicist had enhanced cooperation between his brain hemispheres. As interesting as these findings might be, this type of analysis, and resulting speculation about their relevance to Einstein's genius, suffers from several potential flaws. For a start, in the absence of the brains of other 'geniuses' to compare to, the relevance of findings relating to one individual is unclear. Moreover, the differences identified above were selected as being potentially interesting, yet those that did not fit the picture of a genius – like Einstein's slightly smaller-than-average brain – were largely ignored. Finally, even if the differences identified are unusual compared to the average, it remains to be shown that they have relevance to Einstein's scientific genius. Einstein was an amateur violin player, bilingual, and, it has been suggested, autistic. So any differences found might relate to these other aspects of his character. This latter point is important because another unusual feature of Einstein's brain, his dramatically asymmetric parietal lobes, has also been identified in musicians who use their left hands, and so it could merely be a consequence of the physicist's lifelong playing of the violin and not an indication of his scientific genius.

If this provides one interesting explanation of the creative process, it still does not explain why some people seem to be especially creative and imaginative. In an attempt to understand this issue better, there have been attempts to identify structural differences in the brains of deceased 'geniuses' such as Einstein; brain imaging studies have been conducted on highly creative individuals, and studies have sought to identify regions of the genome linked to high intelligence, but there is little clear evidence of distinctive differences either in brain structure or function or in genetics in particularly gifted individuals.[161]

One potential complicating factor in trying to identify the biological roots of giftedness is that there seems to be a thin line between genius and mental disorder. The belief that creativity and madness are closely related goes back to at least ancient Greek times, with Aristotle noting that 'those who have been eminent in philosophy, politics, poetry, and the arts have all had tendencies towards melancholia.'[162] However, this idea has also received support in recent times from studies that have sought to explore potential links between creativity and mental disorder in terms of neuronal and brain mechanisms. For instance, one recent study imaged the brains of a variety of people, including some prone to schizophrenia.[163] While being imaged, the volunteers were asked to imagine novel uses for everyday objects, this being a common way to assess creativity. The study identified important similarities in the brain images of individuals who showed high evidence of creativity and those prone to schizophrenia, with both showing high activity in the right precuneus, a brain region that is involved in the gathering of information. This is in line with a proposal by psychologist Shelley Carson that creativity and imagination and some forms of mental disorder are both characterised by what she calls 'cognitive disinhibition', the failure to keep off-the-wall images or ideas out of conscious awareness (Fig. 12.2).[164]

In creative individuals, this could be a positive characteristic, being a fertile source of new ideas for the mind. But in people with a tendency to schizophrenia, this might be a basis for delusional thoughts or mental confusion. Of course, there is likely to be far more to schizophrenia than lack of a filter for incoming environmental signals, and in the following chapter, we will look in more detail at this disorder and what we are learning about it and its potential biological and social roots.

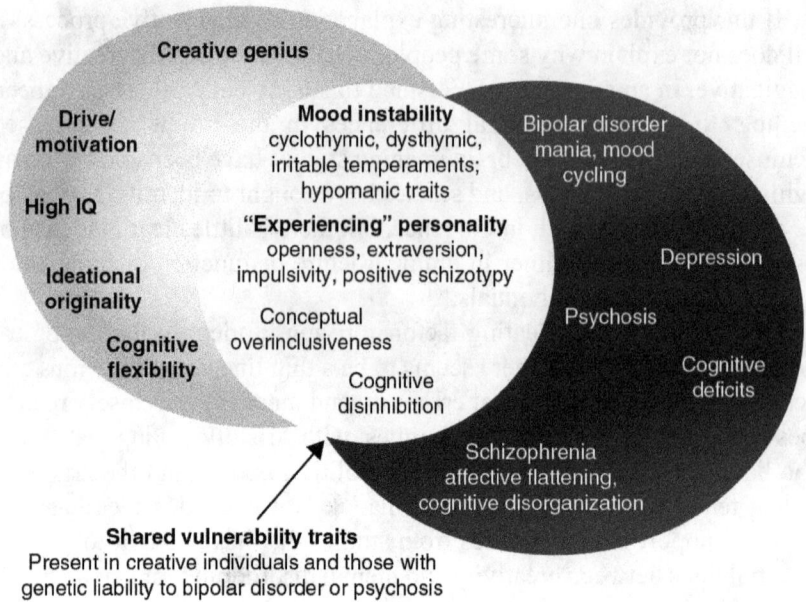

Creative genius

Drive/
motivation

High IQ

Ideational
originality

Cognitive
flexibility

Mood instability
cyclothymic, dysthymic,
irritable temperaments;
hypomanic traits

"Experiencing" personality
openness, extraversion,
impulsivity, positive schizotypy

Conceptual
overinclusiveness

Cognitive
disinhibition

Bipolar disorder
mania, mood
cycling

Depression

Psychosis

Cognitive
deficits

Schizophrenia
affective flattening,
cognitive disorganization

Shared vulnerability traits
Present in creative individuals and those with
genetic liability to bipolar disorder or psychosis

Fig. 12.2. Carson's model of the shared vulnerability between creative genius and psychopathology, summarising the temperament, personality, and cognitive characteristics shared by creative individuals and those with genetic liability to bipolar disorder and/or psychosis. The clinical overlap between bipolar disorder and schizophrenia is also represented, as are the characteristics unique to each disorder.

Source: Reproduced from Greenwood, T. (2016) *Molecular Neuropsychiatry,* 2:198–212, with permission.

Quiz

Which brain region was shown recently to become less active during improvisation?
A. Auditory cortex
B. Visual cortex
C. Dorsolateral prefrontal cortex
D. Anterior cingulate cortex

Brain region recently shown to play an important role in imagination and creativity:
A. Amygdala
B. Hypothalamus
C. Pons
D. Cerebellum

Which of the following was true of Albert Einstein's brain compared to an average brain?
A. Slightly smaller
B. Average size
C. Slightly bigger
D. Much bigger

Chapter 13

Sanity and Psychosis

Key Concepts

- Initial clues as to biological mechanisms that might underlie schizophrenia came from the identification of drugs that alleviate some of its symptoms. This led to the idea that there is too much dopamine activity in the schizophrenic brain.
- One interesting insight that has emerged in recent years based on both genetic analysis and experimental studies is that schizophrenia may be linked to an abnormal immune response, involving a surge in the activity of glial cells in the brain.
- The high and low phases of bipolar disorder are often so extreme that they can greatly interfere with everyday life. However, there is also an association of this mental disorder with great creativity and high levels of intelligence.

For a species with such a unique gift of conscious awareness, it is remarkable how often that gift can turn into a burden. Mental distress is recognised as a major problem in modern society, with around one in four people treated for a psychiatric disorder in Britain and a similar pattern in Northern America and Europe.[165] A continuing debate is whether mental disorders are primarily due to individual biology or a consequence of an adverse environment. In fact, there is reason to believe that even framing the issue in this way is misleading, as increasingly we are beginning to realise that an individual's genetic make-up may only become an important factor in certain social circumstances, while an adverse environment can lead to profound changes in a person's biology, including effects upon the brain and its development.[166]

One thing that everyone should be able to agree on, though, is the misery and suffering that can result from mental disorders. At the very least, such conditions can result in an individual being unable to find the fulfilment and happiness in life that should be a right of every human being; at worst, they can result in the premature ending of lives – both through individual suicide or by the taking of lives in mass shootings.

It is important therefore that science continues to find ways to better understand the basis of mental disorders such as schizophrenia, clinical depression, and bipolar disorder, with the hope that this might not only increase our basic knowledge about these different types of disorders but also lead to new diagnoses and treatments for these conditions. And with such a goal in mind, let us now see what the latest developments in neuroscience and psychology are revealing about schizophrenia and psychosis more generally.

Schizophrenia affects nearly one percent of the world's population, and sufferers typically begin showing symptoms in their early 20s to mid-30s.[167] This condition is characterised by cognitive, behavioural, and emotional abnormalities. To be diagnosed with schizophrenia, individuals need to have two or more of the following negative symptoms for a minimum of six months – disorganised speech, grossly disorganised, or catatonic behaviour – and at least one positive symptom, delusions and hallucinations being typical examples. Despite years of studies, the pathophysiological basis of schizophrenia remains far from clear. However, clues are emerging from a number of different directions.

Some of the first clues as to biological mechanisms that might underlie schizophrenia came from the identification of drugs that can prevent or alleviate some of the symptoms of schizophrenia. Such anti-psychotics are typically chemicals that antagonise the actions of the neurotransmitter dopamine in the brain.[168] In contrast, drugs used to treat Parkinson's disease are dopamine agonists because one cause of the rigidity, tremor, and muscle spasms that are a feature of this disorder is the degeneration of the substantia nigra, a brain region particularly rich in dopamine neurons. That two side effects of such anti-Parkinson's drugs are hallucinations and delusions, these also being characteristic symptoms of schizophrenia, has been pointed to as further evidence that this disorder is primarily due to there being too much dopamine activity in the schizophrenic brain (Fig. 13.1).[169]

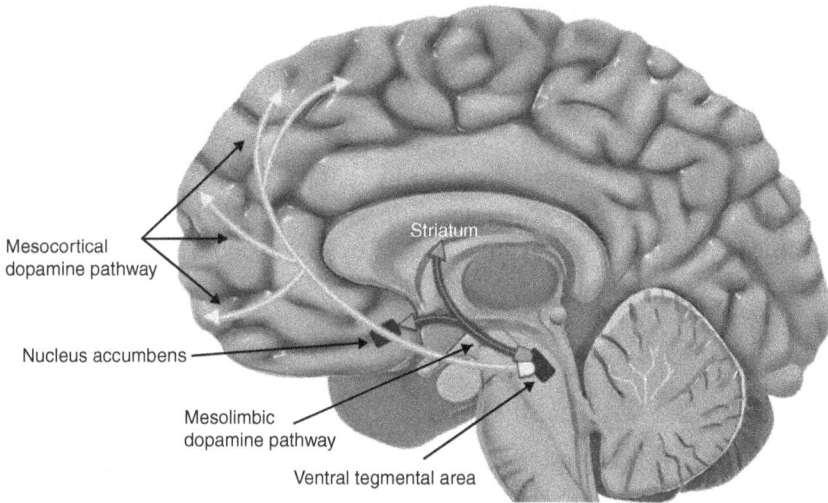

Fig. 13.1.   The dopamine hypothesis of schizophrenia.

Source: Reproduced from Aryutova, K. and Stoyanov, D. (2021) *International Journal of Molecular Sciences*, 22:9309, with permission.

Yet, recent decades have seen increasing criticism of the general idea that mental disorders are primarily due to imbalances in the levels of particular neurotransmitters in the brain as if this organ were a bucket, meant to be filled with just the right amount of a chemical.[170] In the case of schizophrenia, one problem that has been highlighted about such a viewpoint is that the dopamine antagonists used to treat this disorder typically suppress 'positive' symptoms, such as delusions, hallucinations, and hyperactivity, but have little impact on the 'negative' symptoms such as apathy, lethargy, and withdrawal from social situations. This suggests that the schizophrenic condition involves more than simply excessive activity in dopaminergic activity, even if this plays an important role in this disorder.[171]

Another approach to understanding the biological basis of schizophrenia is to look for genetic links. This approach has been bolstered in recent years by the use of genome-wide association studies (GWAS). This approach investigates a large number of people, some of whom have been diagnosed with a human condition, and tries to identify genetic differences that only occur in affected individuals. Initial studies of this type sought to identify links between schizophrenia occurrence and the presence of common genetic variants.

GWAS has identified hundreds of different variants linked to schizophrenia.[172] However, a major problem in making sense of such findings is that each of the variants only seems to contribute a very small amount to the chance of succumbing to the disorder. This raises the important question of how deterministic such a genetic link can be.

Recently, a more convincing line of evidence about genetic links to certain forms of schizophrenia has emerged.[173]

Box 13.1.   GWAS and Other Types of Genomic Analysis

One feature of GWAS findings is that each genomic region identified only appears to increase the risk of succumbing to a common disorder like schizophrenia by a small amount – less than two percent. Equally confusing at first glance is that the vast majority of GWAS hits – around 90 percent – are not even in protein-coding genes but in regions between genes. So, how are we to make sense of this situation? That most associations are not in protein-coding genes is in line with recent findings that have identified four million genetic 'switches' that regulate the activity of the 20,000 or so protein-coding genes in the human genome. Many genomic hits identified through GWAS in schizophrenics are in such regulatory regions. This points to a more subtle influence of such GWAS hits on gene expression and much more possibility of environmental influence than for single-gene disorders, for which there is such a strong link between a gene and the disorder that the latter will always tend to manifest itself, no matter what environment a particular individual is exposed to. One potential flaw of GWAS is its focus on 'common' variations, that is, single-letter differences in the human DNA sequence found in at least five percent of individuals. When this type of analysis was first initiated, there was a good rationale for such a focus. For cost reasons, the only method of analysis for studying a large number of individuals was not to sequence the whole genome but rather to identify the presence, or absence, of common variations, in the genomes of those individuals that were being assessed. But what if the common variations being assessed have no role in a disorder? The geneticist Jonathan Pritchard has argued that many GWAS hits have no particular biological relevance to disease and would not make good drug targets. He believes that GWAS may be detecting 'peripheral' variants because they act through complex regulatory networks to influence the activity of 'core' genes that are more directly connected to an illness. GWAS proponents have countered that by identifying the components of such networks, scientists can build up a clearer picture of how the cell normally works and how it can go wrong during the development of a particular disease. But this does not address the possibility that GWAS may be failing to identify the core genes involved in a disorder. Such a possibility could explain why genomic hits identified by GWAS seem to carry such a small risk of succumbing to the disorder. Rather than representing an actual role in the condition, such associations may reflect the existence of rare variants only present in a small number of individuals but whose presence leads to a much greater risk of those individuals having the disorder; this in turn tends to skew the apparent importance of linked common variants. Until recently, it was impossible to test such a possibility because of the prohibitive costs of identifying such rare variants by sequencing the whole genomes of large numbers of individuals. However, with 'next-generation' methods of DNA sequencing resulting in a dramatic decrease in the cost of analysing a whole genome, it is now becoming feasible to carry out such whole genome sequence analysis for a variety of mental disorders.

This more recent analysis has employed whole genome sequencing (WGS), which makes it possible not only to identify common genetic variants but also very rare mutations that can only be identified by this more detailed approach.

Such analysis has identified mutations in 10 genes that strongly increase – in one case by more than 50-fold – the chance of succumbing to schizophrenia. The findings are important not only because they help us understand why schizophrenia developed in the particular individuals in which they were identified but because it is hoped that they will provide major insights into the biological basis of this disorder as a whole.

Two of the genes identified, GRIN2A and GRIA3, encode parts of the glutamate receptor, which, as we have seen, mediates excitatory neuronal responses. Pharmacological studies had suggested that glutamate signalling may be involved in schizophrenia, but the new findings provide the first genetic evidence of this. Interestingly, GRIN2A activity in the brain peaks during adolescence, around the time people suffering from schizophrenia begin to show symptoms.

However, many of the genes identified have no previous link with a brain disorder or indeed with neuronal function. Such genes include

SETD1A, involved in transcriptional regulation, CUL1, which helps the cell recycle old or unneeded proteins, and XPO7, which chaperones molecules out of the cell's nucleus. A challenge for future studies will be determining how defects in these processes lead to schizophrenia.

Despite the importance of the identification of rare mutations that greatly increase the chances of an individual succumbing to schizophrenia, it remains the case that in the vast majority of people with this disorder, the genetic links are far less clear. This may reflect the fact that schizophrenia is a disorder with a broad spectrum of different symptoms and varying severity of effects in different affected individuals. Indeed, a person may be diagnosed as schizophrenic with a completely different set of symptoms from another affected person. So, we might expect there to be many different contributing genetic factors in schizophrenia, reflecting the biological complexity of this disorder and also the different levels of severity in individuals.

A different approach to identifying the biological roots of schizophrenia involves not looking at the genome but searching for biological differences in the brains of people with this disorder. It is important to note that such differences could be linked to a genetic susceptibility to schizophrenia, but they could equally be a consequence of an adverse environment, as there is increasing evidence that environmental effects can manifest themselves in terms of biology.

One interesting insight that has emerged in recent years is that schizophrenia may be linked to an abnormal immune response (Fig. 13.2).[174]

For instance, in the study mentioned earlier that identified rare mutations linked to schizophrenia, one of the genes identified codes for complement component 4 (C4), part of the innate immune system.

This is far from the only evidence. Thus, a recent study suggested that schizophrenia may be triggered by an inappropriate immune response involving a surge in the number and activity of glial cells in the brain.[175] We have already seen that one role for glial cells is 'pruning' synapses, much as a gardener prunes plants, in order to regulate the numbers of synapses and therefore connections in a neuronal circuit. However, it seems that in some cases of schizophrenia, the pruning is overly aggressive, leading to vital neuronal connections being lost (Fig. 13.3). Other studies show that schizophrenia is often associated with inflammation in the brain, inflammation being an important component of the immune response.

So, what might trigger such inappropriate immune responses in the brain? We have already looked at genetic links that might predispose an

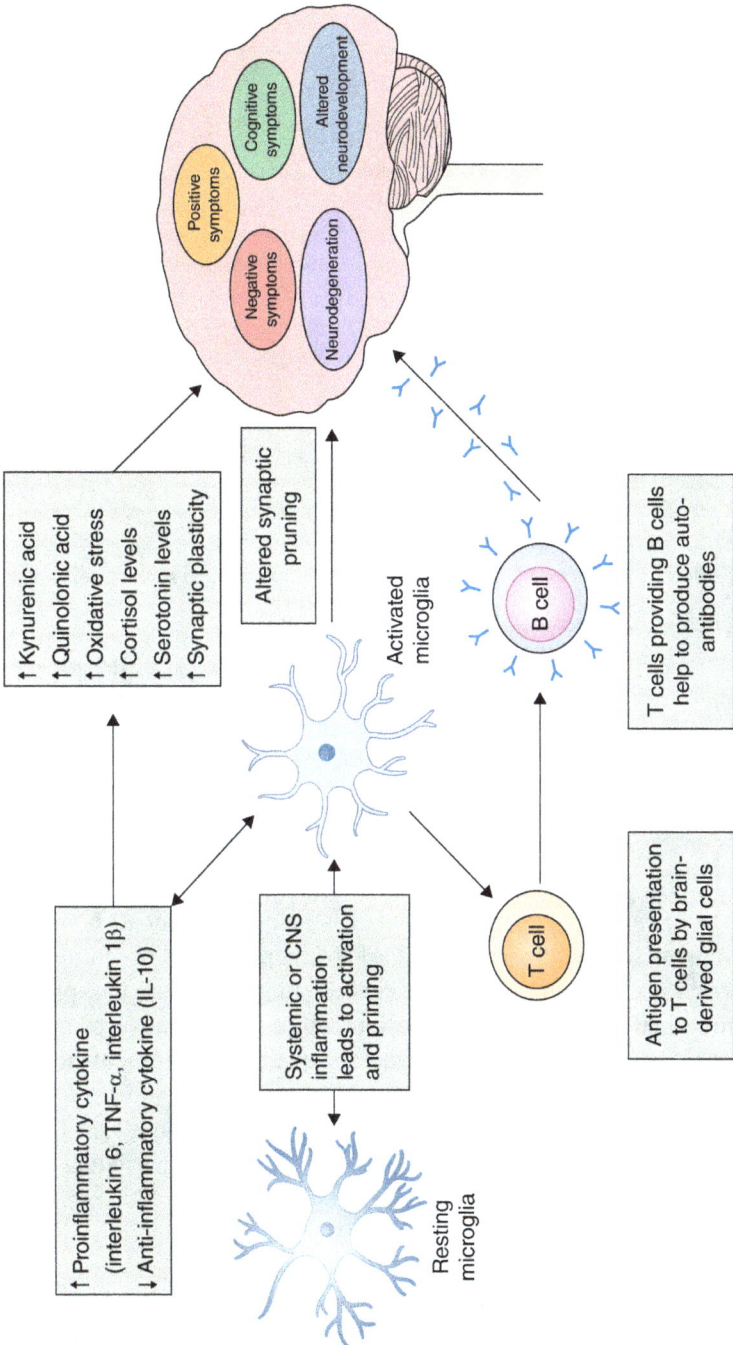

Fig. 13.2.   Possible mechanisms of immune-mediated causation of psychosis. TNFα = tumour necrosis factor α. CNS = central nervous system.

Source: Reproduced from van Mierlo, H.C. *et al.* (2020) *Schizophrenia Research*, 217:114–123, with permission.

(a)

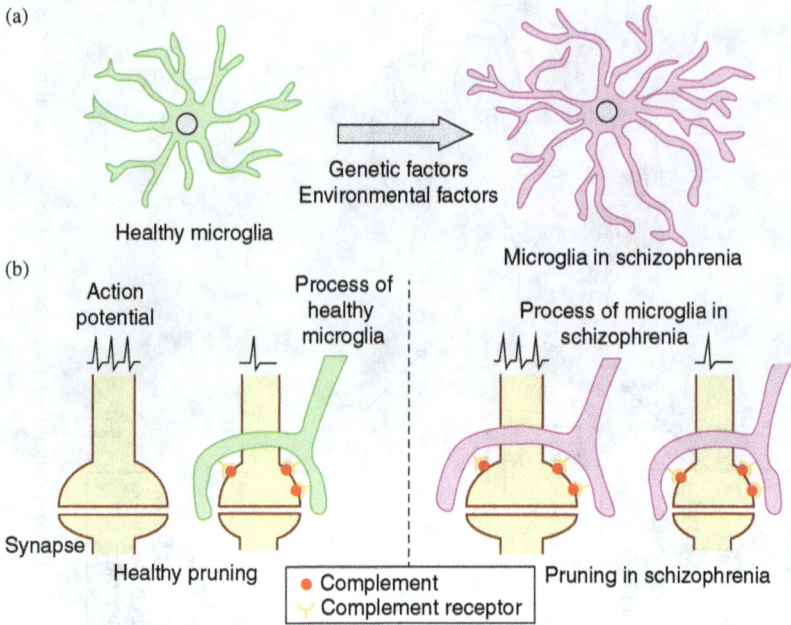

(b)

Fig. 13.3. Microglial synaptic pruning in schizophrenia. (a) Microglia exhibit hyper-ramified morphology in schizophrenia due to genetic and environmental factors. (b) Healthy microglia eliminate complement-tagged synapses with lower activity. In schizophrenia, hyper-ramified microglia prune healthy synapses by excessive activation of complements.

Source: Reproduced from Izuo, N. and Nitta A. (2021) *Journal of Personalized Medicine*, 11:371, with permission.

individual to have such a response. But it is also important to consider the environment's role in the genesis of schizophrenia. For numerous studies carried out over the past few decades suggest that sexual, physical, and emotional abuse, as well as various other types of adverse childhood experiences, may be important factors in the development of this disorder.[176]

Thus, even if an individual does have genetic differences that make them more susceptible, it may still be the case that only in a particular type of environment will their schizophrenia develop into a full-blown condition. This could explain why many of the GWAS genetic links only appear to have a minor contributing role.

Given the importance of social factors in the development of schizophrenia, it is worth considering how these might affect both brain biology and cognitive function. But in order to do so, it would help to have a clearer idea of the nature of such social factors. In this respect, the insights of the psychiatrist R. D. Laing are a useful place to start. Coming to prominence in the 1960s, Laing's interactions with his schizophrenic patients led him to propose that a key factor in the development of this disorder is major problems of communication within the schizophrenic's family.

Typically, the person who becomes schizophrenic is caught in a situation in which messages from other family members are deeply contradictory; however, the contradiction is never brought into the open, and the person is unable to leave the field of interaction with such people. One phenomenon that Laing thought was particularly important was the 'double-bind', a psychological predicament in which a person receives from other family members such conflicting messages that effectively no appropriate response can be made.[177]

In this context, it is interesting that a study by psychologist Bjorn Rund found that non-paranoid schizophrenics, but notably not paranoid schizophrenics, generally came from families with abnormalities in their patterns of communication.[178] Thus, the parents of such schizophrenics were often egocentric in their behaviour and tended to ignore what their children were saying, as well as interrupting them or sending them mixed messages.

Rund's study particularly focused on attention, the process by which an individual's awareness becomes focused on a subset of what is going on in their head or their environment. Normally, voluntary forms of attention emerge as key people in a child's early years begin to use various different means to direct the child's attention in a focused manner. However, in a family situation in which normal communication has broken down, Rund proposed that the child has 'no opportunity to establish a firm situation, because it will never know which are the relevant stimuli in a given situation. Instead, the attentional styles that are internalised will be characterised by a steady wandering from one stimulus to another, in the search for the most relevant one.' Rund also believed that the 'emotional climate' within a family could affect the development of schizophrenia. This is surely particularly likely if physical and sexual abuse is a part of family life. Anxiety, insecurity, and instability thus tend to be a feature of families in which schizophrenics grow up.

Rund's study did not look at how genetics might play a role in the genesis of schizophrenia. But it seems possible that if a tendency towards schizophrenia was linked to genetics, not only could this tendency be passed down directly, but also through the complexity of genetic mechanisms, it might also be the case that apparently unaffected family members might still display abnormal behaviour linked to their genetics, and such behaviour could help trigger the schizophrenic condition in a vulnerable individual within such a family. However, it also seems likely that other factors outside the family might combine to help trigger this disorder.

Studies such as those above are important because they show the importance of social interaction in the normal development of a human being from childhood into adulthood and how a dysfunctional social environment might be an important factor in mental disorder. It would be interesting, therefore, given what we have said about the importance of language in human cognition, to study in more detail the ways that abnormal forms of communication, verbal and otherwise, for instance body language, can play an important role in the development of schizophrenia. Ultimately though, we also need to link this to differences in brain biology.

Schizophrenia is not the only mental disorder associated with psychosis. This is also a feature of bipolar disorder, formerly known as 'manic depression'.[179] Even less is known about the biological basis of this condition than schizophrenia, but it seems to run in families. It affects 1 in 100 people in the developed world and is characterised by periods of depression followed by episodes of mania, during which affected individuals can feel extremely happy, ambitious, and creative, but sometimes in this phase, they can become psychotic (Fig. 13.4).

The high and low phases of bipolar disorder are often so extreme that they interfere with everyday life; consequentially, this can be a highly debilitating disorder. However, there is also an association of this mental disorder with great creativity and high levels of intelligence.[180] For instance, a recent study tested the IQ of individuals at age eight and then assessed for manic traits when aged 22 or 23. The study showed that individuals in the top 10 percent of manic characteristics had a childhood IQ 10 points higher than those who scored in the lowest 10 percent.[181] This correlation was strongest for verbal IQ.

Bipolar disorder entails dramatic mood swings between extreme happiness and severe depression. One feature of interest is that people with bipolar disorder tend to be creative when they are coming out of deep depression. When a bipolar patient's mood improves, their brain activity does too: activity decreases in the lower part of the frontal lobe brain region and increases in a higher part of that lobe. Interestingly, the same shift happens when unaffected individuals have creative bouts.

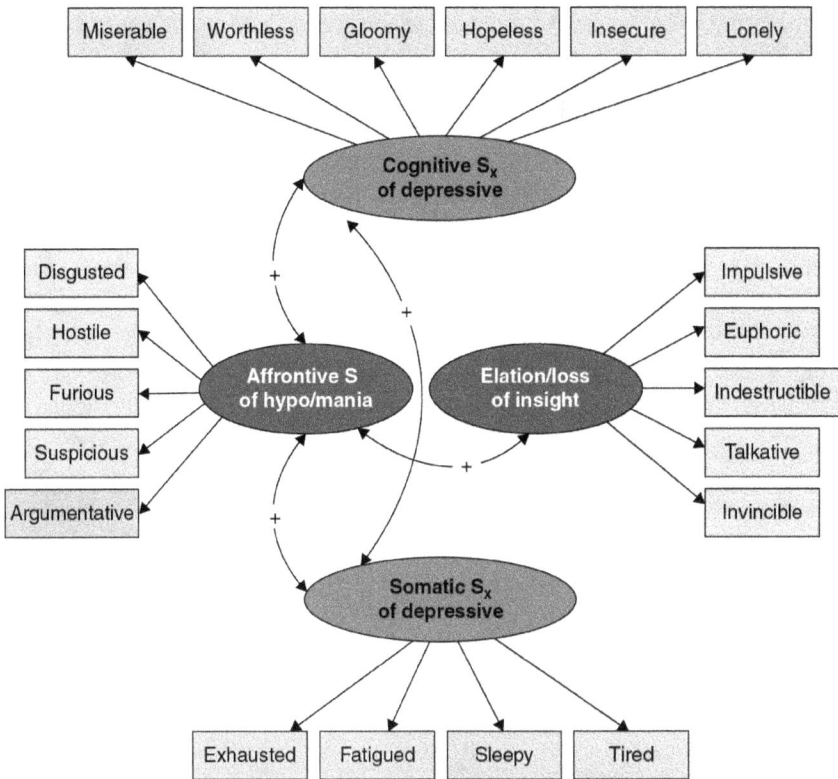

Fig. 13.4. Four-factor model of bipolar disorder symptoms.

Source: Reproduced from Yerushalmi, M. *et al.* (2021) *JMIR Formative Research*, 5: e30472, with permission.

One explanation for the creative aspects of bipolar disorder is that individuals in the manic phase of this disorder do not filter stimuli as well as other people.[182] Instead, they can entertain contradictory ideas simultaneously and become aware of loose associations that most people's unconscious brains would not consider worthy of sending to the surface of our consciousness.

It is possible that while the invasion of multiple stimuli into conscious thought can be overwhelming and disruptive, it can on occasion be quite creative. For example, word association studies, which ask participants to list all the words that come to mind in relation to a stimulus word, have shown that bipolar patients undergoing mild mania can generate three times as many word associations in a given time period as the general population.[183] As for how this leads to strokes of genius, it could be that the sheer bounty of unsuppressed ideas means a greater probability of producing something profound.

Of course, no one is bursting with creative energy during a severe bout of depression. Above all, conditions like bipolar are debilitating and even life-threatening, and although society may benefit from the productivity of tortured geniuses such as Vincent van Gogh, who may have had bipolar disorder,[184] those individuals do not always consider their moments of brilliance to be worth the extensive suffering. This is an important point to make lest it be thought that there is anything glamorous about suffering from a mental disorder. This is particularly true of the depressive side of bipolar disorder, which can lead to sufferers having extremely negative thoughts and contemplating and even committing suicide. This is even more the case for another mental disorder, clinical depression, which can be also linked to extreme anxiety, and we will now look at these linked disorders.

Quiz

Proportion of people treated for a psychiatric disorder in the UK:
A. 1 in 2
B. 1 in 4
C. 1 in 8
D. 1 in 16

An increase in which of these neurotransmitters is most associated with schizophrenia?
A. GABA
B. Serotonin
C. Dopamine
D. Noradrenaline

Former name for bipolar disorder:
A. Psychotic depression
B. Manic depression
C. Clinical depression
D. Cyclical depression

Chapter 14

Anxiety and Depression

Key Concepts

* An apparently major step forward both in our understanding of clinical depression and how to treat it occurred in the 1950s, when evidence emerged that depression might be due to low levels of the neurochemical serotonin.
* An alternative theory of depression is that it is due to defects in neurogenesis. Recent studies have indicated that rather than a shortage of serotonin, a lack of growth of new synapses and reduced generation of new neurons could cause depression.
* A recent study has linked defects in the SIRT1 protein to depression. SIRT1 can protect neurons from ageing and death by destroying free radicals, so loss of its function could affect the brain's ability to regenerate itself through neurogenesis.

More than 100 US citizens commit suicide each day, this being the 10th leading cause of death overall – third among 15–24-year-olds and fourth among 25–44-year-olds.[185] Many people who commit suicide have been diagnosed with clinical depression. Globally, over 300 million people, or 4.4 percent of the world's population, are estimated to be affected by clinical depression,[186] a condition characterised by feelings of sadness, emptiness or hopelessness, angry outbursts, irritability or frustration, loss of interest or pleasure in normal activities, sleep disturbances, tiredness and lack of energy, anxiety, agitation or restlessness, slowed thinking, speaking, or body movements, feelings of worthlessness or guilt, trouble in concentrating, making decisions and remembering things, and frequent or recurrent thoughts of death, suicidal thoughts, suicide attempts, or suicide.

So, how might we better understand depression and hopefully prevent deaths by suicide in the future? One problem we face is the lack of consensus in even defining this disorder. As a human condition, something similar to depression has been recognised for thousands of years. In ancient Greece, people with 'melancholia' were thought to have too much 'black bile' in their bodies, and the condition was treated by altering their diet.[187] In the 19th and early 20th centuries, those wealthy enough to be able to afford treatment for their depression were subjected to 'rest cures', which mainly consisted of being confined to their room in isolation while being grossly overfed.[188] Recently, the social background to this particular approach to depression has been critically assessed.[189]

An apparently major step forward both in our understanding of clinical depression and how to treat it occurred in the 1950s, when evidence emerged that depression might be due to low levels of the neurochemical serotonin.[190] In particular, studies showed that certain chemicals that alleviated the symptoms of depression appeared to work by inhibiting the reuptake of serotonin into certain neurons in the brain. Prevention of such reuptake, after serotonin has been released at neuronal synapses, is thought to enhance the ability of this neurotransmitter to continue having its effects upon the brain.

In line with a role for a deficiency in serotonin levels as a key factor in depression, a 2003 study suggested that people with a variant of the gene that controls serotonin uptake were not as well equipped to deal with stressful life events and were more likely to develop depression.[191] Since its publication, this study has been heavily cited, and many other studies have been published about links between this gene, stressful life events, and depression risk, with some confirming a link while others finding no such evidence. Yet, a 'meta-analysis' of these studies failed to confirm the findings of the original study.[192] As mentioned in the context of schizophrenia, there is increasing criticism of the idea that mental disorders are due to excess, or lack, of a particular brain chemical.

If doubts are being cast on a simplistic 'serotonin deficit' model of depression,[193] are we getting any closer to better understanding this disorder? One recent theory of depression is that it is due to a lack of new neurons being regenerated. We have seen that the idea that such 'neurogenesis' only occurs during the development of the brain in the embryo, foetus, and child, but not in the adult brain, has recently been challenged. Recent studies have indicated that rather than a shortage of serotonin, a lack of growth of new synapses and reduced generation of new neurons could cause depression. For instance, one study found that cells in culture exposed to the SSRI drug paroxetine produce the protein integrin beta-3, which regulates cell adhesion and connectivity, new synapse formation, and neurogenesis.[194] Lower serotonin levels may therefore be more a consequence than a cause of clinical depression, since when the brain stops making new neurons or fewer neuronal connections are formed, this might reduce serotonin release.

Other recent studies have suggested a link between depression and inflammation (Fig. 14.1).[195]

We saw earlier how abnormalities in how glial cells respond to inflammation may be one factor in the development of schizophrenia. In depression, inflammation may affect the brain in a different way, sparking feelings of hopelessness, unhappiness, and fatigue.

Such feelings may be caused by the immune system failing to switch off after a trauma or illness, triggering a severe version of the low mood people can experience when fighting an infection. Indeed, recent studies suggest that treating inflammation can alleviate depression, while treatments that boost the immune system to fight illness can be accompanied by a depressive mood; for instance, people may feel down after a vaccination.

Other studies have supported the idea that in a depressive brain, the ability of neurons to connect appropriately becomes abnormal, creating or enhancing low mood, destructive thinking, and other symptoms.[196] Increasingly, neuroscientists believe that the key to understanding depression lies in identifying how the disorder affects neural circuitry and the way that widely separated brain regions communicate through the long-range projection of nerve fibres.

According to this view, mental disorders result from the disruption of the larger circuit wiring of the brain. In support of this, recent studies have shown that certain people with depression have reduced volume in brain regions used for emotional processing and fewer neural 'couplings' within these regions.

In contrast, other studies have shown an increase in the number of neural connections in the brains of some depressed individuals.[197] Such studies indicate that the limbic and cortical regions of the brain in certain depressed patients, which are related to emotional processing, send neural

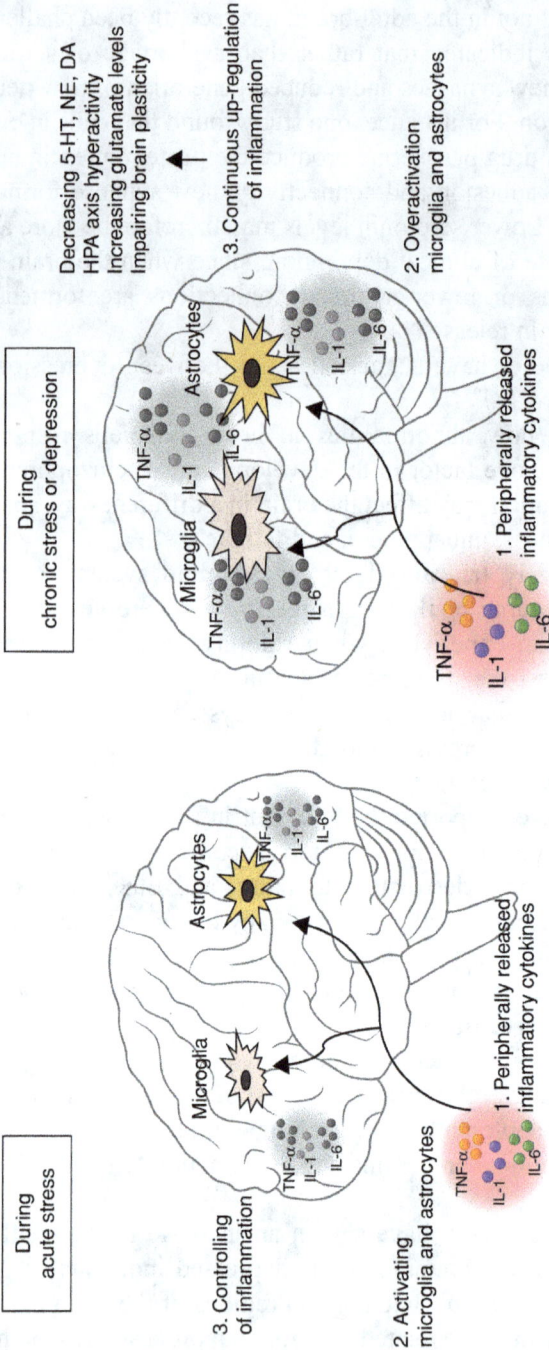

Fig. 14.1. Peripherally released pro-inflammatory cytokines may reach the brain where they drive neuroinflammation by activating microglia and astrocytes modulate brain areas involved with mood regulation, reducing brain monoamine levels, activating neuroendocrine responses, promoting glutamate excitotoxicity, and impairing brain plasticity.

Source: Reproduced from Rhie, S. *et al.* (2020) *Journal of Exercise Rehabilitation*, 16:2–9, with permission.

signals at a much higher volume than normal. Not only are the connections abnormal, so is the information being transmitted. Intriguingly, given evidence mentioned previously showing the importance of brain waves as coordinators of consciousness, there is also evidence that such waves may be abnormal in depressed individuals.

What might we learn from genetics about the biological basis of clinical depression? Similar to the situation with schizophrenia, a major focus in recent years has been to use GWAS to uncover such potential genetic links. Such GWAS findings have implicated hundreds of different genomic regions as making a contribution, each very small, to the chance of someone becoming clinically depressed.[198] However, in terms of furthering our understanding of the biological basis of depression, the situation is proving even more complex than with the findings that have emerged about genetic links to schizophrenia.

One problem for GWAS analysis of depression is that, as already mentioned, this is a very common disorder, with more than 300 million people worldwide affected. The disorder's symptoms and severity can vary widely from one person to the next and also between men and women. This means that there may be a whole spectrum of different conditions that are being grouped together that have quite different biological causes, complicating genetic analysis. There have also been criticisms of the fact that some studies have accepted a self-assessment of depression, rather than a rigorous one by a clinician.[199]

To address some of these problems, a recent study focused on depressed women in China.[200] A motivation for performing the study in this country was that because depression tends to be underdiagnosed in China, women identified as being clinically depressed might have a particularly severe form of the disorder. And indeed, those taking part in the study were at the most severe end of the spectrum. The study identified DNA sequence variations in two genes – LHPP and SIRT1 – as being clearly different in many of the depressed women.

LHPP's function in the cell remains unclear, while SIRT1, one of a class of genes called sirtuins, is known to play a role in mitochondria, which, as already mentioned, are the subcellular structures that produce energy in our cells through aerobic respiration. Although vital for multicellular life, a by-product of such respiration is the production of oxygen free radicals, which can be toxic to cells. Recent studies suggest that SIRT1 can protect neurons from ageing and death by destroying free radicals, so this could be important given that, as we have seen, depression

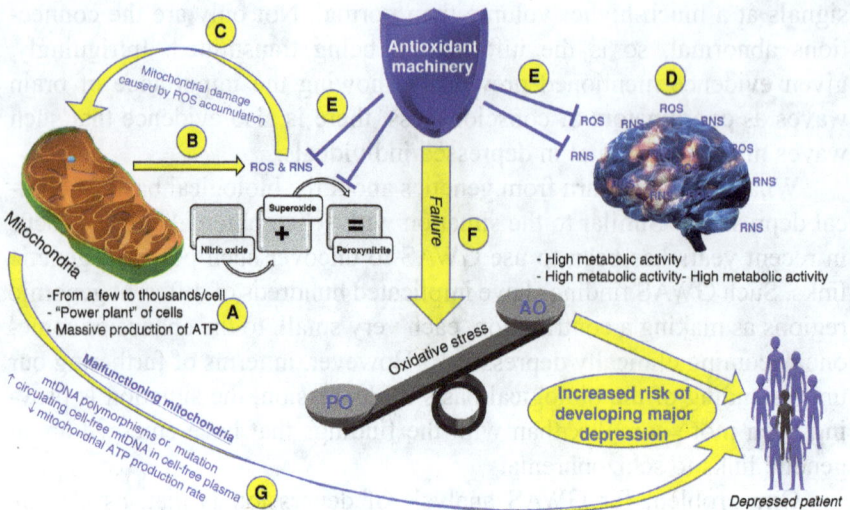

Fig. 14.2. (A) Mitochondrial physiology. (B) Brain mitochondria produce high quantities of reactive oxygen species (ROS) and reactive nitrogen species (RNS) along with adenosine triphosphate (ATP), increasing their own vulnerability (C) and that of the brain (D) to oxidative damage. When the ability of the antioxidant machinery to balance ROS/RNS production (E) fails, oxidative stress develops (F). Both oxidative stress and malfunctioning mitochondria (G) represent risk factors for the development of major depression.

Source: Reproduced from Caruso, G. *et al.* (2019) *Frontiers in Pharmacology*, 10:995, with permission.

has been linked to inflammation and to defects in the brain's ability to regenerate itself through neurogenesis (Fig. 14.2).[201]

A complicating factor for attempts to identify a biological basis to depression, or for that matter any mental disorder, is the role that social factors can play in the genesis of such disorders (Fig. 14.3).

In 1978, psychologists George Brown and Tirril Harris studied the incidence of depression in London and concluded that the best predictor of this disorder is being a working class woman with an unstable income and a child, living in a tower block.[202]

One conclusion is that such a stressful environment is more likely to precipitate depression than a less stressful one. But another factor that might trigger depression, given the importance of social interaction in human society, is disruption to such interaction.

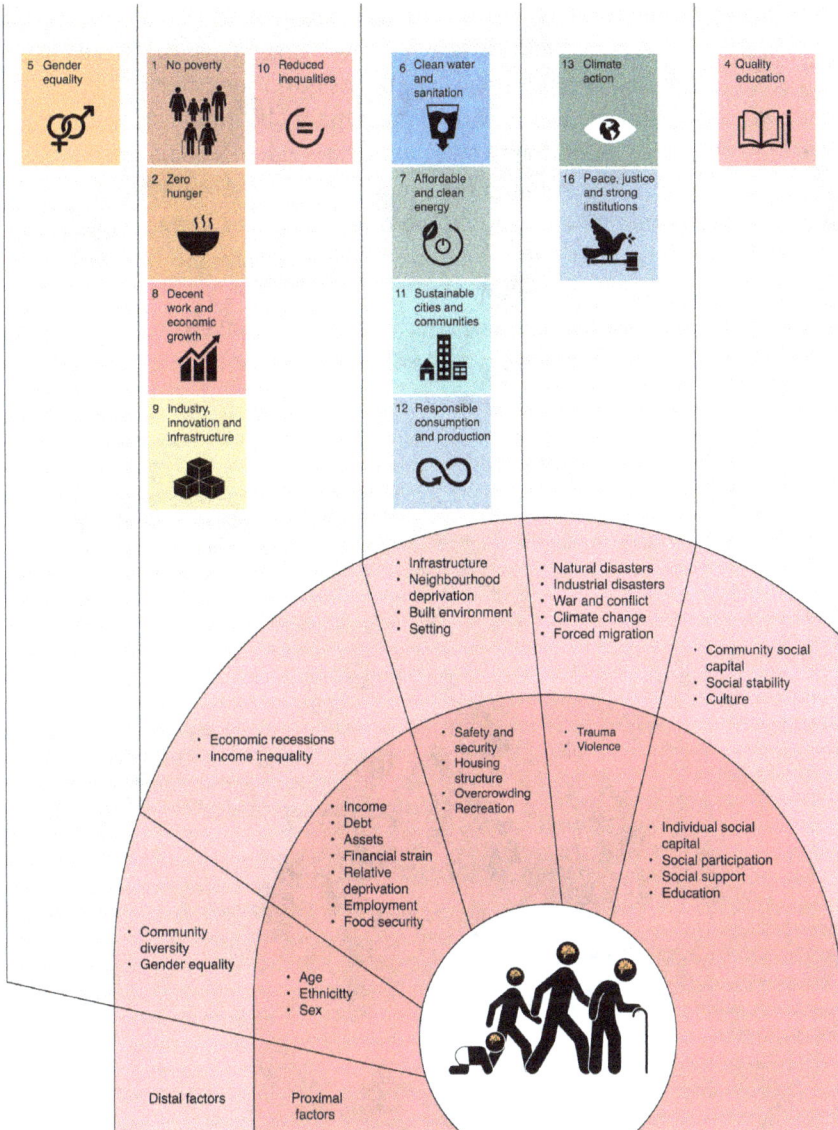

Fig. 14.3. Social and cultural determinants of mental health.

Source: Reproduced from Patel, V. *et al.* (2018) *The Lancet Commissions*, 392:1553–1598, with permission.

Indeed, Brown and Harris found that **89** percent of the depressed women they interviewed had suffered a life-changing event, such as family bereavement, a marriage break-up, or loss of a job after full employment. While all of these events would presumably be highly stressful, they could also lead to a reduction in an affected individual's social interaction. Another study that investigated the incidence of depression in New York in the 1960s found this condition to be more prevalent in people of lower socioeconomic status, but the 'loneliness, the isolation, the lostness … of urban life' was also a key factor.[203]

Anxiety is another mental condition often linked to depression (Fig. 14.4).[204] Anxiety disorders recognised clinically include generalised

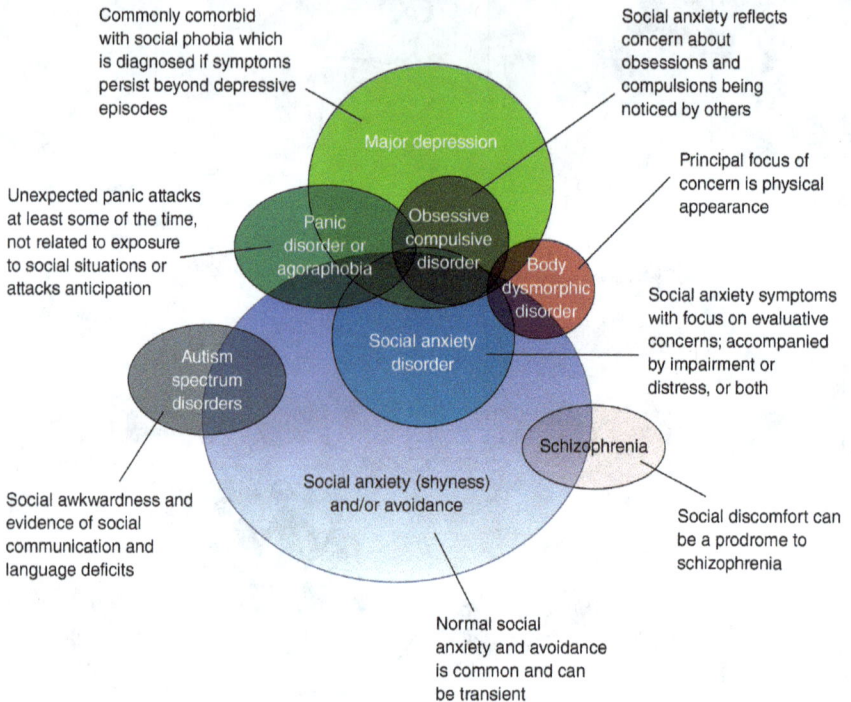

Fig. 14.4.   Conditions that commonly overlap with social anxiety disorder (social phobia) and might be considered in the differential diagnosis of an individual with social anxiety symptoms.

Source: Reproduced from Stein, M.B. and Stein, D.J. (2008) *The Lancet*, 9618:1115–1125, with permission.

anxiety disorder (an ongoing state of excessive anxiety lacking any clear reason or focus), social anxiety disorder (fear of being with and interacting with other people), phobias (strong fears of specific objects or situations), panic disorder (sudden attacks of overwhelming fear that occur in association with symptoms such as sweating, palpitations, chest pains, trembling, and choking), post-traumatic stress disorder (PTSD; distress triggered by recall of past traumatic experiences), obsessive-compulsive disorder (OCD; recurrent obsessive thoughts, images or impulses and physical or mental rituals driven by unfounded anxieties, such as fear of contamination), and illness anxiety disorder (disproportionate preoccupations with acquiring a specific illness).

In some respects, anxiety disorders might be thought of as a disproportionate extension of an important normal physiological response – the 'fright, flight, or fight response' – which as we saw previously, is mediated by adrenaline stimulating G-protein coupled receptors (GPCRs) that act via the second messenger cyclic AMP (cAMP) and also, in the longer term, the influence of stress hormones such as cortisol.[205] This normal response to a threatening situation is a vital survival instinct, which typically involves physiological changes such as increased heart rate, rapid breathing, dilation of the eyes, and increased sweating. However, such changes are only meant to occur in response to a real threat and also to subside once that threat has disappeared or been overcome. In contrast, anxiety disorders involve such changes without a real or serious threat, and in some forms of this type of disorder, they can also persist and become part of a generalised anxiety syndrome.

Despite the similarities between different anxiety disorders in terms of underlying physiological mechanisms, an interesting aspect of these disorders is how different they are in terms of the specific stimulus that triggers the disorder and in the variety of their focus. In this respect, we also have to consider how such differences may be linked to general fears and prejudices in a particular society. For instance, it is surely not surprising that veterans of war are particularly prone to PTSD given what they may have experienced in battle.[206] Similarly, the occurrence of OCD in modern society may be linked to the many messages we grow up with about the need for cleanliness and order in the home.[207] Yet, while noting these potential influences, we still need to explain why anxiety disorders can persist for years even long after a physical threat is no longer present or turn into a pathological version of a normal, everyday behaviour, such as personal hygiene or house-keeping.

Studies that have sought to identify a genetic basis for PTSD have followed a similar route to that followed for other mental disorders, namely approaches such as GWAS. The findings have been similarly complex, with hundreds of genomic regions linked to this condition, but each only apparently contributing a small amount to the likelihood of someone succumbing to this disorder. However, six genomic regions in particular were found to be more strongly associated with PTSD risk, and these are all thought to play a role in inflammatory or immune responses.[208] It may be then that in such individuals, a traumatic event may somehow lead to an inappropriate or exaggerated immune or inflammatory response, and this then becomes propagated, leading to a chronic condition.

Claims about the role of genetics in anxiety or depression compared to those that highlight a role for the environment in a person succumbing to this disorder can suggest that these two types of influences act separately. However, it would be a mistake to believe that the influence of biology and environment are separable in this way, for as we have seen, it is becoming clear that the environment can directly affect the genome through epigenetic mechanisms. Not only can such environmental influence affect the epigenome of a particular individual during their lifetime, but more controversially, there is also evidence that environmental effects can also affect the epigenomes of their offspring.

An illustration of how anxiety might be passed down through the generations in an epigenetic manner comes from a recent study in which male baby mice were exposed to stressful stimuli – such as fox odour or restraint in a conical tube. The study found that the anxiety this induced was transmitted to the offspring of the mice by specific micro RNAs (miRNAs) – one of the classes of regulatory RNAs.[209]

Not only were specific miRNAs found at higher levels in the sperm of the stressed male mice, but injection of purified forms of these miRNAs into a fertilised mouse egg generated from unstressed parent mice led to the birth of anxious mice in the next generation.

Further study showed that stress causes an increase in the hormone cortisol in the blood, which triggers the release of stress-inducing miRNAs from a structure called the epididymis in which sperm are stored after production by the testicles. In an inter-generational feedback loop, the miRNAs transmitted to the next generation affect genes that regulate blood cortisol in that generation.[210]

Of course, people are not mice, and an obvious obstacle in trying to study whether similar molecular mechanisms transmit anxiety across generations in our species is that it would be hardly ethical to induce stress in human baby boys and then see if this is transmitted to the next generation. Instead, investigations of the role of epigenetic mechanisms, acting across generations, as a possible factor in the genesis of human mental disorders have had to focus on individuals who have been exposed to extremely stressful situations and then assess what might be different about their epigenomes and those of their children, compared to unaffected individuals and their offspring.

Undoubtedly, the most horrific event in the 20th century was the Holocaust of World War II, in which the Nazis murdered as many as 15 million people – mainly Jews, but also Slavs, gypsies, LGBT+ individuals, the disabled, and political opponents of Hitler and his party – in concentration camps across Germany and Poland. Those who survived the Holocaust were deeply traumatised by their experience, resulting in an increased incidence of anxious and depressed individuals among the survivors. But it has been claimed that Holocaust survivors' children are also more likely to develop PTSD, depression, and anxiety, despite having grown up in a non-stressful environment.

A recent study claimed to have found evidence that this apparent higher incidence of mental disorder is associated with epigenetic differences in the DNA of Holocaust survivors' children. In particular, it was claimed that the children of male Holocaust survivors who suffered PTSD had higher methylation of a gene involved in the stress response.[211] As we have mentioned previously, such methylation changes can affect the degree to which a gene is turned on or off. Subsequently though, the study's findings and conclusions have come in for criticism from various directions.

One criticism is that only a small number of individuals – 32 survivors and 22 of their offspring – were studied. Another potential flaw is that the study did not consider the possibility that survivors might – deliberately or inadvertently – have communicated the horror of their experience to their children while the latter were growing up, thereby exposing them to stress. Finally, there has been criticism of the fact that the study only investigated a small number of genes and only found a small amount of change in the methylation states of the genes studied.

Claims about the role of epigenetic influences in the genesis of mental disorders in humans will always need to be scrutinised carefully and with consideration of potential alternative explanations. Nevertheless, the increasing number of robust findings emerging from animal studies means that we should pay attention to the possibility that social influences might have impacts reaching beyond the individuals exposed to them. But the ways in which such influences might affect the mental state of an individual, or future generations, also need to take into account the particular structure of current society.

In the last two chapters, we have looked at mental disorders such as schizophrenia and depression with a view to not only understand their material basis but also to identify new ways to treat them. This is in line with the characterisation of these mental states as disorders. But it is now time to consider whether some mental conditions characterised as disorders in the past are purely negative phenomena or whether we run the risk by such a judgement of discounting what may reflect important diversity in the human population and might indeed be a vital component of what makes us human and enriches our species.

Quiz

A deficiency in which of these neurotransmitters has been linked to depression?
A. Dopamine
B. Serotonin
C. Noradrenaline
D. Acteylcholine

Which class of genes has recently been shown to play a role in depression?
A. Fortuins
B. Senilins
C. Sirtuins
D. Kalinins

Type of RNA recently shown to play a role in transmission of anxiety across generations:
A. siRNA
B. miRNA
C. piRNA
D. lncRNA

Chapter 15

Normality and Diversity

Key Concepts

- There may be many different underlying causes for different types of autism. Such complexity is indicated by the multiple regions of the genome linked to autism and by studies of neurons derived from autistic individuals.
- In general, autistic individuals have been perceived as being more rigid in their behaviour. Yet, recent studies have suggested that given the right opportunities people with autistic traits can come up with unusually creative ideas.
- Recent studies show that while ADHD children tend to have lower activity in brain regions linked to attention and lower brain connectivity, when hyperfocused on a task, these parameters are actually higher than in unaffected individuals.

Throughout this book, we have mentioned two main ways of viewing mental disorders. First, there is what is sometimes called the 'biomedical model', which sees such disorders as due to inherent biological differences in individuals and, ultimately, in genetic differences in such individuals.[212] Second, there is the view that mental disorders are a product of disturbing events that happened to an individual in the past or are currently a problem, whether trauma, problematic family relations, or the general pressures of living in modern society.[213] This latter stance on mental disorders takes a number of different forms, ranging from Freudian psychoanalysis, which views such disorders as products of the repression of disturbing feelings – primarily sexual ones – to behaviourism, which sees them as dysfunctional responses to past and current events. To complicate matters further, we have seen that recent findings in epigenetics make it likely that such a separation of biology from environment is an illusion since an individual's environment can not only lead to epigenetic changes in their genomes, but these may even be passed down to future generations.

Despite their differences, these approaches are united in viewing such mental conditions as abnormal. Yet, is it really the case that everything termed a mental 'disorder' is indeed so? Or could it be that in diagnosing conditions that affect the mind, we are ignoring the possibility that some 'disorders' may be part of the normal spectrum of human diversity? To take this argument further, could it even be the case that such diversity is an important component of human society and a source of some of its richness and achievements? In this chapter, we look at these possibilities, with particular reference to autism spectrum disorder (ASD) and attention deficit/hyperactivity disorder (ADHD).

Autistic spectrum disorder is estimated to affect 1 in 100 people of all ages in the UK.[214] ASDs are characterised by impairments in social inter-action and both verbal and non-verbal communication, along with restricted, repetitive, or stereotyped behaviour (Fig. 15.1).[215] There is also evidence that autistic individuals have differences in their 'theory of mind'.[216] This mental ability allows us to anticipate other people's behaviour in terms of their intentions – what they think and/or want another person to do – and more profound mental states: thinking, believing, knowing, dreaming, cheating, and so on. Theory of mind allows us to explain and anticipate the behaviour of those around us.

Autistic individuals appear to find it more difficult to anticipate the behaviour of others. This seems to be due to the fact that most people can infer information about social behaviour that is not explicit, but a person with autism has more difficulty doing so.

Autistic individuals have a tendency to need to break the totality of social behaviour into small units in order to understand and learn its often unstated rules and inconsistencies. Another characteristic of many autistic individuals is that they may display restricted, repetitive, or stereotyped behaviour.[217] To explain this, it has been proposed that the cognitive skills that generally allow human beings to organise themselves, be flexible, anticipate, plan, set objectives and goals, control our impulses, and so on are altered in autistic individuals.

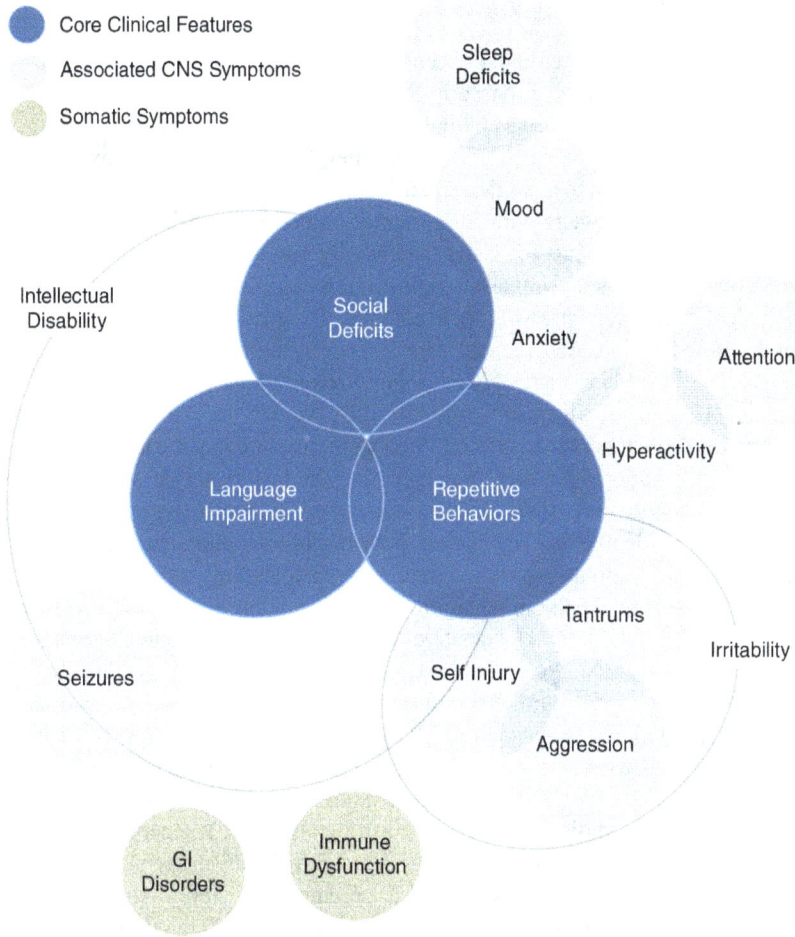

Fig. 15.1. A schematic representation of core clinical features of autism spectrum disorder (ASD), associated central nervous system symptoms and somatic symptoms that are often observed in ASD patients.

Source: Reproduced from Kas, M. *et al.* (2014) *Psychopharmacology*, 231:1125–1146, with permission.

Such individuals seem more attuned to processing local information before global information. Because of this, autistic individuals tend to first focus on specific details of images or objectives rather than on their entirety; the tendency towards repetitive behaviour may also reflect a need

Box 15.1.   Changing Views about Autistic Individuals

Autism was first described independently in 1943 by two paediatricians of Austrian origin: Leo Kanner, based in Baltimore, US, and Hans Asperger, in Vienna. For a long time, it was thought that Kanner's autistic children were far more disabled by their condition since they had delayed or nonexistent speech. In contrast, Asperger described his charges as 'little professors' – fluent if pedantic speakers with idiosyncratic interests. In reality, not all of Asperger's autistic patients were so academically gifted, and they displayed a wide range of deficits as well as strengths, but he chose to focus on the four most talented children, stressing their potential for great achievement, given appropriate education. Asperger may have been trying to protect his autistic charges at a time when Nazi eugenic policy viewed physically and mentally disabled children as 'lives unworthy of life'. Under the T2 'euthanasia' programme, more than 5,000 such children were murdered by means of lethal injection or starvation. However, Asperger's precise historical role is currently a matter of controversy, with recently uncovered evidence suggesting that he also helped identify some children with disabilities and sent dozens to Spiegelgrund, a children's ward in Vienna, where adolescents were euthanised or subjected to brutal experimentation. Notwithstanding these new revelations, Asperger was definitely positive about 'autistic intelligence', seeing traits in both artists and scientists, and observing that 'not everything that steps out of line, and is thus "abnormal", must necessarily be "inferior".' However, his findings languished in largely unread German texts until their translation into English in 1981. In contrast, Kanner's views on autism became well known soon after their publication in the US in 1943 and for a long while dominated discussion about this topic. Initially, Kanner suggested that the basis for the social difficulties associated with autism lay in a child's inability to form emotional ties with their parents. This view – particularly influenced by Freudianism – reflected a long-held assumption in psychology: that children's initial relationship with their parents forms a blueprint for all other relationships. Kanner at first suggested that an autistic child was biologically impaired in this capacity. But subsequently he began laying a large degree of blame for autism on 'toxic' parenting. He described the parents – particularly mothers – who brought their children to him as 'emotional refrigerators', whose lack of warmth contributed to their sons' and daughters' retreat into their own worlds. Although Kanner eventually moved away from this position and acknowledged that autism had a strong inborn element, his initial viewpoint unfortunately shaped ideas about autism for decades. Parents of autistic children had to deal not only with the challenges of bringing up an autistic child in an era when few schools would accept such children but also with battling their guilt on the psychoanalyst's couch.

to look for and create patterns in order to find a safe space within a social world they may find threatening.

Multiple lines of evidence suggest that autism has a strong inborn element. However, it remains unclear to what extent this is due to genetic differences or to epigenetic or other effects on the embryo or foetus in the womb. Such uncertainty may reflect the fact that ASD is exactly that – a spectrum – which may reflect different underlying causes for different types of autism. Such complexity is indicated by the multiple regions of the genome linked to autism in the same type of genome-wide association studies (GWAS), mentioned previously in the context of other disorders, and also by studies of neurons derived from autistic individuals.

By taking a skin cell from an individual and using this to derive first a pluripotent stem cell and then neurons, it is possible to assess how genetic differences in individuals might affect neuronal and brain structure and function. Two recent studies of this type show how varied might be the underlying molecular causes of even a very severe, clearly genetically determined type of autism.

In the first study, neurons were derived from people with a deletion and those with a duplication of the same region of chromosome 16, both types of mutations being associated with severe forms of autism (Fig. 15.2).[218] In both cases, the neurons were found to have fewer synapses than do those from unaffected individuals. But neurons derived from people with the chromosome deletion were found to have unusually large cell bodies and very long dendrites while those from people with a duplication in this region were atypically small and had shortened dendrites. The findings are interesting given that people with a deletion of this chromosome 16 region have macrocephaly (abnormally large heads), whereas those with an extra copy of the region have microcephaly (small heads). It is clear then that, although changes in chromosome 16 lead to some common effects, the specific nature of the changes leads to effects characteristic of a particular type of autism.

In the second study, neurons were derived from three people with a deletion of part of chromosome 15, three with a duplication of this region, and three unaffected individuals.[219] One gene in this region, CHRNA7, codes for a protein channel that allows calcium ions to flow into neurons, with such flow being essential for neuronal function. When the neurons were exposed to compounds that cause the channels to open, less calcium flowed into neurons lacking a copy of CHRNA7 than into normal neurons. This suggests that children with CHRNA7 deletions have too few functional calcium channels on neurons.

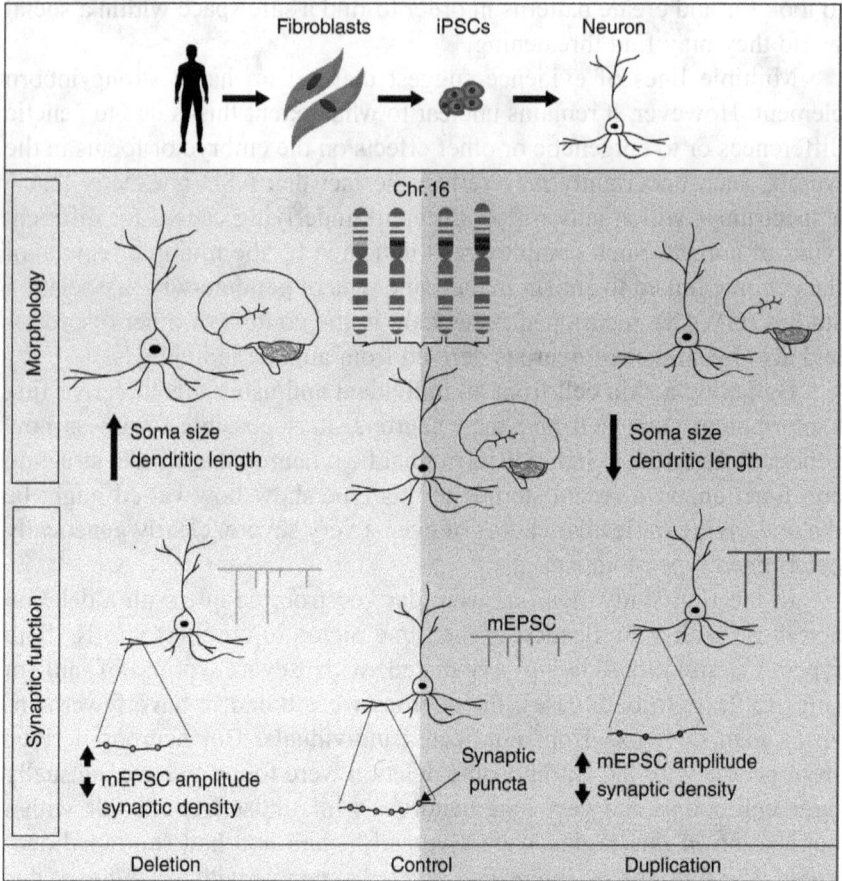

Fig. 15.2.   Neurons derived from individuals harbouring neurodevelopmental disorders caused by the 16p11.2 deletion or duplication manifest contrasting cellular phenotypes that may underlie the macro- or microcephaly observed in carriers, respectively.

Source: Reproduced from Deshpande, A. *et al.* (2017) *Cell Reports*, 21:2678–2687, with permission.

Surprisingly, neurons from children with an extra CHRNA7 gene also show unusually low calcium influx. In this case, too much CHRNA7 protein impairs neurons' ability to assemble the proteins and transport them to the cell surface. The results illustrate that the effects of mutations, even in a single gene disorder, are not always predictable.

Despite these findings, the majority of less severe autistic conditions are not clearly defined genetically. There is therefore the possibility that they have a less obvious biological mechanism underlying them and are more linked to environmental factors. In recent years, there have been highly misleading claims about such a link.[220] Notably, in the late 1990s, claims were made about a link between the vaccine for measles, mumps and rubella (MMR) and autism. This prompted large drops in vaccination rates. One consequence was that measles cases were shown to have risen by 300 percent in Europe in 2017, the result of parents shunning vaccines following such claims. In fact, such claims have been totally refuted.

One reason why there has been a tendency for some parents of autistic children to believe claims about links between vaccination and autism or be taken in by other claims about quack 'remedies' for autism is their desperation about the problems of dealing with a child with autism who can have all sorts of serious behavioural issues that can make it difficult for such children to adapt to school life, or even cope with everyday social routines. This is one of the reasons why autism has traditionally been viewed primarily as a disorder.

Yet, a different approach to autism exists that, far from seeing it as a disorder to be 'cured', instead views at least less severe cases as part of a spectrum of human characteristics. Such an approach highlights the positive, rather than negative, aspects of autism, and the development of the full potential of an autistic individual as an issue for society as a whole, rather than simply a problem for that individual or their parents.

In many ways, the recognition that autism can have positive aspects is not a new one. Ever since Asperger's identification in 1943 of high-achieving, 'gifted' autistic children, there has been recognition that some people with autism can be highly creative.[221] For instance, actor Darryl Hannah has spoken about her struggles with autism since she was a child.[222] Tito Mukhopadhyay is virtually mute, but the eloquent poems he writes by hand or types out have provided a fascinating window into how an autistic person can experience life. The artist Stephen Wiltshire has become well known for his ability to draw landscapes in exact detail even after seeing them only once. And many IT experts in California's 'Silicon Valley' have been noted to have autistic traits.

However, there is a potential problem with a focus only on high-achieving autistic individuals since this can lead to the idea that people who do not succeed in such conventional terms are somehow less worthy of attention. Instead, it is important that we consider ways in which the potential of every autistic individual might be boosted. To do so, it will be necessary to recognise the positive aspects of autism but also consider how educational measures might address the more negative features of the condition. To some extent, this means widening our definition of what it means to be creative.

In general, autistic individuals have been perceived as being more rigid in their behaviour. This rigidity is linked to the difficulty they can have in judging the actions and intentions of others and their tendency towards restricted, repetitive, or stereotyped behaviour. Because of these characteristics, it is often assumed that autistic individuals will also be more rigid in their imaginations. Yet, recent studies have undermined this idea and suggested that given the right opportunities, people with autistic traits can come up with unusually creative ideas.

For instance, one recent study assessed creativity in autistic and non-autistic individuals by asking them to generate ideas about static objects such as paper clips and abstract images.[223] Participants were expected to create their own context; the objects were not defined by their use in society. Those with autistic traits offered fewer responses to problems presented, but their solutions were more original and creative than those without such traits. For instance, when asked to list possible uses for a paper clip, creative responses of autistic individuals included using the wire to support flowers, creating a paper aeroplane weight, or making a token for a board game.

The finding that autistic individuals are better able to display their creativity and imagination in situations that are less dependent on social context makes sense given previous evidence that people with autism often have trouble interpreting their experiences within such a context. The findings indicate that when autistic people are shown images on a context-less background, they can visualise contexts not usually associated with those objects, which may be one, but not the only, explanation for their higher creativity.

It is one thing to recognise the potential of autistic individuals, but this still leaves the question of how we develop such potential. For although discussion of autism often focuses on talented individuals with this condition, in reality only around 20 percent of autistic adults in the UK are in full-time work.[224] This figure has also remained the same for the past decade, showing that autistic people are not benefiting from British employment programmes. A similarly large majority of autistic individuals fail to find full-time work in the US. This suggests that either people with autism are being failed by their schools or something else is preventing them from entering the world of work.

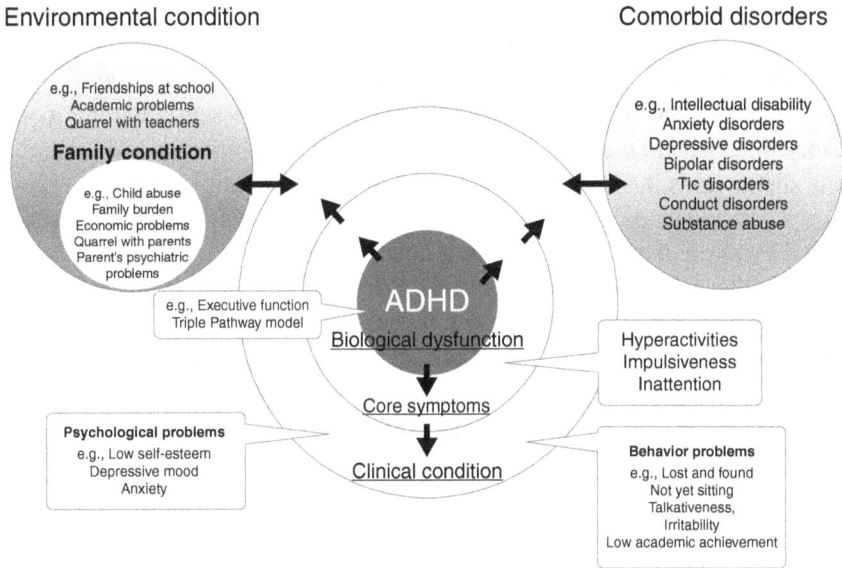

Fig. 15.3. Clinical condition and core symptoms of attention-deficit hyperactivity disorder (ADHD).

Source: Reproduced from Usami, M. (2016) *Psychiatry and Clinical Neurosciences*, 70:303–317, with permission.

Attention deficit/hyperactivity disorder (ADHD) is another condition that traditionally has been associated with problems not only in terms of performance at school but also in the world of work (Fig. 15.3).[225]

For instance, a UK study has shown that people with ADHD tend to have lower incomes and are more likely to be unemployed than the general population. ADHD is a common and increasingly diagnosed condition that has been estimated to affect up to 9 percent of children. Children with ADHD may have trouble paying attention, controlling impulsive behaviours, or be overly active.[226] The disruptive aspects of ADHD and the difficulty concentrating, which is a feature of some types of ADHD, can lead to children with this condition getting into trouble at school, although the increasing recognition of ADHD as a clinical condition may be helping to offset this. Increasingly, ADHD personality characteristics are also being recognised in adults.

Like ASD, ADHD occurs as a spectrum; thus, the extent to which these different behaviours occur in an child may vary, and there is variation too in their continuation into adulthood. In addition, as with ASD, there is increasing evidence that ADHD can have positive aspects.

One positive feature of ADHD is that affected individuals can 'hyperfocus', that is, focus on a task for hours on end, essentially tuning out everything around them.[227] This can allow them to complete a task without any distractions, and the outcome can be of great quality. Typically, such hyperfocusing tends to occur when the individual is doing a task or exercise that they particularly enjoy and find interesting.

Another potentially positive aspect of ADHD is that people with this condition are often talkative, which means they can spark interesting conversations. Their spontaneity and impulsivity means that ADHD individuals may be less afraid to do whatever they enjoy at the moment without concerning themselves with long-term implications or overthinking situations. While such an attitude may prove risky or even dangerous at times, it also means that people with ADHD may be more willing to try new experiences, which can be very valuable in building their life experience and making new friends or acquaintances.

If these are some of the different negative and positive features of ADHD, how does this mental condition arise and how does this relate to neuronal and brain mechanisms? Brain imaging studies have shown that individuals with ADHD have reduced activity in brain regions linked to attention, which is in line with the problems people with this condition can have in terms of concentration upon a task.[228] Imaging studies also show reduced brain connectivity. Other studies suggest that children with ADHD have delayed maturation in connections between different parts of the brain, which may underlie this reduced connectivity.

Such a delay in brain maturation may also help to explain why some ADHD children become better at concentrating as they develop into adults. However, ADHD symptoms can persist into adulthood in some individuals, and it would be interesting in future studies to try and explore the mechanistic reasons for this.

As mentioned, an intriguing aspect of ADHD is the tendency of many individuals with this condition to 'hyperfocus'. This behaviour has the following characteristics. For an ADHD individual to hyperfocus, the task generally must be engaging, that is, fun, interesting, or important. Hyperfocusing is characterised by an intense state of sustained or selective attention. When engaged in this activity, there is a diminished perception by the individual of non-task relevant stimuli. During hyperfocusing, task performance improves.

Such behaviour is intriguing, given the association of ADHD with inattention and impulsivity, and raises questions about whether the latter characteristics might be partly due to context. Thus, if an ADHD child finds it hard to concentrate on tasks they find boring, yet can become completely focused on a task, even to the exclusion of awareness of other things going on around them, if they find the task interesting and stimulating, this suggests that more consideration could be made of ways to keep that interest and stimulation.

From a neurological point of view, it is interesting that while ADHD children tend to have lower activity in brain regions linked to attention and lower brain connectivity, when hyperfocused on a task these parameters are actually higher than in unaffected individuals (Fig. 15.4).

Another finding from brain imaging studies is that during hyperfocusing, there are heightened connections between frontal regions linked to attention and other parts of the brain involved in the reward response. Thus, it may be that when an ADHD individual senses value in a task, goal-directed behaviour reverses their normal inattentiveness and makes them even more focused than someone without ADHD.

In summary, we still have only an incomplete understanding of both the neurological and genetic basis of ASD and ADHD. It is increasingly becoming recognised that not only a condition like ASD that is defined as a spectrum, but all the other conditions mentioned above probably also include a variety of different mental states that can be characterised by different symptoms, and probably also different underlying biological and social determinants. We have also seen that ASD and ADHD can be associated in some individuals with many positive attributes. As we have seen, this can also be the case for a condition like bipolar disorder, which, particularly in its upward phase, may be associated with great creativity and imagination.

It also seems to be the case that the neuronal mechanisms underlying conditions such as schizophrenia and depression may overlap with positive mental characteristics in the human population. Despite this, we should not underestimate the severity of many forms of the conditions mentioned in the last three chapters or the misery that such conditions can cause for both those affected and their families. For this reason, a central

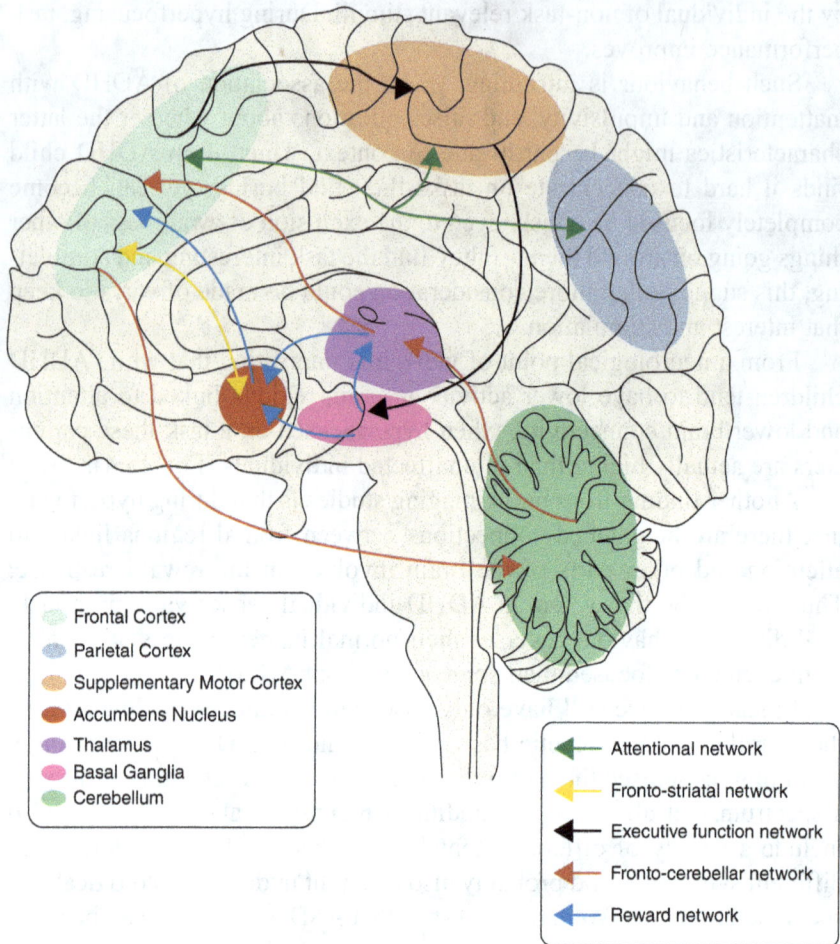

Fig. 15.4. Schematic illustration of the functional circuits involved in ADHD pathophysiology. Shown are the attentional network (green), fronto-striatal network (yellow), executive function network (black), fronto-cerebellar network (red), and reward network (blue).

Source: Reproduced from Purper-Ouakil, D. *et al.* (2011) *Pediatric Research*, 69:69R–76R, with permission.

aspect of both psychiatry and psychology is the search for new ways to treat mental conditions, whether this be via drugs or so-called 'talking therapies', and in the following chapter, we will look at the many different drugs and therapies that have sought to target the mind.

Quiz

What was the phrase Hans Asperger used to describe the autistic children he studied?
A. Little students
B. Little teachers
C. Little professors
D. Little learners

A deletion in which of these chromosomes has been linked to a severe form of autism?
A. Chromosome 1
B. Chromosome 7
C. Chromosome 12
D. Chromosome 16

Percentage of adults with autism spectrum disorder in full-time work in the UK:
A. 10 percent
B. 20 percent
C. 40 percent
D. 60 percent

Chapter 16

Drugs and Therapies

Key Concepts

- One psychotherapy approach that is claimed to have good success in the treatment of schizophrenia is called 'Open Dialogue'. A central feature of Open Dialogue is that, as well as the patient, other family members are involved in therapy sessions.
- While selective serotonin reuptake inhibitors (SSRIs) have become the primary treatment for depression, ketamine has recently been shown to have positive effects in depressed individuals who had not responded to other treatments.
- A common treatment for ADHD is amphetamines. It might seem counterintuitive that an excitatory chemical is used to treat a condition linked to hyperactivity. However, these drugs can help focus the ADHD mind on performing specific tasks.

Since ancient times, human beings have used chemical substances to modulate the brain and nervous system, long before the development of scientific understanding of the molecular and cellular basis of these parts of the body. There is also a long history of humanity using drugs to alter the mind for recreational purposes. As remains the case today, in the past, the division between medicinal and recreational drugs was often blurry.

One of the most basic ways of manipulating the brain and nervous system is pain relief. Some pain-relieving drugs, known as analgesics, that are used clinically today have their origins in ancient remedies. Acetylsalicylic acid, also known as aspirin, is a chemical found naturally in willow bark, an extract of which has been used to provide pain relief since the dawn of history.[229] Acetylsalicylic acid inhibits the enzyme cyclooxygenase, which is involved in the formation of prostaglandins that cause inflammation, swelling, pain, and fever.

Opioids are another commonly used form of pain relief, particularly for severe pain.[230] There is recorded use of opioids as early as 2100 BC. Of course, opioids have also been used as a recreational and substance-of-abuse drug for millennia. An attraction of opioid drugs such as opium or heroin is that, as well as relieving pain, they can produce a feeling of euphoria, well-being, and even hallucinations, which can all serve as a release from the trials and tribulations of everyday life for those who turn to using opioids for these effects.

Opioids are extracted from the opium poppy or synthesised chemically, and commonly used opioids include morphine, heroin, methadone, codeine, and fentanyl. They bind opioid receptors, of which there are four types, all G-protein-coupled receptors (GPCRs),[231] whose evolutionary origins and mechanism of action were mentioned previously. Opioid receptors of course did not evolve to respond to opioids. Instead, they are also the targets for bodily chemicals called endorphins released by the hypothalamus and pituitary gland in response to pain or stress, and these both relieve pain and create a feeling of well-being, of the sort that can often occur after heavy exercise.

Cannabinoids are another class of drugs with an ancient history and both analgesic effects and properties that have led them to be used for millennia as recreational drugs.[232] Such properties include the ability to induce a state of relaxation and well-being, and feelings of heightened sensory awareness, but also sometimes negative feelings like paranoia.

Cannabinoids occur in the hemp plant *Cannabis sativa* and include delta 9-tetrahydrocannabinol (THC), cannabidol, and cannabinol. Like opioid receptors, cannabinoid receptors are GPCRs (Fig. 16.1).

Another similarity to opioid receptors is that cannabinoid receptors did not evolve to respond to cannabis but rather to bodily chemicals called endocannabinoids, which have various effects in the brain and the rest of the body, ranging from neuronal plasticity to pain relief to modulation of appetite and digestion.

Recently, there has been a surge of interest in the therapeutic potential of cannabinoids. A major goal is to identify cannabinoid-like chemicals that have analgesic and other therapeutic properties but lack psychoactive effects and so could be used clinically.

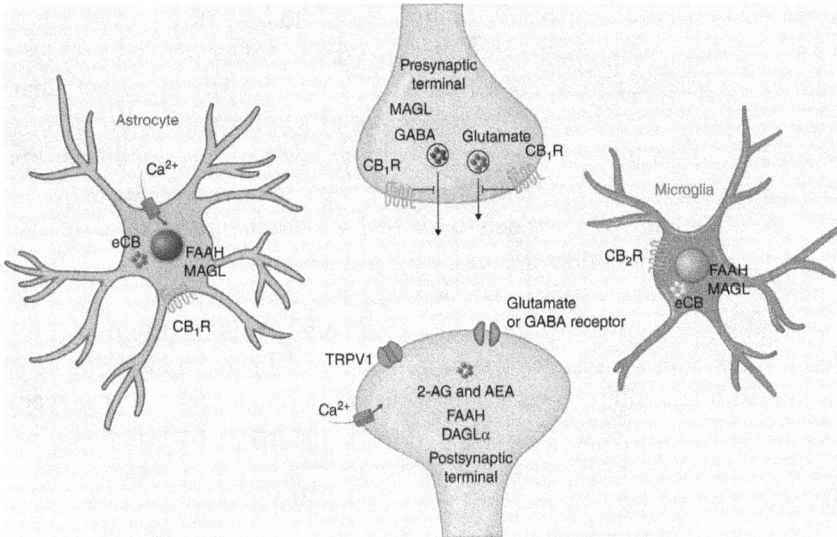

Fig. 16.1. Endocannabinoid (eCB) system shows a distinct anatomical distribution in the central nervous system. On depolarisation of the postsynaptic terminal, 2-arachidonoyl glycerol (2-AG) is present at the postsynaptic terminal and synthesised 'on-demand' by diacylglycerol lipase-α (DAGLα). 2-AG and AEA travel to the presynaptic CB1R to inhibit neurotransmitter release. CB1R is also present in astrocytes, and its activation leads to increased intracellular calcium. AEA can also activate the postsynaptic transient receptor potential cation channel V1 (TRPV1), leading to an increase in the postsynaptic current. CB2RB is present on microglial cells and is involved in immune reactions.

Source: Reproduced from Yin, A. *et al.* (2019) *Acta Pharmacol Sin*, 40:336–341, with permission.

In terms of other drugs that target the brain and nervous system, two other main classes are those that have been developed to treat schizophrenia and clinical depression.

Most drugs used to treat schizophrenia work by blocking dopamine release, which, as mentioned previously, is one reason why this disorder has come to be seen as due to excessive dopaminergic neuronal activity; another reason is that sufferers of Parkinson's disease who are treated with dopaminergic agonists can develop psychosis.

As mentioned previously, drugs that target dopaminergic receptors have shown some success in suppressing 'positive' symptoms, such as delusions, hallucinations, and hyperactivity, but have little impact on the 'negative' symptoms, such as apathy, lethargy, and withdrawal from social situations. This is one reason why the claim that schizophrenia is caused by an excess of dopaminergic activity is likely to only be a partial expla-nation for the underlying basis of this disorder.[233] It has also led to claims that anti-psychotics may be acting as a 'chemical straightjacket' that, while suppressing some of the symptoms of schizophrenia, do little to address the underlying molecular or cellular basis of this condition. For this reason, the search continues for other ways to treat this disorder.

One potential new approach to treating schizophrenia is based on new findings that, as mentioned previously, suggest that one feature of this disorder may be an inappropriate immune response involving a surge in the number and activity of glial cells in the brain. It is therefore possible that further study of the specific biological mechanisms underlying such an inappropriate immune response in the brain might identify new types of drugs that could be used to target not only the psychotic aspects of this condition but also schizophrenia as a whole.[234]

Importantly, not only new drugs but also novel types of 'talking thera-pies' could provide a basis for new and better ways to treat schizophrenia. Previously, we have mentioned that it might be mistaken to view this condition as a single disorder. Indeed, new evidence suggests that schizo-phrenia may be best seen as a collection of different disorders that share symptoms in common but have very different biological bases and deter-mining causes.[235] Other studies have shown that different types of schizo-phrenia appear to not only show distinct responses to different types of drugs, but some may also be more amenable to psychotherapy than to drug treatment. For instance, recent studies have suggested that people with a history of childhood trauma diagnosed with schizophrenia are less likely to be helped by antipsychotic drugs, but others with this disorder can benefit.[236]

One psychotherapy approach claimed to have good success in the treatment of schizophrenia is called 'Open Dialogue'.[237] This approach, pioneered in Finland – which, in the 1980s, had one of the worst inci-dences of schizophrenia in Europe – has, over the past 30 years of applica-tion in this country, led to 74 percent of psychotic patients being back at work within two years, compared with just 9 percent in the UK.

A central feature of Open Dialogue is that, as well as the patient, other family members are involved in therapy sessions.

Such input could be important given the potential role of dysfunctional family relations in the generation of the condition mentioned previously, but also, as we saw previously, individual thoughts may constitute a kind of dialogue. If this is the case, not only conscious but also unconscious thoughts may reflect tensions between an individual and other members of their family. It might therefore be beneficial for an affected individual to undergo therapy with other family members. Engaging in a dialogue with them in a forum mediated by a therapist may provide a space to tackle some of the familial tensions that may underlie schizophrenia.

Another key aspect of Open Dialogue is that it is not anti-medication. Treatment, from drugs to different kinds of psychotherapy, is agreed upon by everyone at the therapy sessions. But whereas the mainstay of standard treatment is usually medication, in the Open Dialogue approach, the core is psychotherapy. Perhaps the most effective aspect of the Open Dialogue approach is the time it affords the patient to develop a dialogue about their condition with the same set of therapists – and also with family members – over an extended period of time. Given the evidence presented in this book for the importance of language in the formation of human conscious awareness and its role in our unique capacities of creativity and imagination, it is maybe not surprising that such enhanced social interactions can have a therapeutic impact. Intriguingly, there is also increasing evidence that psychotherapy can lead to positive changes in the neural chemistry of the brain, suggesting that it is a mistake to only equate such changes with pharmacological interventions.

Another major class of drugs used in clinical psychiatry is those used to treat clinical depression. As mentioned previously, this condition has for many years been thought to be primarily due to reduced levels of serotonin in the brain. This view is partially based on success in treating this condition with drugs designed to boost levels of brain serotonin.

The first set of such drugs was discovered completely by chance. Scientists in the 1950s, searching for a treatment to control the mood swings of schizophrenics, identified a class of drug – called tricyclics because of their three-ring chemical structure – that triggered bouts of euphoria in their patients.[238] This only made the schizophrenic individuals worse, but it suggested that tricyclics might be a treatment for depression. Indeed, when given to depressive patients, some patients became newly sociable and energetic, leading to claims that tricyclics represented a 'miracle cure' for depression.

These drugs, which act by blocking serotonin uptake and thus boosting its levels in the brain, helped about three quarters of depressive patients. However, they had serious side effects such as lethargy, weight gain, and, occasionally, death from overdose. But a search for chemicals with a similar effect led to the discovery of selective serotonin reuptake inhibitors (SSRIs), a particularly well-known one, Prozac, being released onto the market in 1987. As their name implies, these drugs also increase brain serotonin levels by preventing their reuptake into neurons (Fig. 16.2). SSRIs provided relief for the same percentage of patients as tricyclics but with less risk of overdose and fewer side effects.

SSRIs have been a huge success for the pharmaceutical industry, with Prozac earning Eli Lilly, the company that developed it, $1 billion a year by 1990.[239] SSRIs have become so widely used that they have been used to treat far more conditions than clinical depression, with some doctors prescribing them to everyone from pensioners to pre-teens for everything from premenstrual stress to fear of public speaking. Yet recently, doubts

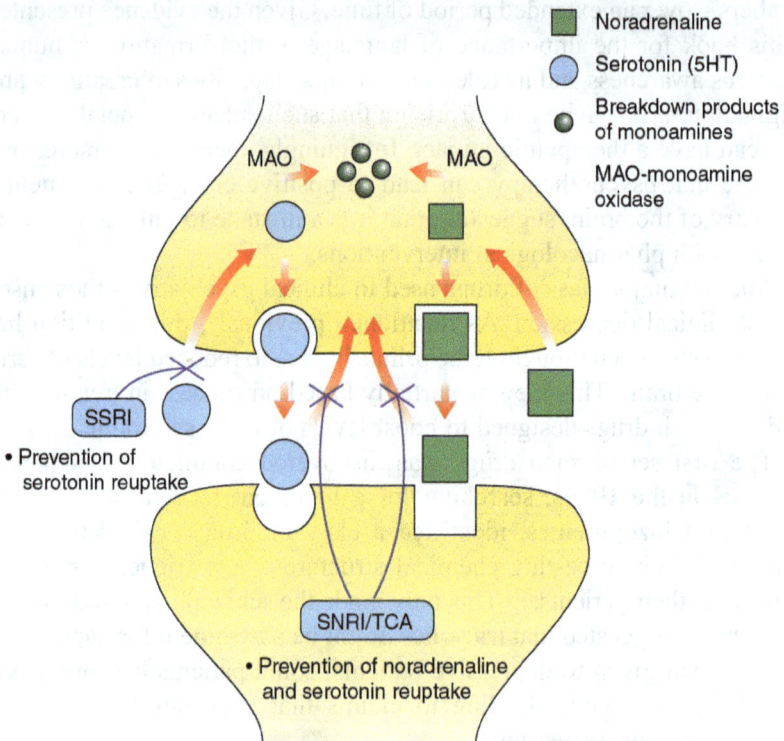

Fig. 16.2.   Mechanism of action of the SNRIs, TCAs, and SSRIs. SNRI – serotonin and noradrenaline reuptake inhibitor; TCA – tricyclic antidepressant; SSRI – selective serotonin reuptake inhibitor.

Source: Reproduced from van Rensburg, R. and Reuter, H. (2019) *South African Family Practice*, 61:59–62, with permission.

have surfaced about the appropriateness of SSRIs being prescribed for such different conditions, the effectiveness of these drugs and the mechanisms by which they affect brain function.

One controversial issue is evidence that SSRIs may not be as effective as claimed. For instance, a recent study found that the ability of SSRIs to combat mild or moderate depression appeared no better than a placebo, although this did not generally appear to be the case if the treated individual was suffering from a more severe form of depression.[240]

Another problematic aspect of SSRIs is that while these drugs are only meant to be taken for a limited period, in practice many patients remain on them for years, and for some, it can be very difficult to stop taking them; such are the severe effects of withdrawal.[241]

One puzzling aspect of SSRIs is why they can take several weeks to have an effect given that their primary mechanism of action is meant to be inhibiting serotonin uptake, which should be a fairly immediate effect. This conundrum is one reason why some scientists have begun to look for other mechanistic explanations for depression and also begun to ask whether SSRIs might be having other actions in the brain besides blocking serotonin uptake. One suggestion, due to various new pieces of evidence, is that depression is caused by abnormalities in neurogenesis, as mentioned previously.[242] This raises the question of whether lower serotonin levels might be more a consequence than a cause of depression, since when the brain stops producing new neurons or fewer neuronal connections are formed, this could lead to a reduction in serotonin release.

The idea that depression is associated with defects in neurogenesis may explain the mechanism of action of a new drug used to treat depression – ketamine. This was developed as an anaesthetic but is also used as a recreational drug, particularly on the nightclub scene, because of its tendency to make users feel 'out of themselves' by producing an apparent dissociation between mind and body. Ketamine has recently been shown to have positive effects in some people with severe depression who had not responded to other treatments.[243] Intriguingly, recent studies suggest that one way that ketamine may act is by triggering neurogenesis in some parts of the brain (Fig. 16.3).

Another suggestion for new potential therapies to treat depression is based on new evidence that depression may be associated with an abnormal inflammatory or immune response.[244] We saw earlier how recent studies suggest that abnormalities in how glial cells respond to brain inflammation may be one factor in the development of schizophrenia. For

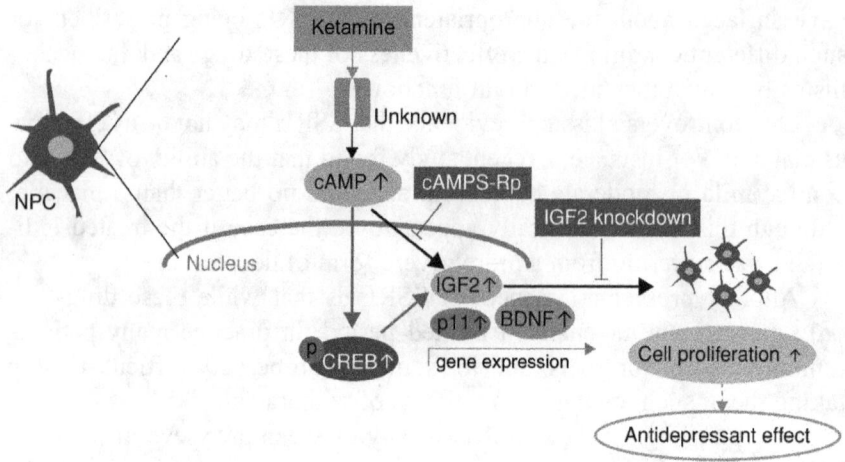

Fig. 16.3. The N-methyl-D-aspartate (NMDA) receptor antagonist ketamine offers promising perspectives for the treatment of major depressive disorder.

Source: Reproduced from van Grossert, A. (2019) *Cells*, 8:1139, with permission.

depression, there is also a potential link with inflammation and immunity, given that vaccinations can induce feelings of depression in some individuals and studies have shown that individuals given the drug interferon, used to treat conditions including cancer by inducing an immune response, often develop depression.

In depression, abnormalities in inflammatory and immune responses may affect the brain in a different way than the situation with schizophrenia, in this case sparking feelings of hopelessness, unhappiness, and fatigue. It may be the case, therefore, that a new approach to treating depression could involve targeting immune and inflammatory responses in the brain. However, there will be a need for a better understanding of the roles that these responses play in conditions as different as schizophrenia and depression and about the likely effects on other immune and inflammatory responses in the body, for such drug treatments to be both specific in their action and not the cause of unwanted or dangerous side-effects.

What about treatments for other mental disorders? Bipolar disorder is a condition that, as mentioned previously, is characterised by periods of depression followed by episodes of mania, during which affected individuals can feel extraordinarily happy, ambitious, and creative, but sometimes in this phase, they can become psychotic. A standard treatment for this condition is the so-called 'mood stabilisers', which include antipsychotic drugs, anti-epileptic drugs, and lithium (Fig. 16.4).[245]

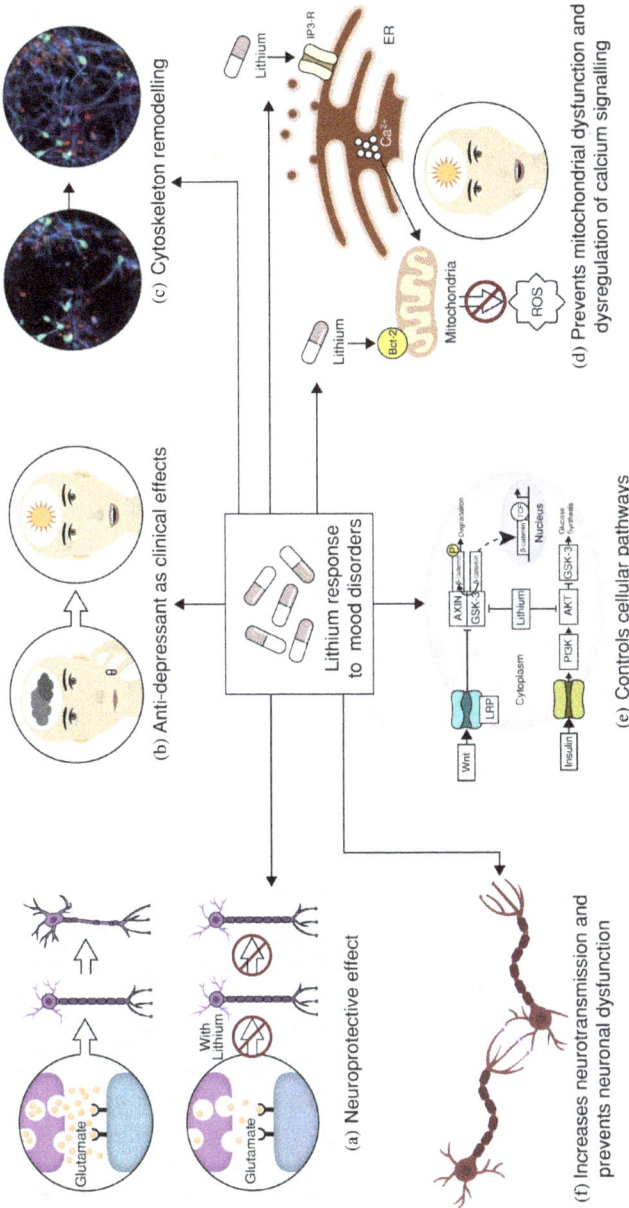

Fig. 16.4. (a) Lithium prevents neuronal dysfunction by inhibiting the activation of apoptotic pathways. (b) Lithium salts have been widely used as anti-manic and anti-depressants. (c) It plays a vital role in cytoskeleton remodelling and neurite outgrowth. (d) It upregulates neuroprotective protein BCl-2, which prevents mitochondrial dysfunction and calcium channel dysregulation. (e) It activates Wnt and insulin pathways by inhibiting constitutively activated glycogen synthase kinase-3 (GSK-3) in both pathways. (f) It also regulates neurotransmission and prevents synaptic dysfunction.

Source: Reproduced from Nayak, R. *et al.* (2021) *International Journal of Molecular Sciences,* 22:9315, with permission.

The latter substance, which is after all a metal ion and administration of which might be expected to have all sorts of effects on the brain and the rest of the body, was identified as a treatment for bipolar disorder after clinical studies showed that it caused rapid improvement in a group of bipolar patients. It has been proposed to alleviate some bipolar symptoms by targeting signalling pathways that regulate brain function. However, it is far from clear how lithium really affects brain function, and the search continues for new treatments.

Another mental condition mentioned in this book is ADHD. As already mentioned, this condition occurs as a spectrum of different behavioural characteristics. We have also discussed how there is an increasing recognition that individuals with this condition can have many positive characteristics, such as greater creativity and imagination. Yet, it also has negative features, and because of this, there has been a search for drugs to treat ADHD, and this has led to a number of treatments that are widely used today.[246] One reason for this is that ADHD can prove very debilitating in schoolchildren in terms of concentration on set tasks and exam performance. There is also increasing recognition of potential negative effects of ADHD in adults.

A common treatment for ADHD is amphetamines. This class of drugs, which includes those used as recreational drugs and substances of abuse, mainly act by stimulating production of the excitatory substances dopamine and noradrenaline. It might seem counterintuitive that an excitatory chemical is used to treat a condition associated with hyperactivity, at least in some of its manifestations. However, amphetamines can also focus the mind on a problem to be solved, and this may be one of the ways that use of amphetamines can help individuals affected by ADHD concentrate on a specific task.

A general problem with many of the drugs that have been developed to treat disorders of the mind is that we have only a very incomplete understanding of how even commonly used drug treatments used to treat conditions ranging from schizophrenia to depression to bipolar disorder to ADHD work in terms of underlying molecular and cellular mechanisms in the brain. A better understanding of such mechanisms and greater insights into how the brain works as a whole will be required for the development of better drugs and therapies. But there is also another emerging potential alternative to the use of traditional small molecule drugs for the treatment of mental disorders, and that is the use of brain implants and gene edits.

Quiz

Acetylsalicylic acid, also known as aspirin, is found naturally in the bark of which tree?

A. Beech
B. Oak
C. Willow
D. Yew

Psychotherapy approach that claimed to have good success in the treatment of schizophrenia:

A. Open Pathway
B. Open Dialogue
C. Open Resolution
D. Open Question

A drug that has recently been used to successfully treat certain types of depression:

A. Ketamine
B. Morphine
C. Interferon
D. Amphetamine

Chapter 17

Implants and Edits

Key Concepts

- As a clinical approach, deep brain stimulation (DBS) has shown success in treating Parkinson's disease, tremor, and dystonia. It is also beginning to show potential for the treatment of Alzheimer's disease and some cases of clinical depression that have failed to respond to drug-based therapy.
- The most obvious targets for gene therapy in the human brain are single-gene disorders, such as Huntington's disease, where there is a clear link between a defect in a specific gene – in this case, the huntingtin gene – and the disorder.
- Restoring sight to blind people is a major challenge. One approach involves linking a camera hidden behind a pair of glasses to the optic nerve, thus bypassing the eye. Cameras have also recently been connected to the brain's visual cortex.

Electricity is key to how the brain works. As such, it raises the possibility that manipulation of the electrical activity of the brain might represent a way to treat mental disorders. Of course, this also raises the possibility that by such an approach it might be possible to modulate consciousness itself. In some respects, drugs used to treat mental disorders, whose primary mode of action is often to alter the production or uptake of specific neurotransmitters, may be seen to be affecting the electrical activity of the brain. However, this is a very indirect effect and also a diffuse one, as it affects all regions in the brain and, indeed, any part of the body as a whole in which the targeted neurotransmitters play a role.

There is another approach to manipulating electrical activity in the brain, and that is to use electricity itself. Such an approach is potentially more direct and focused but raises questions about the practicality and safety of stimulating electrical signals in the brain.

One way to electrically stimulate particular regions of the brain, and indeed specific neurons, is to use stimulating electrodes. As we have seen, in studies using experimental animals, this approach is one of the ways, along with the use of recording electrodes, that neuroscientists learn about the functional properties of particular neurons in the brain.

We have also seen how electrodes are used to both stimulate and record electrical activity in the human brain in studies of patients undergoing brain surgery who have volunteered to take part in such studies. As a clinical approach, deep brain stimulation (DBS) has shown success in treating Parkinson's disease, tremor, and dystonia (Fig. 17.1).

It is also beginning to show potential for the treatment of Alzheimer's disease and some cases of clinical depression that have failed to respond

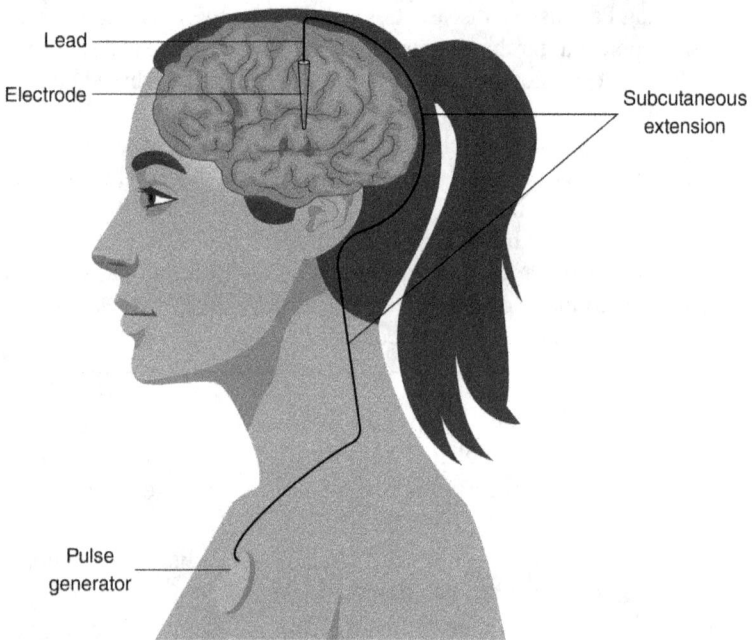

Fig. 17.1.   Deep brain stimulation (DBS).

Source: Reproduced from Rosa, M. and Lisanby, S. (2012) *Neuropsychopharmacology*, 37:102–116, with permission.

to drug-based therapy.[247] However, the invasive nature of DBS limits its general clinical use, not least because the penetration of the skull and brain tissue that it requires carries the risk of intracerebral haemorrhage and infection. Because of such problems, there is interest in developing non-invasive forms of electrical stimulation of the brain.[248]

Two such approaches increasingly used in clinical medicine are transcranial electrical stimulation (TES) and transcranial magnetic stimulation (TMS), which utilise electrodes or coils to apply electric or magnetic forces to the human scalp, resulting in both acute and neuroplastic alterations in cortical excitability.

These approaches have been used to treat epilepsy, stroke, schizophrenia, and depression and have the advantages of being safe, well-tolerated, cost-effective, and easy to operate. However, due to the complex structure of human brains, externally applied electric and magnetic fields often decline dramatically as depth increases, leading to the low spatial resolution of some non-invasive brain stimulation approaches, including TMS and TES. Because of this, there has been a move to develop non-invasive types of electrical stimulation that can penetrate deep into the brain in a focused and more targeted fashion.

One such approach is temporally interfering (TI) electrical stimulation (Fig. 17.2).[249] Although at an early stage of development, TI is showing promise as an approach that, unlike TMS and TES, can stimulate deep brain targets without the need for surgery, thus offering the advantages of both spatial targeting and a non-invasive character.

Approaches such as the ones mentioned above employ external electrical stimulation to stimulate different regions in the brain. But another approach is now available that utilises neurons' own electrical potential to excite, or alternatively inhibit, neurons within the brain. This approach, known as 'optogenetics', has revolutionised the study of brain function and has also excited interest in the possibility of using this approach to treat brain disorders.

Optogenetics was developed based on the realisation that since neurons conduct electrical impulses via changes in their ionic composition and given that, as mentioned previously, some unicellular algae have light-sensitive ion channels in their membranes, introducing such channels into neurons would make these modulatable by light.

In optogenetics experiments, light-sensitive ion channels derived from algae are introduced into neurons in a mouse's brain by injecting a virus engineered to express these ion channels into the brain.[250]

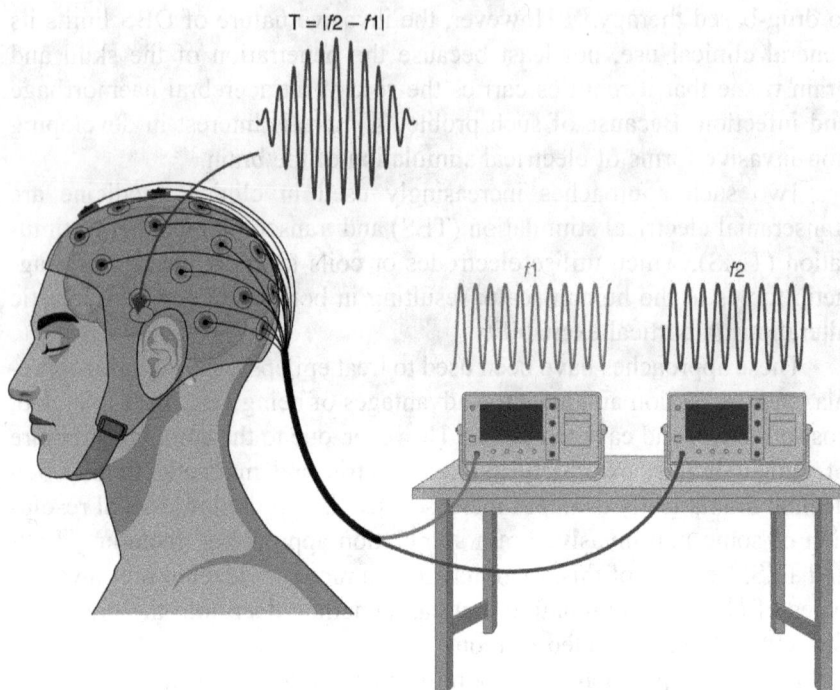

Fig. 17.2.   Two electric fields ($f1$ and $f2$) deliver inhibitory stimulation to a specific brain region at extra-physiological frequencies (e.g. $f1 = 5000\,\text{Hz}$ and $f2 = 5160\,\text{Hz}$), where T is the target frequency representing the difference between the two (e.g. $160\,\text{Hz}$).

Source: Reproduced from Fani, N. and Treadway, M.T. (2024) *Neuropsychopharmacology*, 49:305–306, with permission.

Box 17.1.   The Invention of Optogenetic Technology

Optogenetics uses light to manipulate the positive or negative charge of neurons genetically engineered to behave in this way. Underpinning this technology was the discovery that certain types of bacteria and algae have protein pores on their surface membranes that allow ions into these micro-organisms in response to light. While mainly viewed as merely a curiosity of nature by those studying them, a few scientists began to recognise that such proteins might also form the basis of a revolutionary new biotechnology. In fact, as early as 1979, Francis Crick speculated that 'this seems rather far-fetched, but it is conceivable that molecular biologists could engineer a particular cell type to be sensitive to light.' At the turn of the 21st century, a few scientists decided to test whether opsins provided a solution. One was Gero Miesenbock, who realised that it might be possible to see whether opsins could trigger a light-induced ionic change in neurons and thereby trigger an artificial electrical impulse. Miesenbock demonstrated the potential of such an approach by engineering neurons in the brain of a fruit fly to express opsins and then showing they could respond to light. Few people thought this approach could work in mammals, but Karl Deisseroth decided to see if he could develop this technology in rodents. First, Deisseroth and his team expressed a microbial opsin in rat neurons in culture using a viral carrier. When light was shone on to the cells, this triggered an action potential. The way was open to see if a similar effect could be obtained in the living brain using a transgenic approach. This involved both using transgenic approaches to modify specific cell types in the rodent brain to become responsive to light and finding ways to deliver light deep into the brain. This latter goal was achieved using an ultrathin fibre-optic wire attached to a laser light source, which was surgically implanted into the brain. These approaches allowed Deisseroth's team to make a dramatic demonstration of the power of optogenetics. By stimulating neurons in the motor cortex, they showed that light could be used to make a mouse run in circles, like a remote-controlled toy. But what really convinced neuroscientists of the relevance of optogenetics as a research tool were studies published by Deisseroth's team in 2009. One demonstrated the use of optogenetics to define the precise neuronal connections in Parkinson's disease. Another examined the cellular basis of pleasure and reward. Two other studies by Deisseroth's team used optogenetics to identify neurons that regulate brain activities known to be abnormal in schizophrenia and autism. These studies appeared in quick succession and convinced neuroscientists of the revolutionary potential of the technology.

This leads to expression of the channels in neurons. On its own, this would not lead to changes in the neurons' electrical potential. However, the mice also have surgically inserted fibre-optic cables that are used to shine beams of light onto specific parts of the brain. The fact that different types of light-sensitive ion channels occur naturally in algae that respond to different frequencies of light and that can both increase or reduce the electrical potential of a cell means that in modern optogenetics, it is possible to both activate or inhibit a particular neuron by changing the light frequency shone onto it (Fig. 17.3).

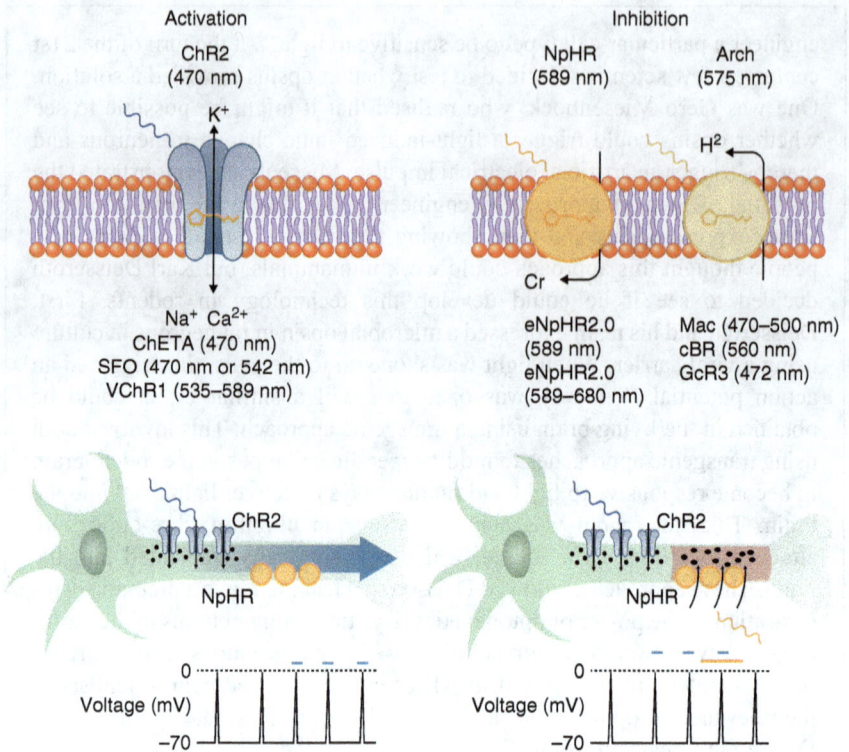

Fig. 17.3.   Neuromodulation with optogenetic technique: blue light activates ChR2 with an excitatory effect, while yellow light activates NpHR and Arch with an inhibitory effect.

Source: Reproduced from Spagnuolo, G. *et al.* (2020) *Applied Sciences*, 10:173, with permission.

Optogenetics has revolutionised the study of brain function by making it possible to artificially modulate the activity of neurons in the brain of a living mouse and then see what effect this has upon behaviour, perception, memory, or some other aspect of cognition.

The success of the optogenetic approach in mice has raised the question of whether this approach might be used clinically in humans. For instance, the fact that in mice this approach has been used to uncover hidden memories or alternatively suppress memories could mean that optogenetics might be used therapeutically in humans to treat conditions such as post-traumatic stress disorder (PTSD) to get to the root of the memories of trauma that might be driving incidents of PTSD or remove these from the mind. For conditions such as schizophrenia or depression, optogenetics might be used to activate or inhibit neural circuits that underlie abnormal brain activity in these disorders. Applied to the rest of the nervous system, optogenetics might be a way to treat chronic pain conditions.

Technical barriers to using optogenetics in humans are twofold.[251] First, optogenetics requires a light source of some sort to activate or inhibit neurons. In mice, as already mentioned, this is achieved by surgically implanting fibre-optic cables into the brain. However, this is highly invasive and causes some damage to the brain; therefore, a central focus for those seeking to develop optogenetics for human use is either to concentrate on developing this technology for the treatment of chronic pain by introducing fibre-optic cables into the spinal cord, which might be achieved with less damage to this tissue, or to develop non-invasive types of light sources that could be used to illuminate the brain. With respect to the latter goal, a current focus is to develop light-sensitive ion channels that can be illuminated by light of a low frequency, for instance infrared light, which can penetrate bone and, therefore, could be beamed into the brain from a source on the skull.

Another barrier to the development of optogenetics for therapeutic purposes in humans is that in mice, neurons only become activatable by light after brain cells have been genetically engineered to express light-sensitive ion channels. This is achieved by injecting viruses expressing such channels into the brain, and this approach would raise many safety issues if it were applied to the human brain. As well as the fact that a person's neurons would be permanently genetically altered, there might be concerns about the potential harmful effects both of introducing gene expression constructs and of the viral particles. However, if these safety issues could be resolved, it might be thought that successfully treating a serious condition like depression or schizophrenia validated this approach.

In fact, we may be on the verge of a revolution in gene therapy in humans, not only to enable optogenetics to be used in the human brain but also as a way to treat disorders that affect the human brain by manipulating the expression of genes in our mental organ.

The impetus for this revolution in gene therapy comes from the development of a form of gene editing known as CRISPR-Cas.[252] In bacteria, 'guide RNAs' recognise sequences in the genomes of invading viruses and direct the Cas enzyme to cut the DNA at the sequences, disabling the virus. By artificially generating guide RNAs and introducing these into a cell, it is possible to use these as tools to cut at any point in the genome of a living cell, be these bacteria or other unicellular species or from a plant or animal, including humans. Generating a cut in the DNA in this way can then trigger two different outcomes: either the cell repairs the damage via a cellular repair mechanism named non-homologous end joining (NHEJ), which can lead to a disabling, or 'knockout', of a gene, or if a piece of DNA similar to the sequence that is being targeted is also introduced into the cell, this can trigger a repair mechanism named homology-directed repair (HDR), leading to more subtle changes being introduced into the genome, for instance, a mutation or correction of a mutation.

Gene editing is revolutionising agriculture because it is now possible to genetically modify both plants and animals to introduce disease resistance or altered characteristics of resulting foodstuffs.[253] In biomedicine, gene editing is also having a big impact because it allows the generation of genetically modified organisms that can be studied as models of human health and disease. But it is particularly in clinical medicine that some of the most exciting scientific developments are occurring because of the potential ways in which gene editing looks set to transform treatments for disease, and this is also the case for disorders of the brain, whether neurodegenerative, developmental, or psychiatric.

The most obvious targets for gene therapy in the human brain are single-gene disorders, such as Huntington's disease, where there is a clear link between a defect in a specific gene – in this case, the huntingtin gene, and the disorder.[254] In Huntington's disease, a single mutant copy of the huntingtin gene causes the disease. There are many important reasons for wanting to use gene therapy to treat Huntington's disease. This is a devastating disorder that occurs in mid-life, in which sufferers first begin to show jerky movements, then odd behaviour and psychosis, followed finally by dementia and death. While there is a test that can identify sufferers of the disorder long before symptoms appear, there is no cure.

A complicating factor for attempts to treat Huntington's disease using gene therapy is that the normal huntingtin gene plays a vital role in brain function. Because of this, any gene-editing approach must disable the mutant huntingtin gene without affecting the normal version of the gene. Another challenge is that gene-editing tools must be introduced into the brain of an affected person in such a way that they penetrate into the different parts of the brain and cross the membranes of its cells. To achieve this, clinical scientists are experimenting with viruses and nanoparticles to transport the editing tools.

Other diseases that affect the brain that might be good targets for gene therapy are versions of neurodegenerative disorders such as Alzheimer's and Parkinson's that occur with an unusually early onset because of a clear link with a defect in a specific gene.[255] For instance, an early-onset form of Alzheimer's is due to a defect in a gene called presenilin, while a defect in the gene parkin is a causal factor in the development of early-onset Parkinson's. In both these cases, if a person possessing a mutant version of these genes were identified early enough, gene therapy might be used to prevent the development of the disease.

Other types of human brain disorders where gene therapy might be employed are types of psychiatric or neurodevelopmental conditions where there are clear links with a specific change in the genome. In general though, as previously mentioned, the genetic basis of most cases of schizophrenia and depression is far from clear. This is also the case for conditions such as ASD and ADHD, and because there is increasing evidence of many positive aspects of these conditions, the idea of trying to 'cure' them is controversial. Despite this, in those rare types of, say, ASD, where there is both a clear genetic link and the condition itself is very severe, as mentioned previously, a case might be made for using gene editing to correct the genetic defect and alleviate some disease symptoms.[256]

A final way to use technology to treat disorders of human cognition would be to focus not on the brain itself but on the inputs into that brain from other parts of the body. We saw earlier how perception of the world outside our bodies through our five 'senses' – sight, hearing, touch, taste, and smell – is based on exquisitely structured organs – the eye, ear, nose, and tongue, as well as a variety of sensory receptors in the skin. However, some people lack one of the senses due to a congenital defect or following injury. For instance, a person may be born or become blind or deaf. Until recently, there was nothing that could be done to reverse such a condition. However, thanks to technological advances, it is now becoming possible to reverse some effects of deafness or blindness via implants.

One type of implant is the cochlear implant.[257] As previously mentioned, the cochlea is a fluid-filled spiral cavity in the inner ear that plays a vital role in the sense of hearing and participates in the process of auditory transduction. Sound waves are transduced into electrical impulses that the brain interprets as individual sound frequencies. However, some individuals are born without a cochlea or it can be damaged through exposure to noise or via another type of injury. A cochlear implant is an electronic device that bypasses damaged portions of the inner ear and directly stimulates the auditory nerve. Hearing through a cochlear implant is different from normal hearing, and it takes time to learn or relearn to hear with this device. However, it can allow people to recognise warning signals, make sense of other sounds in the environment, and understand speech.

Restoring sight to blind people is even more of a challenge than restoring hearing, but there has recently been some progress in this area.[258] One approach involves linking a camera hidden behind a pair of glasses to the optic nerve, thus bypassing the eye. However, some people have no functional optic nerve or the remainder of the brain circuitry that links this to the visual cortex. To deal with this situation, cameras have also recently been connected to the brain's visual cortex (Fig. 17.4). Using such a

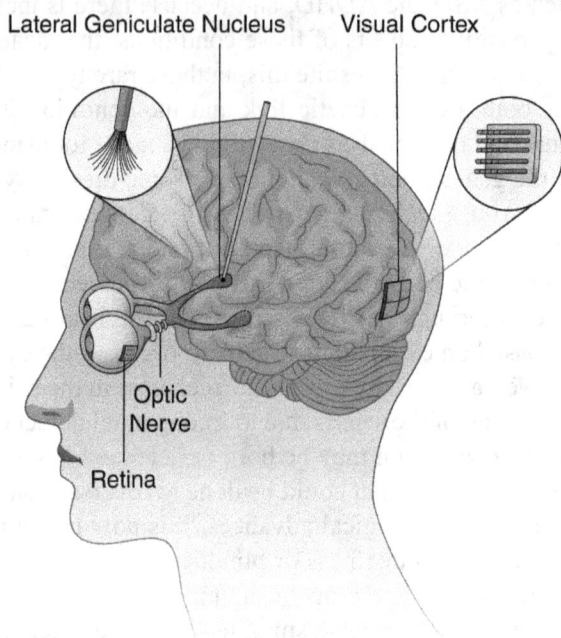

Fig. 17.4. Small arrays of electrodes can be implanted epiretinally, subretinally, or suprachoroidally to stimulate retinal ganglion cells. Similarly, the axons of these cells can be stimulated as they pass along the optic nerve, using 'cuff-style' electrodes. The lateral geniculate nucleus can be accessed using conventional deep-brain stimulation electrodes or newer-generation devices incorporating a 'tuft' of microelectrodes. Lastly, the visual cortex may be stimulated directly using surface (not shown) or penetrating microelectrodes.

Source: Reproduced from Lewis, P. *et al.* (2015) *Brain Research*, 1595:51–73, with permission.

device, treated individuals have become able to identify objects such as ceiling lights, letters, shapes, and people.

There is a long way to go in terms of refining such artificial devices to make them capable of reproducing the environment in anything like the detail of natural perception. In addition, given how important we have seen the role of sensory inputs is in shaping the development of the cortex and other parts of the brain, there may be limits to how much even the most sophisticated external devices can substitute for the natural process. Some individuals born blind or deaf may also choose not to give up this state of affairs because their brains have adapted to their condition and provided them with alternative ways of perceiving the world that do not rely on vision or hearing.

So much for approaches that seek to restore particular senses to people that lack these. What about individuals that, through some congenital disorder or injury, are unable to move or affect the world around them, that is, they lack motor function? We saw previously how the ability to respond to the environment is a vital complement to being able to sense it, even in simple unicellular species such as bacteria. In simple multicellular species, for instance jellyfish, typically a sensory neuron that senses changes in the environment is connected via an interneuron to a motor neuron that triggers some kind of response.

This stimulus–response connection is still a key feature of the cognitive process even in more complex multicellular organisms. In human beings, the ability to respond to changes in the environment, or indeed perform actions characteristic of normal everyday life, may be impaired by congenital disorders, neurodegenerative disorders of the brain and nervous system, or injury. For instance, an accident to a person's spinal cord can lead to complete paralysis below the neck. Other injuries to either the brain or peripheral nerves can lead to varying degrees of partial loss of motor function in different parts of the body.

To help people with total or partial loss of motor function, a number of approaches are currently being pursued. One involves trying to repair damaged nerves using stem cell technology.[259] Another is trying to understand the mechanisms that allow some species to regenerate nerves and other parts of the body to see if this might lead to insights that might be used to develop regenerative therapies for human beings.[260]

Yet another approach seeks to develop electronic devices that might bridge the gap between neurons in the brain and those in the limbs, enabling a paralysed person to walk again.[261]

If too much damage has occurred to the limbs, another approach that has achieved some success is that a paralysed person is encased in some type of exoskeleton; the person is then able to walk and perform all sorts of actions by manipulating the machine via an implant in their brain.[262] Such a person might be considered a kind of cyborg; of course, the machine in this case has a human being at its centre.

Yet, as computers become more advanced, this raises the question of whether machines themselves may one day become capable of performing all the various actions that a human being can currently do, with our brains as well as our bodies, and perhaps even begin to surpass human abilities. To consider this question further, it is time to look at the so-called 'artificial intelligence' and compare this with human cognition.

Quiz

Non-invasive clinical approach used to stimulate electrical activity in the brain:
A. Deep brain stimulation
B. Electroencephalogram
C. Transcranial electrical stimulation
D. Voltage clamp

The Cas enzyme in CRISPR/Cas is guided to its target sequence by which type of molecule?
A. DNA
B. RNA
C. Protein
D. Lipid

Which process was optogenetics first used to stimulate in the brain of a living mouse?
A. Memory
B. Pleasure
C. Reward
D. Movement

Chapter 18

Minds and Machines

Key Concepts

- Claims that computers are close to equalising or even surpassing human intelligence have increased in intensity over recent years, mainly because of the achievements of a type of computer program called a learning system.
- The units of a neural network are named neurons and are supposed to be analogous to biological neurons. Neural networks contain three main layers: an 'input layer', an 'output layer', and in between these are 'hidden layers'.
- Unlike the human brain, there is no evidence that computer programs, including the different types of new machine learning systems, have any sense of the meaning of the data that is fed into them or of the output data received by their operator.

Human beings have the highest form of consciousness not only on planet Earth but also in the known Universe, given that we currently have no knowledge of any life, sentient or otherwise, on other planets.[263] A key feature of human consciousness that we have highlighted which distinguishes it from that of other species is our ability to think conceptually. It is this that allows human beings to recognise the difference between past, present, and future, see ourselves as individuals distinct from other people, understand distance and location, and indeed comprehend a whole number of even more complex concepts, such as laws of mathematics, scientific concepts, or principles of ethics or law.

Previously in this book, we have identified the evolution of language as being central to the development of conceptual thinking, as well as the development of a larger and more complex brain. But we also looked at evidence that the event that first set our ancestors on an evolutionary path to a higher form of consciousness was walking on two feet, which freed the hands to do other things than locomotion and led to the development of tools.

As already noted, *Homo sapiens* are not the only species to use tools. However, only human beings use tools as a systematic part of our everyday life, to the extent that it is hard to think of a human activity that does not involve some kind of tool or technology. Another unique feature of our species is that human tools evolve over time. This was true even of the first stone tools that were developed by our hominin ancestors. However, the evolution of such tools could be measured in thousands or millions of years. In contrast, in modern society, it is characteristic for many new technologies to emerge in the space of a generation. One particularly important one in modern times is the computer. Combined with social media, computers now are central to modern society.

A major current issue of debate is the question of whether computers are close to achieving a form of intelligence that is equal to, and might soon even surpass, that of human beings.[264] This is an issue that is of relevance not only in considering whether human consciousness might not continue to remain the highest form on the planet but also because many of the new types of computer programs that have been making the headlines are said to be modelled on the neural circuits and modes of operation in the human brain.

It is worth saying at this point that claims that computers are close to equalising or even surpassing human intelligence are not a new thing. Ever since the development of the first modern computer systems in the 1940s, claims have been made in this respect.[265]

However, they have particularly increased in intensity over recent years mainly because of the achievements of a type of computer program called a 'machine learning' system. It is this type of program in particular that is said to be modelled on how the human brain works. So, it will be worth looking in detail at such machine learning systems and the claims made about them. Before we do that though, we need to consider in more general terms how computers work. Computers nowadays occupy such a central part of our lives and are involved in performing so many different roles in society that it is easy to forget their basic function, which is to carry out sequences of arithmetical or logical operations.

Box 18.1. Artificial Intelligence and the Singularity

There has been no shortage of predictions recently that an 'artificial intelligence' (AI) based on a computer will soon not only have reached the same mental capabilities as a human being but also surpassed them. Upon reaching such a point, often referred to as a technological 'singularity', AI is then predicted to undergo an exponential technological growth that will transform life as we know it. For instance, the mathematician Vernor Vinge, who first coined this term in 1993, believes that 'we will soon create intelligences greater than our own. When this happens, human history will have reached a kind of singularity, an intellectual transition as impenetrable as the knotted space-time at the centre of a black hole, and the world will pass far beyond our understanding.' Such is the power of this vision that it is now commonplace to hear predictions of not whether, but when, this singularity will occur, and whether an all-powerful AI will save humanity or hasten our extinction. Representing the first point of view, Frank Lansink, European CEO at IPsoft, believes that, 'AI ... has an integral role to play in the workplaces of the future. It will help unleash creativity, create new job activities and new occupations which combine ground-breaking technology with our most human skills.' Others are less convinced about such a rosy future scenario. For instance, in 2017, the biotech entrepreneur Elon Musk stated that, 'I keep sounding the alarm bell. But until people see robots going down the street killing people, they don't know how to react, because it seems so ethereal.' Meanwhile, the physicist Stephen Hawking stated in 2014 that he believed 'the development of full artificial intelligence could spell the end of the human race.' Not surprisingly, such statements can leave many people feeling highly uneasy about the development of increasingly sophisticated computer and robotic systems. But is the prediction that we are close to seeing the rise of an all-powerful AI really such a likely scenario? One reason for caution is that such predictions are far from new. Notably, Alan Turing, one of the first pioneers of computer science, predicted in 1951 that machines would 'outstrip our feeble powers' and 'take control' within the next human generation. In 1965, Turing's colleague Irving Good argued that 'the first ultra-intelligent machine is the *last* invention that man need ever make, provided that the machine is docile enough to tell us how to keep it under control.' Clearly, such predictions were hopelessly misguided in their timescale, but how about their basic substance? Importantly, given that one commentator has described AI as 'all the things that computers still can't do', is it possible that the singularity has been creeping up on us, and computers are already close to reaching that point of all-powerfulness? To address this issue, we need to look carefully at what computing and robotics have achieved in recent years, as well as examine once again the nature of human consciousness and link this to its material basis in the biology of the brain.

Although we think of computers as modern inventions, they have in fact been around for millennia, in the form of simple calculating machines such as the bead abacus. However, while the abacus can only be used for arithmetic, a modern computer is a general-purpose machine that can perform many tasks and does so at such a rapid rate that it has become a revolutionary technology.

What all computers have in common, though, from an abacus to a supercomputer used, say, by the US government, is that information is fed into them; this information is then processed via rule-based, written operations known as algorithms; and then the processed information is received by the computer's operator. Today's electronic computers are also digital, that is, they manipulate and store data in the form of ones or zeros, as these are easily represented with simple on-off electrical states.

As mentioned above, recent claims that computers are close to equalling or even surpassing human intelligence have tended to focus on a new development in computer technology named machine learning systems. These are statistical algorithms that differ from other types of computer programs in that they can learn from supplied data and generalise to other data. Machine learning systems have made headlines because of their success in various spheres. Thus, they underlie facial recognition and language deciphering programs, have beaten human grandmasters at the game Go, made novel predictions about protein 3D structures, composed critiques of literature, and created works of art. It is such achievements that have led to claims they are on the path to sentience.

The development of machine learning systems was stimulated by a desire to mimic some of the processes that occur during learning in the brain.[266] We saw earlier that our brains develop partly through a process that is determined by our genome and partly through the influence of the environment. We also saw that the activity of neuronal circuits that is affected by the type of signals they are receiving from the outside world strengthens or weakens their synaptic connections through processes such as long-term potentiation (LTP) or long-term depression (LTD), which are based on molecular changes to the synapse. And the pioneers of machine learning sought to create something similar in their learning programs. The fact that such systems are sometimes called 'neural networks' is one indication of the desire to recreate the workings of the brain in these computer programs.

Different types of machine learning systems exist (Fig. 18.1).[267]

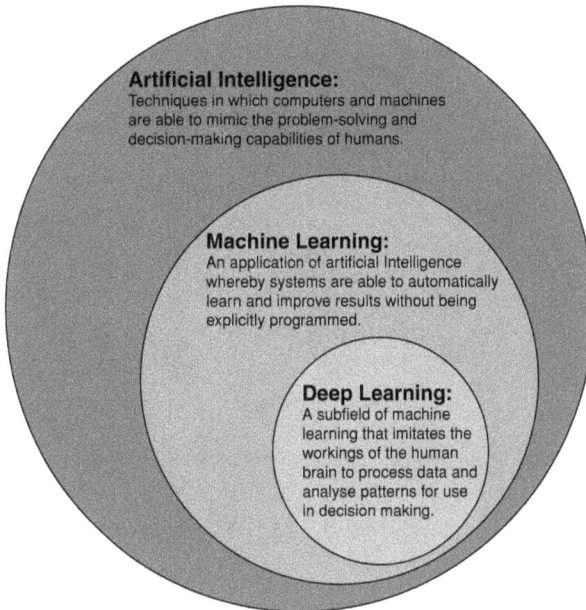

Fig. 18.1.   Subcategories of artificial intelligence.

Source: Reproduced from Bond, A. *et al.* (2023) *Clinical Nutrition ESPEN*, 57:542–549, with permission.

Standard 'machine learning' requires continual human input. Training a machine learning system to, say, identify an image of a particular animal species and distinguish this from other species, typically involves a technician feeding the computer images that have been manually labelled to identify features that distinguish, say, a cat from other species. The computer's ability to distinguish a cat from such species is assessed. If the computer makes incorrect choices, the labels on the inputs are modified until the computer is able to consistently distinguish a cat image from the images of other species that it is shown.

'Deep learning' is a branch of machine learning that requires less continual human input.[268] With a deep learning system, once it is set up, all that is required to teach it how to recognise a cat is to supply it with a large number of cat images, and the system can autonomously learn the features that represent a cat. This type of learning requires a neural network (Fig. 18.2). The units of a neural network are named neurons and are supposed to be analogous to biological neurons. Neural networks contain

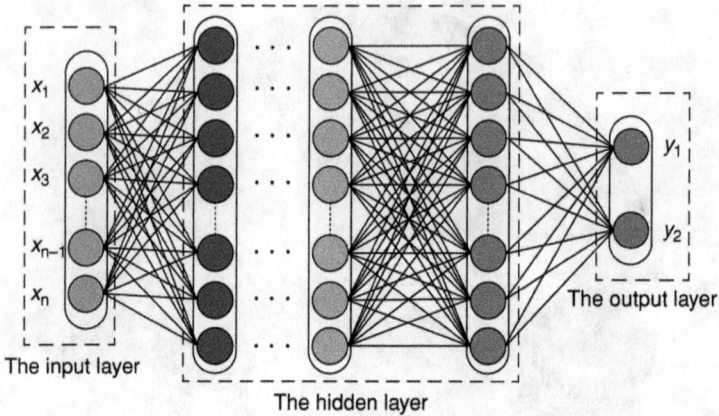

Fig. 18.2. Structure of fully connected neural network (FCNN) with input layer, output layer, and hidden layers.

Source: Reproduced from Yang, X. *et al. Energies*, 13:2975, with permission.

three main layers: an 'input layer', an 'output layer', and in between these what are known as 'hidden layers'.[269]

Hidden layers allow neural networks to learn complex data representations. Deep learning proceeds in both forward and reverse directions. In the forward direction, inputs feed through the network and generate an output. In the backward direction, the difference between the actual and desired outputs generates an error signal that is propagated back through the network to teach it to better produce the desired output.

If this is how computers, including computer learning systems, operate, how does this compare to the operation of the human brain? One potential similarity between our brains and a computer is that both involve circuits. Yet, we have to be careful not to be misled by superficial similarities. Despite 'neural networks' being so named and even their base units referred to as 'neurons', because their circuitry and mode of operation are said to be based on the brain, a crucial difference between these and biological neural circuits is that neurons are not simple on-off switches but complex biological entities that evolve in a molecular fashion in terms of their structure, gene expression, and so on.[270]

In addition, as we have seen, far from brains only consisting of electrical circuits of connected neurons, glial cells also contribute in fundamental ways to brain function, and as we also saw, new evidence from recent studies indicates that brain waves of different frequencies mediate important interactions within and between brain regions.

It is not merely a question of different operating systems; there are fundamental differences in how brains and computers process information. As noted above, human operators input meaningful information into a computer, and the computer then transforms this information by subjecting it to various programmed algorithms. This hopefully then produces a meaningful, useful answer. But there is no evidence that computer programs, including the different types of new machine learning systems, have any sense of the meaning of the data that is fed into them or of the output data received by their operator.[271]

In contrast, a human brain receives many incoming signals from the environment that in themselves are not meaningful information, yet the brain is then able to extract meaning from them in ways that have been highlighted in previous chapters of this book.

Currently, when a deep learning system produces a critique of a poem or creates a work of art, it might seem superficially that it is aware of what it is doing. For the critique can make sense and appear to offer novel insights, or the artwork can appear to express new ideas or emotions. However, what the computer is actually doing is recognising patterns among the huge amount of text or art it has been fed and used these as a basis to create new pieces of text or art. The interesting aspect of this process is that our human ability to see meaning in things allows us to judge the computer's creations in terms of quality, creativity, and insight, yet the computer itself has no awareness of what it is creating.

Could a computer ever become aware of its actions? For this to happen, it would have to become able to see meaning in what it does. To examine this issue further, it is worth looking again at how meaning might arise in our brains. This means re-looking at the question of how human consciousness relates to that of other species, and how different types of species might extract meaning from the world around them.

It could be argued that even a simple bacterium has self-awareness, in that, as we have seen, it can both sense changes in its environment, via protein receptors and channels on the surface of its outer membrane, and respond to these, through changes in its intracellular environment and also sometimes through movement via its motile flagellum. However, these actions are unconscious, reflex changes, and it might be seen as stretching the concept of consciousness too far to ascribe this characteristic to a bacterium.

In fact, it is an interesting question to ask how much we are justified in ascribing consciousness to non-human species if we take this to mean self-conscious awareness. For, as discussed previously, our human ability to view ourselves as individual entities and, therefore, distinct from the rest of the world, including other human beings, is strongly linked to the fact that our consciousness has been transformed by language. It is this that gives us conceptual thought and the ability to distinguish not only the past, present, and future or distance and location but also the idea of self versus other. And therefore, it could be argued that only human beings can be truly self-aware, and thus only our species can have a sense of meaning in the things around us, including our actions.

Not everyone would accept such a human-centric view, though. An alternative viewpoint might accept the special aspects of human consciousness based on our unique language capacity, yet see some other species, particularly 'higher' species, as possessing some measure of self-conscious awareness. Such a viewpoint could point, for instance, to the behaviour of our primate cousins, the great apes, who have been shown to have a sophisticated awareness of the relationships between different members of their primate group and their position within it.

Thus, it might be said to be the case that a kind of conceptual understanding may exist even in the absence of human language, with its system of abstract symbols linked together by grammatical rules, and that might also imply that other primate species do possess a sense of meaning of the world around them. Such a viewpoint might go further and state that even in 'lower' organisms than primates, there may be a measure of pre-conceptual self-awareness linked to a sense of meaning.

While we can pose these sorts of possibilities, it remains the case that in the absence of being able to ask other species for their thoughts about their place in the world, we may never truly understand what it means to be a non-human being. But one factor that unites our species, and every other lifeform on the planet, is our evolutionary origins, and this has relevance for thinking about potential similarities and differences between what has become known as 'artificial intelligence' and biologically based forms of consciousness, which includes that of human beings.

A crucial difference between a biological brain and a computer is that the former has evolved, while the latter has been designed.[272] One consequence of the evolutionary origins of the human brain is that it may continue to be a challenge to understand exactly how such a brain works as a whole. One of the most revolutionary insights of Charles Darwin's theory of evolution by natural selection is that this proceeds by blind chance; there is no designer. Because of this, there is no design principle guiding why our brains happen to work the way they do; this is simply the way they evolved. Of course, an important goal within neuroscience is to use observation and experiment to try and uncover the workings of the human mind, but as we have seen, while our understanding of many molecular and cellular processes in the brain increases every year, how the human brain works as a unified whole to produce consciousness is one of the biggest unresolved mysteries of science.

In contrast, a computer is designed by people. This is not only true of its hardware but also its software. The latter point is worth making, as in some discussions about deep learning systems, accompanied by terms like 'hidden layers', it can sometimes seem as if the process by which the computer arrives at its output is so mysterious that it is opaque to human understanding, and this can add to the idea that the computer is somehow creating outputs such as critiques of poems or works of art in a manner similar to human creativity.

In fact, the particular 'architecture', that is, the character of the 'neurons' and their interconnections, of the hidden layers in the neural network is crucial to the process of deep learning. It is for instance the case that the type of architecture makes a difference in whether a deep learning system can produce a critique of a poem or win at the game Go against a person. But it also means that comparisons between standard machine learning systems and deep learning ones that stress that the latter need no human input are potentially misleading in that the human input is there in deep learning – it is simply more a part of the initial setup, not an input that needs to be continually added.

But if this human input is a requirement of all computer systems, even deep learning ones, it remains unclear how a computer could ever develop a sense of awareness, as it will always be an object designed to fulfil a specific task, rather than an autonomous entity that can begin to make its own decisions and fulfil its own needs in a self-aware manner.

The issue of there being different optimum hidden layer architectures for different end goals in deep learning systems also raises another problem with the idea that such systems are well on the way towards sentience. A person might write a critique of a poem, produce a work of art, play a game of Go, and do all of these tasks to a degree that might not appear to match up to a specialist deep learning system. However, the person's brain can allow them to do all of these things, as well as drive a car, make a table, and swim across a river.

Like a human being, a deep learning system has to learn to fulfil a particular task. However, unlike humans, if a deep learning system that can play Go is now required to fulfil a different task, for instance writing a critique of a poem, not only must the Go-playing learning be erased and a new learning set begun, but even the software architecture often needs to be changed. In other words, there is little sense that deep learning systems, for all their proficiency at particular specialised tasks, are approaching the kind of general intelligence we assume in talking about human intelligence.[273] If we add this to the lack of evidence that computer program possess any self-awareness or sense of meaning in what they do, there is little validity at present to claims that so-called 'artificial intelligence' has any similarity to what we mean when we talk about human intelligence or even this quality in an animal. However, it would be rash to predict that this will necessarily always be the case, given both the continuing increase in our understanding of brain function, and of computing technology, and potential future interactions between these.

Quiz

Name of the hypothetical event in which computers surpass the intelligence of humans:
A. Singularity
B. Potentiality
C. Disparity
D. Linearity

Which of these different layers is NOT a component of artificial neural networks?
A. Input layer
B. Output layer
C. Hidden layer
D. Extra layer

Which game did a Google DeepMind deep learning system beat a human grandmaster at?
A. Chess
B. Go
C. Backgammon
D. Draughts

Conclusion

The aim of this book has been to provide a concise overview of the latest scientific evidence, ideas, and insights in cognitive science, with a particular emphasis on human cognition. On the one hand, we have seen how any understanding of the material basis of human consciousness must be firmly linked to the recognition that our species is merely one part of the amazing, diverse phenomenon that we call life on Earth. We saw how this relationship to other lifeforms is shown not only by the many similarities in structure and function between the human brain and those of other species but also by the fact that many molecular and cellular mechanisms that underlie human brain function have their roots in processes that first came into being at the very dawn of life itself.

We have also seen that a proper understanding of human cognition must recognise not only these molecular relationships but also that the adult human brain is a product of a developmental process during embryogenesis which has much in common with that occurring in other species, the process as a whole being the result of millions of years of evolution. It is for these reasons that many insights about human cognition continue to emerge from studies of the structure, function, and development of the brains of other species, which include mammals, as well as many other 'lower' organisms, such as zebrafish and fruit flies.

At the same time, this book has drawn attention to the unique aspects of human consciousness, particularly our capacity for conceptual thought, which gives our species the ability to understand the difference between past, present, and future, the concepts of distance and location, self versus other, as well as even more complex ideas, such as scientific concepts, the rules of ethics and law, and the principles of art and aesthetics.

We have seen how this capacity for conceptual thought, although now centrally linked to the size and complexity of the human brain that distinguishes this from the brains of other species, has its origins in a more straightforward event, the transition by our ape-like ancestors to a bipedal mode of existence, that fortuitously freed the hands to use and design tools, which led to human language and, finally, the growth and development of the human brain. Such were the contributions of tools and language to our evolution into the first species on Earth capable of recognising and discussing its particular place on our planet.

As we have also seen, our capacity for language and designing and using new tools and technologies continues to be highly central to human consciousness, and we have looked at how new technologies such as computers and the internet pose opportunities but also challenges for our species today. Importantly, we have seen that, despite all the amazing potential that has been unleashed by the human brain in terms of science, technology, art, literature, and culture in general, a major problem for our species is the significant proportion of our species that currently succumb to serious mental disorders.

We have discussed different mechanistic explanations for these disorders partly because this is an important way of understanding how a breakdown in normal human brain function may lead to such a disorder but also hopefully lead to new ways to diagnose and treat such conditions. We have also looked at the possibility that conditions such as ASD and ADHD, while traditionally defined as disorders, may not only include many positive features but, existing as a spectrum, may include conditions that have been grouped together but are both quite different in their symptoms and severity and have different underlying causes.

Discussions about not only mental disorders, but human consciousness as a whole, often counterpose 'nature versus nurture' as opposing factors that determine our character, personality, abilities, and also whether we are likely to succumb to a mental disorder. Although the focus in this book has been on the role of genetic and other biological factors in the genesis of mental disorders and other conditions relating to the mind, it would be a mistake to ignore the influence of society as an equally important factor. A unique feature of humans is the complex nature of our society and the way this evolves over time; thus, a complete discussion of human cognition would also need to bring in fields like sociology, economics, and politics, which we have only touched on.

What we can say is that the tendency in the past to talk about the respective influences of 'nature' and 'nurture', as if these two factors act in some kind of additive way, is not supported by new findings in new scientific fields such as epigenetics. For these have shown that the effect a particular genetic polymorphism might have on an individual is highly related to their specific environment, both exterior and interior, while changes in a person's environment can have profound effects on their epigenetic profile. And such considerations are highly important when we consider the so-called mental 'disorders', both in terms of their origins and the link to a person's place in society and how we seek to treat them.

The fact remains that despite huge strides over recent decades in how the human brain works, particularly in terms of underlying molecular and cellular mechanisms, we are still probably only scratching the surface in terms of understanding how the human brain functions as a whole and how this relates to the phenomenon we call consciousness.

What we can say is that our unique human capacity for designing new types of tools and technologies will be critical to this endeavour, as we have seen just how illuminating some of the insights made possible by approaches like electrophysiology, imaging, optogenetics, and gene editing have been. Computer technologies are already of great importance in terms of analysing the huge amounts of data involved in modern neuroscience. In the future, as their sophistication grows through new approaches such as 'deep learning', they are likely to contribute increasingly to modelling consciousness.

Recently, there have been claims that computers may soon achieve their own kind of consciousness equalling or even surpassing our own. While this book has adopted a sceptical position with regard to such claims based on the actual reality of current 'artificial intelligence', we should not underestimate the potential of AI systems to continue to develop in the future. Our aptitude for designing new technologies is what has allowed our species to progress from hunter-gatherers to space pilots in such a short space of evolutionary time. But our technologies may also be our downfall, and AI is just one area of human endeavour in which we will need to keep a close eye on unintended adverse consequences if we are to continue to progress and use our great powers of cognition to further the health and well-being of humanity and the Earth of which we are the custodian.

References

1. Dennett, D. C. Facing up to the hard question of consciousness. *Philos Trans R Soc Lond B Biol Sci, 373*, 0170342 (2018).
2. Burne, T., *et al.* Big ideas for small brains: What can psychiatry learn from worms, flies, bees and fish? *Mol Psychiatry, 16*, 7–16 (2011).
3. Doyle, N. Neurodiversity at work: A biopsychosocial model and the impact on working adults. *Br Med Bull, 135*, 108–125 (2020).
4. White, M., Mackay, M., & Whittaker, R. Taking optogenetics into the human brain: Opportunities and challenges in clinical trial design. *Open Access J Clin Trials, 2020*, 33–41 (2020).
5. Schrum, J. P., Zhu, T. F., & Szostak, J. W. The origins of cellular life. *Cold Spring Harb Perspect Biol, 2*, a002212 (2010).
6. Kalappurakkal, J. M., Sil, P., & Mayor, S. Toward a new picture of the living plasma membrane. *Protein Sci, 29*, 1355–1365 (2020).
7. Granato, E. T., Meiller-Legrand, T. A., & Foster, K. R. The evolution and ecology of bacterial warfare. *Curr Biol, 29*, R521–R537 (2019).
8. Gordeliy, V., *et al.* Microbial rhodopsins. *Methods Mol Biol, 2501*, 1–52 (2022).
9. Judge, A., & Dodd, M. S. Metabolism. *Essays Biochem, 64*, 607–647 (2020).
10. Papke, R. L. Merging old and new perspectives on nicotinic acetylcholine receptors. *Biochem Pharmacol, 89*, 1–11 (2014).
11. Krishnan, A., & Schioth, H. B. The role of G protein-coupled receptors in the early evolution of neurotransmission and the nervous system. *J Exp Biol, 218*, 562–571 (2015).
12. Sears, S. M., & Hewett, S. J. Influence of glutamate and GABA transport on brain excitatory/inhibitory balance. *Exp Biol Med (Maywood), 246*, 1069–1083 (2021).

13. Hohmann-Marriott, M. F., & Blankenship, R. E. Evolution of photosynthesis. *Annu Rev Plant Biol, 62*, 515–548 (2011).

14. Day, B. J. Antioxidant therapeutics: Pandora's box. *Free Radic Biol Med, 66*, 58–64 (2014).

15. Archibald, J. M. Endosymbiosis and eukaryotic cell evolution. *Curr Biol, 25*, R911–R921 (2015).

16. Dacks, J. B., & Field, M. C. Evolution of the eukaryotic membrane-trafficking system: Origin, tempo and mode. *J Cell Sci, 120*, 2977–2985 (2007).

17. Portin, P. The birth and development of the DNA theory of inheritance: Sixty years since the discovery of the structure of DNA. *J Genet, 93*, 293–302 (2014).

18. Feuerborn, A., & Cook, P. R. Why the activity of a gene depends on its neighbors. *Trends Genet, 31*, 483–490 (2015).

19. Hombach, S., & Kretz, M. Non-coding RNAs: Classification, biology and functioning. *Adv Exp Med Biol, 937*, 3–17 (2016).

20. Blumenthal, S. A. Earl Sutherland (1915–1974) [corrected] and the discovery of cyclic AMP. *Perspect Biol Med, 55*, 236–249 (2012).

21. Kandel, E. R. The molecular biology of memory: cAMP, PKA, CRE, CREB-1, CREB-2, and CPEB. *Mol Brain, 5*, 14 (2012).

22. Wright, C. J., Smith, C. W. J., & Jiggins, C. D. Alternative splicing as a source of phenotypic diversity. *Nat Rev Genet, 23*, 697–710 (2022).

23. Weiss, K., Antoniou, A., & Schratt, G. Non-coding mechanisms of local mRNA translation in neuronal dendrites. *Eur J Cell Biol, 94*, 363–367 (2015).

24. Kim, K. M., Abdelmohsen, K., Mustapic, M., Kapogiannis, D., & Gorospe, M. RNA in extracellular vesicles. *Wiley Interdiscip Rev RNA, 8*, 10.1002/wrna.1413 (2017).

25. Zhang, L., Lu, Q., & Chang, C. Epigenetics in health and disease. *Adv Exp Med Biol, 1253*, 3–55 (2020).

26. Fitz-James, M. H., & Cavalli, G. Molecular mechanisms of transgenerational epigenetic inheritance. *Nat Rev Genet, 23*, 325–341 (2022).

27. Jeon, I., & Kim, T. Distinctive properties of biological neural networks and recent advances in bottom-up approaches toward a better biologically plausible neural network. *Front Comput Neurosci, 17*, 1092185 (2023).

28. Iijima, T., Hidaka, C., & Iijima, Y. Spatio-temporal regulations and functions of neuronal alternative RNA splicing in developing and adult brains. *Neurosci Res, 109*, 1–8 (2016).

29. Hutten, S., Sharangdhar, T., & Kiebler, M. Unmasking the messenger. *RNA Biol, 11*, 992–997 (2014).

30. Lizarraga-Valderrama, L. R., & Sheridan, G. K. Extracellular vesicles and intercellular communication in the central nervous system. *FEBS Lett, 595*, 1391–1410 (2021).

31. Lewis, M. Allostery and the lac operon. *J Mol Biol, 425*, 2309–2316 (2013).
32. Oster, G., & Wang, H. Rotary protein motors. *Trends Cell Biol, 13*, 114–121 (2003).
33. Mackie, G. O. Central neural circuitry in the jellyfish Aglantha: A model 'simple nervous system'. *Neurosignals, 13*, 5–19 (2004).
34. Butler, A. B. Chordate evolution and the origin of craniates: An old brain in a new head. *Anat Rec, 261*, 111–125 (2000).
35. Takano, T., Xu, C., Funahashi, Y., Namba, T., & Kaibuchi, K. Neuronal polarization. *Development, 142*, 2088–2093 (2015).
36. Raghavan, M., Fee, D., & Barkhaus, P. E. Generation and propagation of the action potential. *Handb Clin Neurol, 160*, 3–22 (2019).
37. Carroll, S. L. The molecular and morphologic structures that make saltatory conduction possible in peripheral nerve. *J Neuropathol Exp Neurol, 76*, 255–257 (2017).
38. Antunes, G., & Simoes de Souza, F. M. Olfactory receptor signaling. *Methods Cell Biol, 132*, 127–145 (2016).
39. Rolls, E. T. Taste and smell processing in the brain. *Handb Clin Neurol, 164*, 97–118 (2019).
40. Sudhof, T. C. The cell biology of synapse formation. *J Cell Biol, 220*, e202103052 (2021).
41. Nutt, D. J., *et al.* Mechanisms of action of selective serotonin reuptake inhibitors in the treatment of psychiatric disorders. *Eur Neuropsychopharmacol, 9 Suppl 3*, S81–S86 (1999).
42. Hughes, B. W., Kusner, L. L., & Kaminski, H. J. Molecular architecture of the neuromuscular junction. *Muscle Nerve, 33*, 445–461 (2006).
43. von Bernhardi, R., Eugenin-von Bernhardi, J., Flores, B., & Eugenin Leon, J. Glial cells and integrity of the nervous system. *Adv Exp Med Biol, 949*, 1–24 (2016).
44. Oyarce, K., *et al.* Neuroprotective and neurotoxic effects of glial-derived exosomes. *Front Cell Neurosci, 16*, 920686 (2022).
45. Rutten, G. J. Broca-Wernicke theories: A historical perspective. *Handb Clin Neurol, 185*, 25–34 (2022).
46. LeDoux, J. E. Emotion circuits in the brain. *Annu Rev Neurosci, 23*, 155–184 (2000).
47. Fiddes, I. T., *et al.* Human-specific NOTCH2NL genes affect Notch signaling and cortical neurogenesis. *Cell, 173*, 1356–1369.e22 (2018).
48. Liu, J., Mosti, F., & Silver, D. L. Human brain evolution: Emerging roles for regulatory DNA and RNA. *Curr Opin Neurobiol, 71*, 170–177 (2021).
49. Jones, D. T., & Graff-Radford, J. Executive dysfunction and the prefrontal cortex. *Continuum (Minneap Minn), 27*, 1586–1601 (2021).
50. Rilling, J. K., & van den Heuvel, M. P. Comparative primate connectomics. *Brain Behav Evol, 91*, 170–179 (2018).

51. Deco, G., *et al.* Rare long-range cortical connections enhance human information processing. *Curr Biol, 31*, 4436–4448.e5 (2021).
52. Akyuz, E., *et al.* Revisiting the role of neurotransmitters in epilepsy: An updated review. *Life Sci, 265*, 118826 (2021).
53. Kullmann, D. M., Moreau, A. W., Bakiri, Y., & Nicholson, E. Plasticity of inhibition. *Neuron, 75*, 951–962 (2012).
54. Fries, P. A mechanism for cognitive dynamics: Neuronal communication through neuronal coherence. *Trends Cogn Sci, 9*, 474–480 (2005).
55. Oteiza, P., & Baldwin, M. W. Evolution of sensory systems. *Curr Opin Neurobiol, 71*, 52–59 (2021).
56. Walsh, C. M., Bautista, D. M., & Lumpkin, E. A. Mammalian touch catches up. *Curr Opin Neurobiol, 34*, 133–139 (2015).
57. Catani, M. A little man of some importance. *Brain, 140*, 3055–3061 (2017).
58. Launay, G., Sanz, G., Pajot-Augy, E., & Gibrat, J. F. Modeling of mammalian olfactory receptors and docking of odorants. *Biophys Rev, 4*, 255–269 (2012).
59. Lamb, T. D., Collin, S. P., & Pugh, E. N., Jr. Evolution of the vertebrate eye: Opsins, photoreceptors, retina and eye cup. *Nat Rev Neurosci, 8*, 960–976 (2007).
60. Marin, N., Lobo Cerna, F., & Barral, J. Signatures of cochlear processing in neuronal coding of auditory information. *Mol Cell Neurosci, 120*, 103732 (2022).
61. Carroll, J., & Conway, B. R. Color vision. *Handb Clin Neurol, 178*, 131–153 (2021).
62. Mastrangelo, A., Bonato, M., & Cinque, P. Smell and taste disorders in COVID-19: From pathogenesis to clinical features and outcomes. *Neurosci Lett, 748*, 135694 (2021).
63. Lyon, A. M., & Tesmer, J. J. Structural insights into phospholipase C-beta function. *Mol Pharmacol, 84*, 488–500 (2013).
64. Schulman, H. Nitric oxide: A spatial second messenger. *Mol Psychiatry, 2*, 296–299 (1997).
65. Litvina, E. Y., & Chen, C. An evolving view of retinogeniculate transmission. *Vis Neurosci, 34*, E013 (2017).
66. Espinosa, J. S., & Stryker, M. P. Development and plasticity of the primary visual cortex. *Neuron, 75*, 230–249 (2012).
67. Lee, C. C., & Sherman, S. M. On the classification of pathways in the auditory midbrain, thalamus, and cortex. *Hear Res, 276*, 79–87 (2011).
68. Mori, K., & Sakano, H. Olfactory circuitry and behavioral decisions. *Annu Rev Physiol, 83*, 231–256 (2021).
69. Elam, J. S., *et al.* The human connectome project: A retrospective. *Neuroimage, 244*, 118543 (2021).

70. Ding, Z., *et al.* Functional connectomics reveals general wiring rule in mouse visual cortex. *bioRxiv* 2023.03.13.531369 (2023).

71. Robertson, J. M. Astrocytes and the evolution of the human brain. *Med Hypotheses, 82*, 236–239 (2014).

72. Leggio, M., & Molinari, M. Cerebellar sequencing: A trick for predicting the future. *Cerebellum, 14*, 35–38 (2015).

73. Sunavsky, A., & Poppenk, J. Neuroimaging predictors of creativity in healthy adults. *Neuroimage, 206*, 116292 (2020).

74. Sereno, M. I., *et al.* The human cerebellum has almost 80% of the surface area of the neocortex. *Proc Natl Acad Sci USA, 117*, 19538–19543 (2020).

75. Haas, L. F. Hans Berger (1873–1941), Richard Caton (1842–1926), and electroencephalography. *J Neurol Neurosurg Psychiatry, 74*, 9 (2003).

76. Hughes, J. R. A review of the usefulness of the standard EEG in psychiatry. *Clin Electroencephalogr, 27*, 35–39 (1996).

77. D'Esposito, M., & Postle, B. R. The cognitive neuroscience of working memory. *Annu Rev Psychol, 66*, 115–142 (2015).

78. Miller, E. K. The "working" of working memory. *Dialogues Clin Neurosci, 15*, 411–418 (2013).

79. Cromer, J. A., Roy, J. E., & Miller, E. K. Representation of multiple, independent categories in the primate prefrontal cortex. *Neuron, 66*, 796–807 (2010).

80. Miller, E. K., Lundqvist, M., & Bastos, A. M. Working memory 2.0. *Neuron, 100*, 463–475 (2018).

81. Buschman, T. J., & Miller, E. K. Working memory is complex and dynamic, like your thoughts. *J Cogn Neurosci, 35*, 17–23 (2022).

82. Fries, P. Rhythms for cognition: Communication through coherence. *Neuron, 88*, 220–235 (2015).

83. O'Rahilly, R., & Muller, F. Significant features in the early prenatal development of the human brain. *Ann Anat, 190*, 105–118 (2008).

84. Le Douarin, N. M., & Dupin, E. The neural crest in vertebrate evolution. *Curr Opin Genet Dev, 22*, 381–389 (2012).

85. Leibovitz, Z., Lerman-Sagie, T., & Haddad, L. Fetal brain development: Regulating processes and related malformations. *Life (Basel), 12* (2022).

86. Paidas, M. J., & Cohen, A. Disorders of the central nervous system. *Semin Perinatol, 18*, 266–282 (1994).

87. Northcott, P. A., *et al.* Medulloblastoma. *Nat Rev Dis Primers, 5*, 11 (2019).

88. Maden, M. Retinoic acid in the development, regeneration and maintenance of the nervous system. *Nat Rev Neurosci, 8*, 755–765 (2007).

89. Lamouille, S., Xu, J., & Derynck, R. Molecular mechanisms of epithelial-mesenchymal transition. *Nat Rev Mol Cell Biol, 15*, 178–196 (2014).

90. Allen, N. J., & Lyons, D. A. Glia as architects of central nervous system formation and function. *Science, 362*, 181–185 (2018).

91.   Omotade, O. F., Pollitt, S. L., & Zheng, J. Q. Actin-based growth cone motility and guidance. *Mol Cell Neurosci, 84*, 4–10 (2017).

92.   Seiradake, E., Jones, E. Y., & Klein, R. Structural perspectives on axon guidance. *Annu Rev Cell Dev Biol, 32*, 577–608 (2016).

93.   Lin, T. Y., Chen, P. J., Yu, H. H., Hsu, C. P., & Lee, C. H. Extrinsic factors regulating dendritic patterning. *Front Cell Neurosci, 14*, 622808 (2020).

94.   Sudhof, T. C. Towards an understanding of synapse formation. *Neuron, 100*, 276–293 (2018).

95.   Zatkova, M., Bakos, J., Hodosy, J., & Ostatnikova, D. Synapse alterations in autism: Review of animal model findings. *Biomed Pap Med Fac Univ Palacky Olomouc Czech Repub, 160*, 201–210 (2016).

96.   Hirsch, H. V. The role of visual experience in the development of cat striate cortex. *Cell Mol Neurobiol, 5*, 103–121 (1985).

97.   Fine, I., & Park, J. M. Blindness and human brain plasticity. *Annu Rev Vis Sci, 4*, 337–356 (2018).

98.   Huber, E., *et al.* Early blindness shapes cortical representations of auditory frequency within auditory cortex. *J Neurosci, 39*, 5143–5152 (2019).

99.   Bola, L., *et al.* Task-specific reorganization of the auditory cortex in deaf humans. *Proc Natl Acad Sci USA, 114*, E600–E609 (2017).

100. Ismail, F. Y., Fatemi, A., & Johnston, M. V. Cerebral plasticity: Windows of opportunity in the developing brain. *Eur J Paediatr Neurol, 21*, 23–48 (2017).

101. Vijayakumar, N., Op de Macks, Z., Shirtcliff, E. A., & Pfeifer, J. H. Puberty and the human brain: Insights into adolescent development. *Neurosci Biobehav Rev, 92*, 417–436 (2018).

102. Miller, D. J., *et al.* Prolonged myelination in human neocortical evolution. *Proc Natl Acad Sci USA, 109*, 16480–16485 (2012).

103. Whalley, K. Revealing silent synapses in the adult brain. *Nat Rev Neurosci, 24*, 59 (2023).

104. Tonegawa, S., Liu, X., Ramirez, S., & Redondo, R. Memory engram cells have come of age. *Neuron, 87*, 918–931 (2015).

105. Bailey, C. H., Kandel, E. R., & Harris, K. M. Structural components of synaptic plasticity and memory consolidation. *Cold Spring Harb Perspect Biol, 7*, a021758 (2015).

106. Lee, D. Global and local missions of cAMP signaling in neural plasticity, learning, and memory. *Front Pharmacol, 6*, 161 (2015).

107. Nicoll, R. A. A brief history of long-term potentiation. *Neuron, 93*, 281–290 (2017).

108. Durkee, C., Kofuji, P., Navarrete, M., & Araque, A. Astrocyte and neuron cooperation in long-term depression. *Trends Neurosci, 44*, 837–848 (2021).

109. Robertson, L. T. Memory and the brain. *J Dent Educ, 66*, 30–42 (2002).

110. Dossani, R. H., Missios, S., & Nanda, A. The legacy of Henry Molaison (1926–2008) and the impact of his bilateral mesial temporal lobe surgery on the study of human memory. *World Neurosurg, 84*, 1127–1135 (2015).

111. Terry, A. V., Jr. In *Methods of behavior analysis in neuroscience. Frontiers in neuroscience* (Ed J. J. Buccafusco) (2009).

112. Woollett, K., & Maguire, E. A. Exploring anterograde associative memory in London taxi drivers. *Neuroreport, 23*, 885–888 (2012).

113. Langer, K. G. The history of amnesia-a review. *Curr Neurol Neurosci Rep, 21*, 40 (2021).

114. Quiroga, R. Q., Reddy, L., Kreiman, G., Koch, C., & Fried, I. Invariant visual representation by single neurons in the human brain. *Nature, 435*, 1102–1107 (2005).

115. Rudebeck, P. H., & Rich, E. L. Orbitofrontal cortex. *Curr Biol, 28*, R1083–R1088 (2018).

116. Plassmann, H., O'Doherty, J., Shiv, B., & Rangel, A. Marketing actions can modulate neural representations of experienced pleasantness. *Proc Natl Acad Sci USA, 105*, 1050–1054 (2008).

117. Lee, D., & Seo, H. Mechanisms of reinforcement learning and decision making in the primate dorsolateral prefrontal cortex. *Ann N Y Acad Sci, 1104*, 108–122 (2007).

118. Barbey, A. K., Koenigs, M., & Grafman, J. Dorsolateral prefrontal contributions to human working memory. *Cortex, 49*, 1195–1205 (2013).

119. Burgos-Robles, A., Gothard, K. M., Monfils, M. H., Morozov, A., & Vicentic, A. Conserved features of anterior cingulate networks support observational learning across species. *Neurosci Biobehav Rev, 107*, 215–228 (2019).

120. Sakagami, M., & Pan, X. Functional role of the ventrolateral prefrontal cortex in decision making. *Curr Opin Neurobiol, 17*, 228–233 (2007).

121. Evrard, H. C. The organization of the primate insular cortex. *Front Neuroanat, 13*, 43 (2019).

122. Brewer, J. A., Garrison, K. A., & Whitfield-Gabrieli, S. What about the "Self" is processed in the posterior cingulate cortex? *Front Hum Neurosci, 7*, 647 (2013).

123. Gonzalez, M., & Green, S. Evolution of the human hand from early hominid to today. *Bull Hosp Jt Dis (2013), 81*, 34–39 (2023).

124. Maravita, A., & Romano, D. The parietal lobe and tool use. *Handb Clin Neurol, 151*, 481–498 (2018).

125. Tattersall, I. A tentative framework for the acquisition of language and modern human cognition. *J Anthropol Sci, 94*, 157–166 (2016).

126. Larsson, M. Tool-use-associated sound in the evolution of language. *Anim Cogn, 18*, 993–1005 (2015).

127. Stringer, C. The origin and evolution of *Homo sapiens*. *Philos Trans R Soc Lond B Biol Sci, 371*, 20150237 (2016).

128. Kolodny, O., & Edelman, S. The evolution of the capacity for language: The ecological context and adaptive value of a process of cognitive hijacking. *Philos Trans R Soc Lond B Biol Sci, 373*, 20170052 (2018).

129. Thibault, S., *et al.* Tool use and language share syntactic processes and neural patterns in the basal ganglia. *Science, 374*, eabe0874 (2021).

130. Tremblay, P., & Dick, A. S. Broca and Wernicke are dead, or moving past the classic model of language neurobiology. *Brain Lang, 162*, 60–71 (2016).

131. de Haan, E. H. F., *et al.* Split-brain: What we know now and why this is important for understanding consciousness. *Neuropsychol Rev, 30*, 224–233 (2020).

132. Baumard, J., Osiurak, F., Lesourd, M., & Le Gall, D. Tool use disorders after left brain damage. *Front Psychol, 5*, 473 (2014).

133. den Hoed, J., Devaraju, K., & Fisher, S. E. Molecular networks of the FOXP2 transcription factor in the brain. *EMBO Rep, 22*, e52803 (2021).

134. Nasios, G., Dardiotis, E., & Messinis, L. From Broca and Wernicke to the neuromodulation era: Insights of brain language networks for neurorehabilitation. *Behav Neurol, 2019*, 9894571 (2019).

135. McLachlan, N. M., & Wilson, S. J. The contribution of brainstem and cerebellar pathways to auditory recognition. *Front Psychol, 8*, 265 (2017).

136. Turker, S., Kuhnke, P., Eickhoff, S. B., Caspers, S., & Hartwigsen, G. Cortical, subcortical, and cerebellar contributions to language processing: A meta-analytic review of 403 neuroimaging experiments. *Psychol Bull, 149*, 699–723 (2023).

137. Hansotia, P. A neurologist looks at mind and brain: "The enchanted loom". *Clin Med Res, 1*, 327–332 (2003).

138. Kalan, A. K., Nakano, R., & Warshawski, L. What we know and don't know about great ape cultural communication in the wild. *Am J Primatol*, e23560 (2023).

139. Rivas, E. Recent use of signs by chimpanzees (Pan Troglodytes) in interactions with humans. *J Comp Psychol, 119*, 404–417 (2005).

140. McGrew, W. C. Is primate tool use special? Chimpanzee and New Caledonian crow compared. *Philos Trans R Soc Lond B Biol Sci, 368*, 20120422 (2013).

141. Langland-Hassan, P. Inner speech. *Wiley Interdiscip Rev Cogn Sci, 12*, e1544 (2021).

142. Perrone-Bertolotti, M., Rapin, L., Lachaux, J. P., Baciu, M., & Loevenbruck, H. What is that little voice inside my head? Inner speech phenomenology, its role in cognitive performance, and its relation to self-monitoring. *Behav Brain Res, 261*, 220–239 (2014).

143. Barresi, J. From 'the thought is the thinker' to 'the voice is the speaker': William James and the dialogical self. *Theory & Psychology, 12*, 237–250 (2002).

144. Burnell, D. P. Egocentric speech: An adaptive function applied to developmental disabilities in occupational therapy. *Am J Occup Ther, 33*, 169–174 (1979).

145. Brinthaupt, T. M., & Morin, A. Self-talk: Research challenges and opportunities. *Front Psychol, 14*, 1210960 (2023).

146. Pratts, J., Pobric, G., & Yao, B. Bridging phenomenology and neural mechanisms of inner speech: ALE meta-analysis on egocentricity and spontaneity in a dual-mechanistic framework. *Neuroimage, 282*, 120399 (2023).

147. Borghi, A. M., & Fernyhough, C. Concepts, abstractness and inner speech. *Philos Trans R Soc Lond B Biol Sci, 378*, 20210371 (2023).

148. Loh, K. K., & Kanai, R. How has the Internet reshaped human cognition? *Neuroscientist, 22*, 506–520 (2016).

149. Bailey, A. M., McDaniel, W. F., & Thomas, R. K. Approaches to the study of higher cognitive functions related to creativity in nonhuman animals. *Methods, 42*, 3–11 (2007).

150. Pelaprat, E., & Cole, M. "Minding the gap": Imagination, creativity and human cognition. *Integr Psychol Behav Sci, 45*, 397–418 (2011).

151. Garcia-Pelegrin, E., Wilkins, C., & Clayton, N. S. The ape that lived to tell the tale. The evolution of the art of storytelling and its relationship to mental time travel and theory of mind. *Front Psychol, 12*, 755783 (2021).

152. Delafield-Butt, J. T., & Trevarthen, C. The ontogenesis of narrative: From moving to meaning. *Front Psychol, 6*, 1157 (2015).

153. Harris, P. L. Early constraints on the imagination: The realism of young children. *Child Dev, 92*, 466–483 (2021).

154. Bodrova, E., & Leong, D. J. Vygotskian and post-Vygotskian views on children's play. *Am J Play, 7*, 371–388 (2015).

155. Gray, P. Play as a foundation for hunter-gatherer social existence. *Am J Play, 1*, 476–522 (2009).

156. Limb, C. J., & Braun, A. R. Neural substrates of spontaneous musical performance: an FMRI study of jazz improvisation. *PLoS One, 3*, e1679 (2008).

157. McPherson, M. J., Lopez-Gonzalez, M., Rankin, S. K., & Limb, C. J. The role of emotion in musical improvisation: An analysis of structural features. *PLoS One, 9*, e105144 (2014).

158. Schlegel, A., *et al.* Network structure and dynamics of the mental workspace. *Proc Natl Acad Sci USA, 110*, 16277–16282 (2013).

159. Saggar, M., *et al.* Pictionary-based fMRI paradigm to study the neural correlates of spontaneous improvisation and figural creativity. *Sci Rep, 5*, 10894 (2015).

160. Stachel, J. Einstein and Michelson — The context of discovery and the context of justification. *Astronomische Nachrichten, 303,* 47 (1982).
161. Oerter, R. Biological and psychological correlates of exceptional performance in development. *Ann N Y Acad Sci, 999,* 451–460 (2003).
162. Toohey, P. Some ancient histories of literary melancholia. *Ill Class Stud, 15,* 143–161 (1990).
163. Fink, A., Benedek, M., Unterrainer, H. F., Papousek, I., & Weiss, E. M. Creativity and psychopathology: Are there similar mental processes involved in creativity and in psychosis-proneness? *Front Psychol, 5,* 1211 (2014).
164. Carson, S. Leveraging the "mad genius" debate: Why we need a neuroscience of creativity and psychopathology. *Front Hum Neurosci, 8,* 771 (2014).
165. Steel, Z., *et al.* The global prevalence of common mental disorders: A systematic review and meta-analysis 1980–2013. *Int J Epidemiol, 43,* 476–493 (2014).
166. McGowan, P. O., & Roth, T. L. Epigenetic pathways through which experiences become linked with biology. *Dev Psychopathol, 27,* 637–648 (2015).
167. McCutcheon, R. A., Reis Marques, T., & Howes, O. D. Schizophrenia-An overview. *JAMA Psychiatry, 77,* 201–210 (2020).
168. Howes, O. D., & Kapur, S. The dopamine hypothesis of schizophrenia: Version III–the final common pathway. *Schizophr Bull, 35,* 549–562 (2009).
169. Zahodne, L. B., & Fernandez, H. H. Pathophysiology and treatment of psychosis in Parkinson's disease: A review. *Drugs Aging, 25,* 665–682 (2008).
170. Ang, A., Horowitz, H., & Moncrieff, J. Is the chemical imbalance an 'urban legend'? An exploration of the status of the serotonin theory of depression in the scientific literature. *SSM – Mental Health, 2,* 100098 (2022).
171. Miyamoto, S., Miyake, N., Jarskog, L. F., Fleischhacker, W. W., & Lieberman, J. A. Pharmacological treatment of schizophrenia: A critical review of the pharmacology and clinical effects of current and future therapeutic agents. *Mol Psychiatry, 17,* 1206–1227 (2012).
172. Legge, S. E., *et al.* Genetic architecture of schizophrenia: A review of major advancements. *Psychol Med, 51,* 2168–2177 (2021).
173. Nakamura, T., & Takata, A. The molecular pathology of schizophrenia: An overview of existing knowledge and new directions for future research. *Mol Psychiatry, 28,* 1868–1889 (2023).
174. Ermakov, E. A., Melamud, M. M., Buneva, V. N., & Ivanova, S. A. Immune system abnormalities in schizophrenia: An integrative view and translational perspectives. *Front Psychiatry, 13,* 880568 (2022).

175. Bloomfield, P. S., *et al.* Microglial activity in people at ultra high risk of psychosis and in schizophrenia: An [(11)C]PBR28 PET brain imaging study. *Am J Psychiatry, 173*, 44–52 (2016).

176. Popovic, D., *et al.* Childhood trauma in schizophrenia: Current findings and research perspectives. *Front Neurosci, 13*, 274 (2019).

177. Beels, C. Family Process 1962–1969. *Fam Process, 50*, 4–11 (2011).

178. Rund, B. R. Attention, communication, and schizophrenia. *Yale J Biol Med, 58*, 265–273 (1985).

179. Lane, N. M., & Smith, D. J. Bipolar disorder: Diagnosis, treatment and future directions. *J R Coll Physicians Edinb, 53*, 192–196 (2023).

180. Greenwood, T. A. Positive traits in the bipolar spectrum: The space between madness and genius. *Mol Neuropsychiatry, 2*, 198–212 (2017).

181. Smith, D. J., *et al.* Childhood IQ and risk of bipolar disorder in adulthood: Prospective birth cohort study. *BJPsych Open, 1*, 74–80 (2015).

182. Greenwood, T. A. Creativity and bipolar disorder: A shared genetic vulnerability. *Annu Rev Clin Psychol, 16*, 239–264 (2020).

183. Tu, P. C., Kuan, Y. H., Li, C. T., & Su, T. P. Structural correlates of creative thinking in patients with bipolar disorder and healthy controls-a voxel-based morphometry study. *J Affect Disord, 215*, 218–224 (2017).

184. Wolf, P. Creativity and chronic disease. Vincent van Gogh (1853–1890). *West J Med, 175*, 348 (2001).

185. Turecki, G., *et al.* Suicide and suicide risk. *Nat Rev Dis Primers, 5*, 74 (2019).

186. Liu, Q., *et al.* Changes in the global burden of depression from 1990 to 2017: Findings from the Global Burden of Disease study. *J Psychiatr Res, 126*, 134–140 (2020).

187. Hoppe, C. Citing Hippocrates on depression in epilepsy. *Epilepsy Behav, 90*, 31–36 (2019).

188. Frye, C. B. Using literature in health care: Reflections on "the yellow wallpaper". *Ann Pharmacother, 32*, 829–833 (1998).

189. Martin, D. The rest cure revisited. *Am J Psychiatry, 164*, 737–738 (2007).

190. Lopez-Munoz, F., & Alamo, C. Monoaminergic neurotransmission: The history of the discovery of antidepressants from 1950s until today. *Curr Pharm Des, 15*, 1563–1586 (2009).

191. Caspi, A., *et al.* Influence of life stress on depression: Moderation by a polymorphism in the 5-HTT gene. *Science, 301*, 386–389 (2003).

192. Culverhouse, R. C., *et al.* Collaborative meta-analysis finds no evidence of a strong interaction between stress and 5-HTTLPR genotype contributing to the development of depression. *Mol Psychiatry, 23*, 133–142 (2018).

193. Moncrieff, J., *et al.* The serotonin theory of depression: A systematic umbrella review of the evidence. *Mol Psychiatry, 28*, 3243–3256 (2023).

194. Oved, K., *et al.* Genome-wide expression profiling of human lymphoblastoid cell lines implicates integrin beta-3 in the mode of action of antidepressants. *Transl Psychiatry, 3*, e313 (2013).

195. Beurel, E., Toups, M., & Nemeroff, C. B. The bidirectional relationship of depression and inflammation: Double trouble. *Neuron, 107*, 234–256 (2020).

196. Hamann, S. Blue genes: Wiring the brain for depression. *Nat Neurosci, 8*, 701–703 (2005).

197. Zhu, X., *et al.* Evidence of a dissociation pattern in resting-state default mode network connectivity in first-episode, treatment-naive major depression patients. *Biol Psychiatry, 71*, 611–617 (2012).

198. Kendall, K. M., *et al.* The genetic basis of major depression. *Psychol Med, 51*, 2217–2230 (2021).

199. Flint, J. The genetic basis of major depressive disorder. *Mol Psychiatry, 28*, 2254–2265 (2023).

200. CONVERGE Consortium. Sparse whole-genome sequencing identifies two loci for major depressive disorder. *Nature, 523*, 588–591 (2015).

201. Liu, L., Xia, G., Li, P., Wang, Y., & Zhao, Q. Sirt-1 regulates physiological process and exerts protective effects against oxidative stress. *Biomed Res Int, 2021*, 5542545 (2021).

202. Brown, G. W., & Harris, T. O. *Social origins of depression: A study of psychiatric disorder in women.* Tavistock Press (1978).

203. Fischer, A. K., & Srole, L. *Mental health in the metropolis: The midtown Manhattan study.* Harper & Row (1975).

204. Szuhany, K. L., & Simon, N. M. Anxiety disorders: A review. *JAMA, 328*, 2431–2445 (2022).

205. Canteras, N. S., Resstel, L. B., Bertoglio, L. J., Carobrez, A. P., & Guimaraes, F. S. Neuroanatomy of anxiety. *Curr Top Behav Neurosci, 2*, 77–96 (2010).

206. Deahl, M. P., Klein, S., & Alexander, D. A. The costs of conflict: Meeting the mental health needs of serving personnel and service veterans. *Int Rev Psychiatry, 23*, 201–209 (2011).

207. Campbell, N., & Deane, C. Bacteria and the market. *Market Theory, 19*, 237–257 (2019).

208. Nievergelt, C. M., *et al.* International meta-analysis of PTSD genome-wide association studies identifies sex- and ancestry-specific genetic risk loci. *Nat Commun, 10*, 4558 (2019).

209. Hughes, V. Sperm RNA carries marks of trauma. *Nature, 508*, 296–297 (2014).

210. Short, A. K., *et al.* Elevated paternal glucocorticoid exposure alters the small noncoding RNA profile in sperm and modifies anxiety and depressive phenotypes in the offspring. *Transl Psychiatry, 6*, e837 (2016).

211. Yehuda, R., *et al.* Holocaust exposure induced intergenerational effects on FKBP5 methylation. *Biol Psychiatry, 80*, 372–380 (2016).

212. Deacon, B. J. The biomedical model of mental disorder: A critical analysis of its validity, utility, and effects on psychotherapy research. *Clin Psychol Rev, 33*, 846–861 (2013).

213. Boyle, M., & Johnstone, L. Alternatives to psychiatric diagnosis. *Lancet Psychiatry, 1*, 409–411 (2014).

214. Solmi, M., *et al.* Incidence, prevalence, and global burden of autism spectrum disorder from 1990 to 2019 across 204 countries. *Mol Psychiatry, 27*, 4172–4180 (2022).

215. Lord, C., *et al.* Autism spectrum disorder. *Nat Rev Dis Primers, 6*, 5 (2020).

216. Andreou, M., & Skrimpa, V. Theory of mind deficits and neurophysiological operations in autism spectrum disorders: A review. *Brain Sci, 10*, 393 (2020).

217. Tian, J., Gao, X., & Yang, L. Repetitive restricted behaviors in autism spectrum disorder: From mechanism to development of therapeutics. *Front Neurosci, 16*, 780407 (2022).

218. Deshpande, A., *et al.* Cellular phenotypes in human iPSC-derived neurons from a genetic model of autism spectrum disorder. *Cell Rep, 21*, 2678–2687 (2017).

219. Gillentine, M. A., *et al.* Functional consequences of CHRNA7 copy-number alterations in induced pluripotent stem cells and neural progenitor cells. *Am J Hum Genet, 101*, 874–887 (2017).

220. DeStefano, F., & Shimabukuro, T. T. The MMR vaccine and autism. *Annu Rev Virol, 6*, 585–600 (2019).

221. Barahona-Correa, J. B., & Filipe, C. N. A concise history of Asperger syndrome: The short reign of a troublesome diagnosis. *Front Psychol, 6*, 2024 (2015).

222. Cha, A. E. Study: Autism, creativity and divergent thinking may go hand in hand, *Washington Post* 25 August (2015).

223. Best, C., Arora, S., Porter, F., & Doherty, M. The relationship between subthreshold autistic traits, ambiguous figure perception and divergent thinking. *J Autism Dev Disord, 45*, 4064–4073 (2015).

224. Howlin, P., & Magiati, I. Autism spectrum disorder: Outcomes in adulthood. *Curr Opin Psychiatry, 30*, 69–76 (2017).

225. Erskine, H. E., *et al.* Long-term outcomes of attention-deficit/hyperactivity disorder and conduct disorder: A systematic review and meta-analysis. *J Am Acad Child Adolesc Psychiatry, 55*, 841–850 (2016).

226. Posner, J., Polanczyk, G. V., & Sonuga-Barke, E. Attention-deficit hyperactivity disorder. *Lancet, 395*, 450–462 (2020).

227. Ashinoff, B. K., & Abu-Akel, A. Hyperfocus: The forgotten frontier of attention. *Psychol Res, 85*, 1–19 (2021).

228. Albajara Saenz, A., Villemonteix, T., & Massat, I. Structural and functional neuroimaging in attention-deficit/hyperactivity disorder. *Dev Med Child Neurol, 61,* 399–405 (2019).

229. Montinari, M. R., Minelli, S., & De Caterina, R. The first 3500 years of aspirin history from its roots — A concise summary. *Vascul Pharmacol, 113,* 1–8 (2019).

230. Trescot, A. M., Datta, S., Lee, M., & Hansen, H. Opioid pharmacology. *Pain Physician, 11,* S133–153 (2008).

231. Sanchez-Reyes, O. B., Zilberg, G., McCorvy, J. D., & Wacker, D. Molecular insights into GPCR mechanisms for drugs of abuse. *J Biol Chem, 299,* 105176 (2023).

232. Crocq, M. A. History of cannabis and the endocannabinoid system. *Dialogues Clin Neurosci, 22,* 223–228 (2020).

233. Yang, A. C., & Tsai, S. J. New targets for schizophrenia treatment beyond the dopamine hypothesis. *Int J Mol Sci, 18,* 1689 (2017).

234. Muller, N. Inflammation in schizophrenia: Pathogenetic aspects and therapeutic considerations. *Schizophr Bull, 44,* 973–982 (2018).

235. Arnedo, J., *et al.* Uncovering the hidden risk architecture of the schizophrenias: Confirmation in three independent genome-wide association studies. *Am J Psychiatry, 172,* 139–153 (2015).

236. Morkved, N., *et al.* Impact of childhood trauma on antipsychotic effectiveness in schizophrenia spectrum disorders: A prospective, pragmatic, semi-randomized trial. *Schizophr Res, 246,* 49–59 (2022).

237. Bergstrom, T., *et al.* Retrospective experiences of first-episode psychosis treatment under open dialogue-based services: A qualitative study. *Community Ment Health J, 58,* 887–894 (2022).

238. Hirschfeld, R. M. History and evolution of the monoamine hypothesis of depression. *J Clin Psychiatry, 61 Suppl 6,* 4–6 (2000).

239. Wong, D. T., Perry, K. W., & Bymaster, F. P. Case history: The discovery of fluoxetine hydrochloride (Prozac). *Nat Rev Drug Discov, 4,* 764–774 (2005).

240. Mayor, S. Meta-analysis shows difference between antidepressants and placebo is only significant in severe depression. *Br Med J, 336,* 466 (2008).

241. Kendrick, T. Strategies to reduce use of antidepressants. *Br J Clin Pharmacol, 87,* 23–33 (2021).

242. Kraus, C., Castren, E., Kasper, S., & Lanzenberger, R. Serotonin and neuroplasticity — Links between molecular, functional and structural pathophysiology in depression. *Neurosci Biobehav Rev, 77,* 317–326 (2017).

243. Colla, M., Scheerer, H., Weidt, S., Seifritz, E., & Kronenberg, G. Novel insights into the neurobiology of the antidepressant response from ketamine research: A mini review. *Front Behav Neurosci, 15,* 759466 (2021).

244. Troubat, R., *et al.* Neuroinflammation and depression: A review. *Eur J Neurosci, 53*, 151–171 (2021).

245. Geddes, J. R., & Miklowitz, D. J. Treatment of bipolar disorder. *Lancet, 381*, 1672–1682 (2013).

246. Mechler, K., Banaschewski, T., Hohmann, S., & Hage, A. Evidence-based pharmacological treatment options for ADHD in children and adolescents. *Pharmacol Ther, 230*, 107940 (2022).

247. Dougherty, D. D. Deep brain stimulation: Clinical applications. *Psychiatr Clin North Am, 41*, 385–394 (2018).

248. Antal, A., *et al.* Non-invasive brain stimulation and neuroenhancement. *Clin Neurophysiol Pract, 7*, 146–165 (2022).

249. Guo, W., *et al.* A novel non-invasive brain stimulation technique: "Temporally interfering electrical stimulation". *Front Neurosci, 17*, 1092539 (2023).

250. Duebel, J., Marazova, K., & Sahel, J. A. Optogenetics. *Curr Opin Ophthalmol, 26*, 226–232 (2015).

251. Bansal, A., Shikha, S., & Zhang, Y. Towards translational optogenetics. *Nat Biomed Eng, 7*, 349–369 (2023).

252. Villiger, L., *et al.* CRISPR technologies for genome, epigenome and transcriptome editing. *Nat Rev Mol Cell Biol, 25*, 464–487 (2024).

253. Saini, H., Thakur, R., Gill, R., Tyagi, K., & Goswami, M. CRISPR/Cas9-gene editing approaches in plant breeding. *GM Crops Food, 14*, 1–17 (2023).

254. Alkanli, S. S., Alkanli, N., Ay, A., & Albeniz, I. CRISPR/Cas9 mediated therapeutic approach in Huntington's disease. *Mol Neurobiol, 60*, 1486–1498 (2023).

255. De Plano, L. M., *et al.* Applications of CRISPR-Cas9 in Alzheimer's disease and related disorders. *Int J Mol Sci, 23*, 8714 (2022).

256. Weuring, W., Geerligs, J., & Koeleman, B. P. C. Gene therapies for monogenic autism spectrum disorders. *Genes (Basel), 12*, 1667 (2021).

257. Naples, J. G., & Ruckenstein, M. J. Cochlear implant. *Otolaryngol Clin North Am, 53*, 87–102 (2020).

258. Nowik, K., Langwinska-Wosko, E., Skopinski, P., Nowik, K. E., & Szaflik, J. P. Bionic eye review — An update. *J Clin Neurosci, 78*, 8–19 (2020).

259. Zipser, C. M., *et al.* Cell-based and stem-cell-based treatments for spinal cord injury: Evidence from clinical trials. *Lancet Neurol, 21*, 659–670 (2022).

260. Morales, II, Toscano-Tejeida, D., & Ibarra, A. Non pharmacological strategies to promote spinal cord regeneration: A view on some individual or combined approaches. *Curr Pharm Des, 22*, 720–727 (2016).

261. Torregrosa, T., & Koppes, R. A. Bioelectric medicine and devices for the treatment of spinal cord injury. *Cells Tissues Organs, 202*, 6–22 (2016).

262. Colucci, A., *et al.* Brain-computer interface-controlled exoskeletons in clinical neurorehabilitation: Ready or not? *Neurorehabil Neural Repair, 36*, 747–756 (2022).

263. Pastur-Romay, L. A., Porto-Pazos, A. B., Cedron, F., & Pazos, A. Parallel computing for brain simulation. *Curr Top Med Chem, 17*, 1646–1668 (2017).

264. Buttazzo, G. Rise of artificial general intelligence: Risks and opportunities. *Front Artif Intell, 6*, 1226990 (2023).

265. Grzybowski, A., Pawlikowska-Lagod, K., & Lambert, W. C. A history of artificial intelligence. *Clin Dermatol, 42*, 221–229 (2024).

266. Hassabis, D., Kumaran, D., Summerfield, C., & Botvinick, M. Neuroscience-inspired artificial intelligence. *Neuron, 95*, 245–258 (2017).

267. Greener, J. G., Kandathil, S. M., Moffat, L., & Jones, D. T. A guide to machine learning for biologists. *Nat Rev Mol Cell Biol, 23*, 40–55 (2022).

268. LeCun, Y., Bengio, Y., & Hinton, G. Deep learning. *Nature, 521*, 436–444 (2015).

269. Roudi, Y., & Taylor, G. Learning with hidden variables. *Curr Opin Neurobiol, 35*, 110–118 (2015).

270. Bernaez Timon, L., *et al.* How to incorporate biological insights into network models and why it matters. *J Physiol, 601*, 3037–3053 (2023).

271. Chatila, R., *et al.* Toward self-aware robots. *Front Robot AI, 5*, 88 (2018).

272. Barrett, H. C. A hierarchical model of the evolution of human brain specializations. *Proc Natl Acad Sci USA, 109 Suppl 1*, 10733–10740 (2012).

273. Bengio, Y. On the challenge of learning complex functions. *Prog Brain Res, 165*, 521–534 (2007).

Index

experimental animals, xi, 3, 36, 80,
86, 92–93, 96, 114, 186
external speech, 117–119
extracellular vesicles (EVs), 18, 20,
32
eyes, 48, 51, 67, 73, 86, 108, 155,
185, 193–194

F
face, 46, 89, 128
facial recognition, 89, 200
Falk, Dean, 130
families, 143–144, 161, 169, 177,
180
fatigue, 100, 149, 180
fear, 39, 155, 178
fentanyl, 174
fertilised egg, 67, 156
feudalism, 120
fever, 174
fibre-optics, 189, 191
fibroblast growth factor, 68
fiction, 127
film, 127
flagellum of bacterium, 203
fluidity of thought, 43, 92, 113, 117,
119, 124
functional magnetic resonance
imaging (fMRI), 73, 127
foetus, 68, 73, 149, 163
forebrain, 29, 35, 38, 68
fossils, 104–105
FoxP2, 110
free radicals, 151
Freudianism, 159, 162
friendships, 75, 119–120, 168
fright, flight, or fight response,
15–16, 46, 50, 80, 155
frogs, 26
frontal lobes, 40, 59, 75, 59–60, 95,
127, 144
fruit flies, xi, 80, 189, 207

functional magnetic resonance
imaging (fMRI), 37, 73, 127
future, xii–xiii, 3, 60, 75, 85, 100,
104, 113, 115, 140, 148, 158, 160,
168, 197, 199, 204, 206–207, 209

G
G-protein coupled receptors
(GPCRs), 1, 4, 28, 47, 50, 155, 174
G-proteins, 4
Gα class, 50
Gage, Phineas, 95
Galeazzi Galvani, Lucia, 26
Galvani, Luigi, 26
game of Go, 200, 205
gamma brain waves, 57, 61, 63–64
gamma hydroxybutyrate (GHB), 6
gamma-aminobutyric acid (GABA),
1, 4–6
gastrulation, 68
gene editing, xiii, 191–192, 209
gene expression, 11, 13–15, 18–20,
68, 110, 138, 191, 202
gene 'knockout', 192
gene promoter, 13–14
gene therapy, 187, 191–193
general intelligence, 200, 206
general memory, 85–86
generalisation, 155, 200
genes, ix, 9, 13–16, 19–20, 24, 47,
49, 68, 71–72, 80, 103, 110,
138–140, 151, 156–157, 191, 193
genetic links, 140, 143, 151, 193
genetic mutations, 68, 107, 110, 139,
163–164, 192
genetic variants, 110, 138–139, 147
genetically modified organisms,
191–192
genius, 129–131, 146
genomes, xiii, 9, 11, 14–15, 18–20,
40, 110, 131, 133, 137–140, 153,
156, 159–160, 163, 191–193, 200

nociceptors, 46
nodes of Ranvier, 28
Noggin, 68
non-declarative memory, 84
non-homologous end joining (NHEJ),
   192
non-invasive brain imaging, 36–37
non-paranoid schizophrenia, 143
non-verbal communication, 160
noradrenaline, 4, 6, 182
nose, 28, 193
NOTCH2, 40
NOTCH2NL, 35, 40, 110
notochord, 67–68
nuclear pores, 15
nucleic acid, 11, 13

O
obsessive-compulsive disorder
   (OCD), 100, 155
odours, 45, 48, 54
oesophagus, 47
olfactory bulb, 29, 54
olfactory cortex, 29
olfactory receptors, 28, 47
oligodendrocytes, 31
oncogenes, 71
open dialogue therapy, 173,
   176–177
opioid receptors, 176
opioids, 174
opium poppy, 174
opsin proteins, 48–49, 189
optic nerve, 51, 185, 194
optogenetics, xiii, 187–191, 209
orbitofrontal cortex (OFC), 91, 93,
   96–97, 100
orbitofrontal prefrontal cortex, 41
organelles, 7–9
origin of life, xiv, 1–2, 7, 207
oscillating brain waves, 42, 54, 57,
   62–64, 86, 92–93, 98, 151, 202

output layer of neural network, 197,
   202
oxygen, 2, 7, 24, 37, 151

P
'packets' of memorised information,
   63
pain, 4, 46, 100, 155, 173–174, 191
panic disorder, 155
paralysis, 195–196
paranoia, 174
paranoid schizophrenia, 143
parasympathetic nervous system, 71
parental love, 100
parietal lobes, 130
parkin gene, 193
Parkinson's disease, 136, 175,
   185–186, 189, 193
paroxetine, 149
past, xii, 84, 89, 93, 96, 104, 113,
   115, 119, 160, 197, 204, 207, 209
perception, x, xiv, 38, 42, 45, 49, 54,
   96, 98, 100, 124, 168, 193, 190,
   195
peripheral nervous system, 26, 68,
   71, 195
personality disorders, ix, xiii, 64, 95,
   167, 208
pharmacology, x, 139, 177
pharynx, 47
philosophy, ix–x, xii, 49, 79, 113,
   131
phobias, 155
phonetics, 112
phosphate chemical group, 19
photosynthesis, 7
Piezo receptors, 46
pituitary gland, 174
placebo effect, 179
planning, 38, 41, 75, 92, 127
Plato, 79
play, 123, 125–127